The Psychopath
the Gothic Ror

The Psychopathology of the Gothic Romance

Perversion, Neuroses and Psychosis in Early Works of the Genre

ED CAMERON

McFarland & Company, Inc., Publishers
Jefferson, North Carolina, and London

LIBRARY OF CONGRESS CATALOGUING-IN-PUBLICATION DATA

Cameron, Ed, 1966–
    The psychopathology of the Gothic romance : perversion,
neuroses and psychosis in early works of the genre / Ed
Cameron.
        p.   cm.
    Includes bibliographical references and index.

    ISBN 978-0-7864-4771-8
    softcover : 50# alkaline paper ∞

    1. Gothic fiction (Literary genre), English — History and
criticism.   2. Psychology, Pathological, in literature.
3. Deviant behavior in literature.   4. Neuroses in literature.
5.   Psychoses in literature.   6. Psychoanalysis and literature.
I. Title.
PR830.T3C38   2010
823'.0873309353 — dc22   2010030950

British Library cataloguing data are available

Front cover image ©2010 Pictures Now

Manufactured in the United States of America

McFarland & Company, Inc., Publishers
  Box 611, Jefferson, North Carolina 28640
  www.mcfarlandpub.com

Acknowledgments

An earlier version of Chapter 6 appeared in *Studies in the Humanities* 32.2 (2005). Thanks to Indiana University of Pennsylvania Press for permission to reprint that material here. An earlier version of Chapter 1 appeared in *Gothic Studies* 10.2 (2008), and partial versions of chapters 3, 5, and 6 appeared in *Gothic Studies* 5.1 (2003). Thanks to Manchester University Press for permission to reprint portions of that material. For their assistance and support in getting this project past its initial pre–Oedipal phase, I wish to express gratitude to my graduate professors Christopher Fynsk, Brett Levinson, and the late Frederick Garber. I would also like to give sincere thanks to Linda Belau for her meticulous, supportive, and insightful comments on all aspects of the text. Lastly, I would like to thank those whom I surely owe an unconscious debt: Alex Howe, Catherine Peebles, Petar Ramadanovic, Patrick Dove, Sean Kelly, Kevin Cameron, and Todd Lemke.

"The imagination, by thus embodying and turning them to shape, gives an obvious relief to the indistinct and importunate cravings of the will." — William Hazlitt

Table of Contents

Introduction: The Gothic on the Couch

Since Gothic fiction focuses on the seamy side of human behavior, it lends itself to — and begs for — psychoanalytic investigation. As Michelle Massé claims, both the Gothic and psychoanalysis explore the "ostensibly irrational and distempered" passions.[1] Although Freud and Freudian terminology are mentioned in much Gothic criticism, there remains a real lack of any informed analysis of the irrational libidinal passions that are dramatized within the conventions of the Gothic romance. Jokingly, Diane Hoeveler has complained about how the Gothic has been subjected to too many sessions on the psychoanalytic couch.[2] But, in all actuality, there lacks any sustained analysis of the Gothic with regard to the actual clinical side of psychoanalysis — that side of psychoanalysis burdened with the study of the psychopathologies (perversion, the neuroses and psychosis). There is no doubt that time and again, many Gothic villains have been labeled psychopaths and many Gothic heroines have been dubbed hysterics, but the underlying structures of these distinct pathologies are always ignored, producing interpretations ranging from armchair psychology to literary wild psychoanalysis.

However, filling this critical lacuna leads to certain complications. If the following pages offer a psychoanalytic analysis of late eighteenth and early nineteenth-century Gothic fiction, the analysis will lack the transferential relation necessary for a proper analysis because Gothic fiction is text, not subject. As Freud noted years ago, one cannot interpret an analysand's dreams without the analysand's free associations. The process would be, in the words of Jacques-Alain Miller, "disjointed from the analytic experience," as the suitable forum for psychoanalysis.[3] This, of course, doubles the problem. Not only am I, in the following pages, analyzing texts, not analysands, but I am not a trained analyst, at least not a clinically trained psychoanalyst. However, what this study does offer is a close examination and literary analysis of the

1

underside of the Gothic with detailed attention to and a focused knowledge of the clinical categories of psychoanalysis, especially the structures of perversion, neurosis, and psychosis. So, even though my use of the clinical categories will be largely divorced from their originally conceived purpose, they will help me expose what I am figuratively calling the psychopathological structure of the Gothic. This structure, I will argue, is tied to the Gothic's inherent and incessant haunting by its lost past, much in the manner that Freud's most pathological patients were haunted by their own obscure histories.

Paralleling Freud's eventual discovery of the painful and pathological compulsion to repeat in his patients, my analysis attempts to offer a new appreciation of the repetitive nature of a literary genre known for its recurring, overwrought conventions. The present text, therefore, offers a literary analysis of a literary subject by converting the clinical categories of psychoanalysis, with all the potential trouble this might introduce, into fresh tools for understanding what some would consider a diseased and distressed literary genre. It will be remembered that Freud himself credits literary writers with discovering the unconscious, reserving for himself the modest discovery of the method for scientifically studying what had already been revealed by literature.[4] Psychoanalysts have always relied on existing aesthetic narratives, from *Oedipus* and "The Purloined Letter" to *Finnegans Wake*, when presenting their theoretical concepts.[5] This is most likely because, as Robert Rogers has argued, literary writers, just like the neurotic on the couch, think archaically. In other words, literary writers' mental processes "resemble in their content the magical conceptions of primitive superstition."[6] He also claims that this primary-process "mentation" of the literary artist "is largely responsible for the concreteness of symbolic representation which so distinguishes the literary imagination from that of the analytic, discursive thinker."[7] Psychoanalysis, it seems, remains latent within the literary text. Therefore, my text offers a psychoanalytic study of the unconscious as it is revealed by Gothic fiction, that fiction most interested in revealing what is darkly seen. It will also be remembered that even though the unconscious and literature have much in common (especially a penchant for metaphor, metonymy, synecdoche, and the use of tropes in general), they are not identical. As Lionel Trilling has shown, in between "supervenes the social intention."[8] The Gothic writer, in the following study, is revealed as one who objectifies certain aspects of the unconscious, sublimates them, and makes them available for a psychoanalytically-informed literary examination. In the end, this study offers an analysis of several early Gothic romances in the form of literary case studies, revealing their unconscious dimension, even if this dimension is just something of which Gothic authors and Gothic critical studies have been largely unconscious.

Since this study purports to be a textual analysis of the early British Gothic romance, as if the Gothic were itself an analysand, it takes three phenomena seriously: the clinical side of psychoanalysis, the generic conventions of romance, and psychopathology. Of relative importance, therefore, and deserving special attention here, are three recent studies of the Gothic: Dale Townshend's *The Orders of the Gothic*, Fred Botting's *Gothic Romanced*, and David Punter's *Gothic Pathologies*. While the current study is not directly influenced by and does not directly stem from these three important texts, I do retroactively see *The Psychopathology of the Gothic Romance* in an indirect dialogue with these three, especially given their similar interests. Therefore, as part of this introduction, I'd like to briefly distinguish these three Gothic critical studies from the present study.

Dale Townshend's recent text *The Orders of the Gothic: Foucault, Lacan, and the Subject of Gothic Writing, 1764–1820* covers the same historical period as the present study and purports to be the only sustained Lacanian analysis of Gothic fiction. Even though critics like Robert Miles, Jerrold Hogle, Anne Williams, and others have offered psychoanalytically-informed studies of the Gothic, Townshend has indeed broken ground in his study by giving equal seriousness to Lacanian psychoanalysis as he does to the Gothic fiction he examines. Townshend's text shares this interest in Lacanian psychoanalytic theory with the current study, but from my perspective, his text suffers from its institutionalized phobia of anachronism. And this may partially be responsible for his elision of Lacan's clinical categories. His desire to keep his psychoanalytic tendencies reined in by a Foucauldian understanding of historical transformation — his desire, in other words, to wed psychoanalysis and historicism — leads, unfortunately, to a watering down of his text's psychoanalytic energy.[9] In the end, this further leads to some unnecessary confusion of key Lacanian concepts. Not only does his text conflate the subject with subjectivity, but it also erroneously understands the Lacanian notion of the gaze much in the same way that film studies has.[10] In addition, Townshend also seems to conflate the Other *jouissance* with the *jouissance* of the Other and mistakenly translates Lacan's *plus-de-jouir* (surplus *jouissance*) as "excessive" *jouissance*. These misunderstandings help Townshend fit Lacan's concepts into his overriding Foucauldian paradigm, but they fail to remain rigorously honest to the Lacanian field.[11] The Foucauldian paradigm puts too many restrictions on what can be revealed through a Lacanian analysis. My present study hopes to rectify these reductions by maintaining a more dogmatic relation to Lacanian psychoanalytic theory.

Much like the current study, Fred Botting's *Gothic Romanced* is interested in what he calls the "dark, destructive and monstrous elements of the Gothic."

But more importantly, as a point of comparison, Botting's study is dedicated to an analysis of the romance dimension of the Gothic. In his study, Botting notes how Gothic fiction has almost single-handedly revitalized the romance form: "gothic seems to offer curious substance to an almost empty form."[12] Although Botting is also interested in romance's ability to take the reader elsewhere, an "elsewhere at odds with the present," his study differs significantly from the present one in two major ways.[13] First, Botting's text is mostly concerned with current modes of the Gothic (horror film, science fiction, etc.) than it is with the original genre of Gothic literature. Second, his study is not concerned with how the Gothic strategically incorporates the possibilities of romance into its own genre, as is my present study. Rather, he is mostly interested in how different post-modern Gothic writers have taken the Gothic mode and forced a romantic plot onto its otherwise potentially disturbing subject matter, thereby taming its subversive potential. In this manner, Botting is not really concerned with the generic properties and possibilities of romance. For his study, romance is not really a generic category at all; it remains a plot device, pushing and propagating the romantic heterosexual couple as the ideal, normalized union.[14] My study, on the other hand, takes seriously the generic potential of romance and how early Gothic writers used this potential to figuratively mark out a domain — an elsewhere, to use Botting's terminology — to which contemporary novelistic realism remained unconscious.

David Punter's text, *Gothic Pathologies*, is, like my study, fascinated with the madness, paranoia, and other pathologies that seem to run rampant throughout Gothic fiction. Punter believes that the Gothic and psychoanalysis share an interest in dark backgrounds and argues that pathology contaminates order. He focuses on the narcissism of Frankenstein, the vengeance of Heathcliff, the psychosis of Norman Bates, the paranoia of Caleb Williams, the hatred of Ligeia, amongst other Gothic pathological disturbances, and sees these pathological elements as symptoms of social anxieties. Unlike the present study, however, Punter's examination of the pathological remains largely Jungian and is explicitly anti-Lacanian. Also, Punter's understanding of the pathological lacks any clinical precision, as he equates pathology to the passions in general but not to any clinical structures.[15] Rather than focusing on the passions in general, this current study attempts to link the narrative structures of certain early Gothic romances to recognizable clinical psychoanalytical structures, of which the passions are just symptomatic.

Chapter 1 begins with an examination of the "Preface" to the second edition of *The Castle of Otranto*. My objective in the first chapter is to demonstrate how the Gothic is inherently split between allegorical-realist and romance-imaginative strains. To this end, I consider how the divided nature of the

Gothic was built into the very structure of the text that founded the genre. Focusing on Horace Walpole's "Preface," where he inaugurates a new form of hybrid narrative — a combining of ancient improbability with modern realism — I argue that this distinction has led to the current division in the critical reception of the Gothic novel between allegory and romance. The allegorical appreciation is carried out most effectively by well-known critics like Franco Moretti, Judith Halberstam, and other representatives of Marxist and New Historical critical approaches. These allegorical critics treat allegory as a mode and argue that, because of their intrinsic outlandishness, Gothic narratives suggest a doubleness of intention and an encoded meaning lurking beneath the literal surface of the plot. As with most allegory, this double meaning inevitably relates to the social importance of Gothic themes. With this approach, Frankenstein's creature can be allegorically interpreted as the monstrous emergence of the organized proletariat, Dracula can be understood as the monopolized consolidation of capital taking place throughout late nineteenth-century Europe, and Mr. Hyde can be construed as the "foreigner" that fuels xenophobia.

After summarizing the allegorical reception of the Gothic, I argue that, since this type of reception favors a reading of the Gothic along the parameters of modern realism (one of the halves of Walpole's hybrid formula), it unavoidably reduces Gothic excess and uncanniness to a realist understanding and, thereby, dismisses what is sublime and anxiety-producing about the romance side of the Gothic. Therefore, this chapter further argues that only a critical reception that interrogates how the spirit of romance (the other half of Walpole's formula) lies embedded in these narratives can achieve a truly aesthetic appreciation of the Gothic. Taking seriously the claim made by most early Gothic novelists that their works were "romances," Chapter 1 highlights the essential sublime uncanniness of the Gothic novel as figuring that which makes all realistic interpretation falter, what Freud referred to as *das Ding*. Finally, this chapter illustrates the crucial connection between the Gothic's use of the sublime and the artistic practice of sublimation by showing how the crucial exploitation of the past and use of the sublime in Gothic romance figures a pre-symbolic mode of significance that pays homage to a fundamental anxiety that is best revealed through the Gothic dramatization of psychopathological behavior.

Chapter 2 focuses on the structure of the early British Gothic romance and how this structure parallels Freud's notion of the uncanny. The chapter begins with an examination of Freud's notion and essay on *das Unheimlich* in order to concentrate on the Gothic's obsession with the past. In order to further consider the Gothic romance's divergence from the more realistic novel, this chapter primarily draws out the implications of the role of medieval romances in the make-up of the Gothic universe. Following Northrop Frye's claim that every Gothic is always already a Gothic revival, Chapter 2 argues that the Gothic romance's obsession with the past should be viewed as anticipating Freud's aesthetics of the frightening that he outlines in "The 'Uncanny.'" This chapter, therefore, details how the past functions in the Gothic's structurally uncanny universe as a figure signifying not something other but reality's own inconsistency with itself.

While laying out this argument, I also detail the change in aesthetic taste that slowly took place in British thought and literature during the course of the eighteenth century, highlighting the move away from an adoration of Horatian order and probability toward a growing interest in a Longinian celebration of enthusiasm and the marvelous. By detailing the writings of Joseph Addison, Edmund Burke, Richard Hurd and the general renewed interest in the medieval and the barbarous, I illustrate how the dismissive claim that the literature of the Middle Ages was childish, immature, and unpolished was rearticulated throughout the eighteenth century into an esteem for these so-called antiquated romances' ability to recall archaic images and feelings from childhood. This esteem for the uncivilized eventually led to a desire for more imaginative literature and for a desire on the part of the Gothic romancers to return to an earlier age which should have remained dead and buried (Freud's definition of the uncanny).

Chapter 3 is the first chapter devoted to the Gothic's relation to psychopathology. Focusing on the inaugural Gothic romance, Horace Walpole's *The Castle of Otranto*, this chapter illustrates how Walpole's attempt to blend fanciful romance with contemporary novelistic technique creates a narrative where the past cannot be separated from the present. This type of confluence enacted by Walpole's narrative parallels the very structure of perversion in which repression is too weak to delineate a strongly demarcated past. Because of the perverse structure of Walpole's romance, his narrative overflows with a chaotic and infantile use of the sublime. In a sense, *Otranto*'s use of the supernatural and sublime remains polymorphously perverse, in the Freudian sense of the term. Not until the Gothic matures in the writings of Ann Radcliffe and Matthew Lewis is the overflowing enjoyment of Walpole's early Gothic romance regulated into a more meaningful pattern; that is, the Gothic's *jouissance* gets sublimated into *jouis*sense (enjoyment into enjoy*meant*).

In order to aid the reader in understanding the Gothic sublime's relation to perversion in Walpole's romance, I discuss the details of perversion both as a Freudian pathology and as a Lacanian structure, specifically perversion's relation to enjoyment. Paradoxically, *The Castle of Otranto* is often seen as a romance that is both an immature Gothic narrative and the one Gothic narrative that possesses all the gadgets and machinery that sustained the genre for the following 60 years. This first Gothic romance seems to have it all, but its sublime machinery remains undeveloped and chaotic. As with the perverse subject, enjoyment seems to run rampant. Without a firm anchoring point, Walpole's romance remains an immature jumble of all the future Gothic symbols, symbols that as of 1764 do not yet signify because of their undeveloped nature. I end the chapter by arguing that Walpole's Gothic romance appears to exist in a sort of pre-genital phase in comparison to the more mature romances of Ann Radcliffe and Matthew Lewis.

Chapter 4 focuses on the early development of the Gothic romance as it matured in the 1790s. Following the Freudian claim that sexual differentiation is prompted by the completion of the Oedipal complex, this chapter draws a parallel between the development of Gothic romance and the development of the psyche. Focusing on the Lacanian notion of sexual difference, this chapter illustrates how the two fundamental sublime affects of the 1790s — terror and horror — are two separate reactions to the completion of the Oedipal complex necessary for maturation. Exploring the significance of the difference between terror and horror, I argue that the Gothic aesthetic, which split into these two fairly distinct schools of writing during the genre's maturation period of the 1790s, occurs along the lines of sexual difference.

I begin this examination with an analysis of Anna Laetitia Barbauld's essay "On the Pleasure Derived from Objects of Terror" and Ann Radcliffe's posthumously published essay "On the Supernatural in Poetry" in order to demonstrate how the terror/horror aesthetic split became more pronounced within both late eighteenth-century criticism and literature. From here, the chapter draws a correlation between this split and the Gothic sublime in general. Starting with Edmund Burk's early text on the beautiful and the sublime (the text most Gothic romancers were familiar with), this chapter ultimately turns to Immanuel Kant's *Critique of Judgment* in order to more convincingly situate the dual complexities of the 1790s Gothic sublime. Because Kant formulates both the mathematical and the dynamical sublime, I forge a connection between these two modalities, the Gothic sublime split between terror and horror, and the split between the feminine and masculine sides of sexual difference as outlined in Lacan's *Seminar XX*. From here, the chapter concludes by illustrating precisely how these parallel antinomies, for my purposes, ultimately correlate to a gendered psychopathological separation in neurosis between hysteria and obsessional neurosis.

Turning specifically to the terror Gothic, Chapter 5 centers primarily on Radcliffe's early Gothic romance *The Sicilian Romance*. I read the "explained supernatural," which Radcliffe mastered, as a manifestation of the inherent impossibility pertaining to the logic of the mathematical sublime that Kant details. My point is to illustrate how the "non-existent" supernatural of the terror Gothic points to what could be formulated as a feminine logic of the sublime. Within my close analysis of Radcliffe's early romance, I detail how her narrative moves from hysteria to a signifying of feminine enjoyment; that is, what Lacan calls the Other *jouissance*.

After elucidating the specific structure of hysteria from a psychoanalytic perspective, the chapter interprets Ann Radcliffe's early Gothic *The Sicilian Romance* (a Radcliffe work that has yet to receive much critical attention) within Freud's comments on "family romance" and alongside his famous case study *Dora*. By drawing on the parallels between Dora and Julia, Radcliffe's heroine, the chapter highlights Radcliffe's staging of her narrative as a fantasy made to supplement the insufficiency of the paternal law. Pursuing a Lacanian reading, I argue that it is precisely this insufficiency from which the typical hysteric suffers. Ultimately, my discussion demonstrates that the real sublime terror both haunting and personified by the typical Gothic heroine revolves around her persistence beyond the signifiers that define her being in relation to man ("daughter," "wife," "whore," "mother," etc.).

Chapter 6 focuses on Matthew Lewis's role in perfecting horror Gothic. In this chapter, I place the horror Gothic alongside Kant's formulation of the dynamical sublime as I attempt to illustrate how this particular Gothic form erupted as a reaction to the uncertainties of the terror school of Gothic romance. The chapter, therefore, focuses on Matthew Lewis's *The Monk*. This 1796 romance's shift from terror to horror parallels the classic transference from impossibility to prohibition enacted by the obsessional neurotic. By housing the sublime in the actual supernatural, I argue, Lewis attempts to cover over the indetermination opened up by Radcliffe and the terror Gothic. Following the logic of the dynamic sublime, Lewis's horror Gothic externalizes the sublime's indeterminateness into specific supernatural entities and grue-some details that can be located outside the proper boundaries of the self. In order to supplement this argument, Chapter 6 further considers how Lacan's notion of phallic enjoyment functions as a compromise of the Other enjoy-ment, which is documented in Chapter 5.

After discussing the specific clinical structure of obsessional neurosis, the form of neurosis from which most male neurotics suffer, this chapter analyzes Lewis's Gothic romance in relation to Freud's "Rat Man" case study, his most important analysis of obsessional neurosis. Throughout this analysis, Chapter 6 ultimately argues that *The Monk*'s protagonist is actually Lorenzo, a character who plays a seemingly tangential role within the narrative. I argue that the lusty monk Ambrosio and the faithful brother-in-law Raymond, who play the more active roles within the romance's split narrative, signify Lorenzo's obsessional conflict between his sensual drives and his affectionate desires. Chapters 5 and 6, in the end, illustrate how the early English Gothic romance of the 1790s constructed an aesthetic form rooted in an internal antinomy between feminine hysteria and masculine obsession brought to light by Radcliffe's and Lewis's particular strategic use of the Gothic sublime.

Chapter 7, the concluding chapter, develops the relation between the Gothic and psychosis through an examination of the main character and the structure of the narrative of James Hogg's Gothic romance *The Private Memoirs and Confessions of a Justified Sinner*. After providing a general account of the clinical structure of psychosis by introducing some insights from Freud's case study on Schreber, this chapter argues that the confusion between self and other that characterizes psychosis is sublimely dramatized by Hogg's narrative through the relation between Robert Wringhim and his hallucinatory doppelgänger, Gil-Martin.

Because of his viciously pious mother, his strict Calvinist upbringing, and his lack of a strong father, Wringhim falls into a psychotic state shortly after finding himself one of the predestined. During his psychotic break, Wringhim's ego defenses break down and Gil-Martin acts as the uncastrated Wringhim, committing all the heinous crimes Wringhim documents. Since castration never separates Wringhim from the Other's desire, he is constantly bombarded by the Other's enjoyment, which takes the form of Gil-Martin's sublime crime spree. Within this virtual narrative of a psychotic, Hogg indirectly reveals the underlying cause of such Gothic behavior.

By illustrating how early Gothic writers provided an artistic glimpse into the irrational passions most of us keep hidden, this study privileges an aesthetic appreciation of the titillating psychological insights of early Gothic romance over a strictly historical appreciation. Through critical attention to the romance dimension of the Gothic, this study opens up the possibility of envisioning how the Gothic intimates a feeling beyond the pleasure regulated by the reality principle toward the type of pathological and paradoxically painful pleasure associated with the sentiment of the sublime and what Jacques Lacan would call enjoyment (*jouissance*). Through a Lacanian analysis of the use of the sublime by Horace Walpole, Ann Radcliffe, Matthew Lewis, and James Hogg, this text attempts to uncover the latent structures of perversion, hysteria, obsessional neurosis, and psychosis, respectively, in order to argue that the romance strain of the genre reveals the Gothic sublimation of irrational libidinal drives.[16]

Freud claims that sublimation provides a socially acceptable escape valve for libidinal energy that would otherwise materialize in socially inappropriate ways. The Gothic, therefore, provides one avenue in which socially unacceptable drives are elevated and sublimated into socially acceptable literary artworks. So, rather than reading the hidden, repressed meaning behind the surface façade of Gothic romances, this study interprets the structure of various early Gothic romances as sublimations of the very drives that take center stage in the various psychopathologies. In this way, I hope to illustrate Lacan's claim that literature not only paves the way for the psychoanalyst, it also advances psychoanalytic theory.[17] Drawing a parallel between the Freudian and Lacanian analysis of psychical development and the rise of the Gothic as a genre, this study illustrates not only that the emergence and maturation of the Gothic can be viewed from Freudo-Lacanian insights, but also that different romances within the genre reflect certain psychopathological structures depending on their relation to the genre's origin.

Through a critical approach sensitive to the aesthetic dimension of Gothic romance, this text ultimately argues that criticism should recognize the sublimatory capacity of Gothic fiction and of literature in general, a capacity that extends to the reader the opportunity to view what is normally hidden and only darkly seen.

1

The Two-Headed
Gothic Monster

Critics have always noted the close relation between the sublime monstrosity of Gothic fiction and the uncanny as a particular form of the frightening. Not only did Freud develop his understanding of the uncanny directly from his interpretation of E.T.A. Hoffman's Gothic tale "The Sandman,"[1] but Harold Bloom blatantly claims both that Freud's essay "The 'Uncanny'" outlines Freud's theory of the sublime and "is the only major contribution that the twentieth century has made to the aesthetics of the sublime."[2] Likewise, David Morris has argued that relative to Burke, Freud's speculation on the uncanny "offers us a much improved theory of terror" that "helps to explain why sublimity is a vital, integral part of the gothic novel."[3] Following Morris's famous claim that the Gothic functions as an explicit critique of Burke's empirical understanding of the sublime, Vijay Mishra contends that "the Gothic rewrites the sublime and prefigures its theorization as the uncanny."[4] In addition, Andrew Smith has convincingly maintained that the Gothic sublime "represents a nascent form of the uncanny."[5] Dale Townshend has asserted the psychological importance of the Gothic sublime by claiming that the Gothic "modifies the sublime into something altogether more psychological, something entirely less corporeal, indeed something more conceptually akin with the Freudian uncanny."[6] And most recently, Kathy Justice Gentile has referred to the sublime as the uncanny's "more revered sibling."[7]

Along with all these arguments in favor of understanding the Gothic sublime as at least a latent form of the uncanny lies the supposition that the late eighteenth century fostered a favorable environment for the literary development of the uncanny. Terry Castle, in fact, maintains that the uncanny as an aesthetic trope originates in the eighteenth century: "The very psychic and cultural transformations that led to the subsequent glorification of the period as an age of reason or enlightenment — the aggressive rationalist imperatives of the epoch — also produced, like a kind of toxic side effect, a new human experience of strangeness, anxiety, bafflement, and intellectual impasse."[8] She essentially follows Freud's argument that literature offers more uncanny effects than life itself because in real life "natural causes and the laws of probability" (the reality principle) tend to be in control.[9] In his analysis of the uncanny, however, Freud intentionally focuses on a Gothic text precisely because of Gothic literature's capability and drive to produce and present fictive excess. The Gothic's fictive excess, therefore, is sublime because, even like Longinus's "loftiness" or John Dennis's "enthusiasm," it represents that which is by nature beyond representation. However, unlike, the pre–Gothic sublime, the Gothic sublime as a "toxic side effect" demarcates the distorted form of the return of the transcendental realm once it has been supposedly surmounted by reason. Unlike the religious sublime of John Dennis and many Graveyard poets from earlier in the century, which, through its failure to represent, evokes God as that which is both transcendental and inaccessible, the Gothic sublime negatively reveals that which is immanent but inaccessible, that which has been repressed through "the historic internalization of rationalist protocols."[10] With the Gothic, the aesthetic mode of the sublime no longer articulates the otherworldly; rather, it reveals the inherent inconsistency and incompletion of the newly emerging immanent-oriented view of the world. As Castle concludes, the Gothic sublime plunges us into a "hag-ridden world of the unconscious."[11] Or, in the words of Morris, the Gothic sublime is "utterly without transcendence," and it "takes us deep within rather than beyond the human sphere."[12]

From the uncanny resemblance between the huge helmet that mysteriously falls from the sky and the helmet on the statue of Alfonso in *The Castle of Otranto*, as well as the uncanny resemblance between Theodore and Alfonso himself, to the terrifying "explained-supernatural" perfected by Ann Radcliffe and the birth of the sci-fi creature that acts out Victor's unconscious desires in *Frankenstein*, there is no shortage of uncanny elements even within the early history of the Gothic.[13] The most sublime moments of Gothic fiction occur when something that should have remained in the past, something that should have remained dead and buried, has returned in the present, bewildering characters and creating disequilibrium in the narrative itself. The opening prophesy in *Otranto*, the "dead" mother in Radcliffe's narratives, Victor's missed "mummy" in *Frankenstein*, the aristocracy in *Dracula*, youth in *Dorian Gray*, vaguely medieval settings in early Gothic narratives, and Catholic superstition in many more Gothic tales all testify to the Gothic sublime's drive to return to an earlier state of things. The Gothic has always used alien figures that are obscure yet somehow intimate in order to produce its sublime effects.

This baffling yet intimate nature of the uncanny sublime in Gothic fiction produces a seductive craving in both characters and critics alike to tame its radical uncertainty with rational understanding. And even though, in the words of Mishra, Gothic texts "project a vision of the world that the mind can grasp only if it forgoes for the moment the law of reason,"[14] many critical approaches to Gothic fiction have concerned themselves with interpretations that reduce the Gothic's uncanny sublime dimension to a biographical, political, historical, or psychological understanding, thereby minimizing any aesthetic impact. But how should we understand the critic's desire to assign meaning onto the uncanny sublime when it appears in the aesthetic productions of the Gothic? How many of us have, for instance, left the theater after viewing a horror movie and immediately, or at least before the still of bedtime, spread a symbolic meaning onto the central uncanny elements of the film?[15] "*The Exorcist* is clearly about teenage rebellion and the horrors of rearing an adolescent girl." "John Carpenter's *People Under the Stairs* is clearly about the rising rate of poverty and the increasing number of people living under the poverty line during the Reagan/Bush years." "*Poltergeist* is clearly about ex-hippie guilt over joining the Reagan corp." Since the point where the uncanny sublime emerges is always immediately seized by an overwhelming amount of meaning, it can stand for everything culture has to repress: the proletariat, sexuality, other cultures, alternative ways of living, heterogeneity, the other. It is, after all, a site where the ideological battle for the hegemony of meaning takes place. But, because there is a certain arbitrariness to the content that can be projected onto this uncanny element, any projection of meaning results from the reduction of the uncanny (as that to which symbolization is structurally inadequate) to symbolic meaning. Therefore, because it is possible to give a multifarious array of meanings to these uncanny sublime elements, meaning itself may not be the point.

The suggestion that the uncanny elements of Gothic works of literature contain insights and convey meaning beyond the text itself actually predates the formation of the Gothic proper. For example, as early as 1732 in an edition of the anti–Walpole journal *The Craftsman*, an anonymous writer, in his essay "Political Vampyres," reports how a one Mr. D'anvers solved a dispute between a "beautiful young Lady" and a "grave Doctor of Physick" over the existence of vampires.[16] While the former disputant, who is described as "an Admirer of strange Occurrences," adamantly insists on the existence of such monstrous creatures, the enlightened physician simply claims that such marvelous creatures are contrary to all known philosophical principles and in violation of "the Laws of Nature."[17] In a seeming paradox, Mr. D'anvers solves the quarrel, according to the reporter, by agreeing with the Lady as far as the very existence of vampires goes, but also by agreeing with the physician "that an inanimate

Corpse cannot perform any vital Functions."[18] Since tales of vampires emanate from the Eastern region of the world, D'anvers argues, outlandish supernatural tales are the result of the East's "Allegorical Style": "The States of Hungary are in subjection to the Turks and Germans, and are governed by a pretty hard Hand; which obliges them to couch all their Complaints under Figures."[19] Therefore, D'anvers concludes, the tale of the Eastern vampire that recently made it into the British press must be a symbolic representation of a corrupt minister who "carries his oppression beyond the Grave" by "entailing a Per-petuity of Taxes, which must gradually drain the Body politick of its Blood and Spirits."[20] The anonymous reporter's readers would not have overlooked the similar financial corruption of Sir Robert Walpole and other British min-isterial tyrants so shortly after the South Sea bubble. However, in 1732 this manner of taming the fabulous tale by spreading a symbolic meaning onto the supernatural content is undoubtedly a neoclassical endeavor, especially the reduction of the supernatural literary tale to anti–Whig political allegory. But how should one treat the similar symbolic spreading of meaning onto the Gothic uncanny after the establishment of the Gothic in the second half of the eighteenth century when writers were actively, if only indirectly, devaluing the neo-classical literary value given to wit, which cannot offer us more than is possible to know, in favor of the sentiment of the uncanny sublime, which itself stages emptiness?

In our own period of Gothic critical revival, the allegorical interpretation of the strange case of the Hungarian vampire by Mr. D'anvers is itself most insightfully revived by various new historical and cultural approaches that attempt to highlight the ideological dimension of Gothic literature. However, unlike D'anvers' interpretation of the Hungarian vampire above, current Gothic criticism does not bother to categorize its object of investigation as generically allegorical. Rather, these numerous critics partake in the interpre-tive art of allegoresis, the technique where critics or readers assert a meaning to a literary work as if it is an allegory, regardless of any hints or explicit state-ments by the author that the work is indeed generically an allegory.[21] Although Northrop Frye maintains that all literary interpretation (precisely because lit-erature speaks indirectly) amounts to allegorical interpretation,[22] there is also an interpretive strategy common within the last few decades that exists, to use Peter Berek's words, "not simply as a way of preserving canonical texts, but as a way of displaying the explanatory power of a system of ideas which the critic holds to be more important."[23] Whether the system of ideas is Marx-ist, psychoanalytic, postcolonial, poststructuralist, feminist, or queer is less important than the fact that the system of ideas exists independently of the literary text under investigation. In this manner, allegoresis both assumes that there exists a general meaning beyond the particular meaning of the literary text and attempts to modernize the literary text.[24]

In various ways critics have lately come up with some ingenious ways of interpreting the uncanny monstrosity endemic in the Gothic form. Most famously, Franco Moretti, using a straightforward Marxist analysis, has illustrated how the uncanny monsters of *Frankenstein* and *Dracula* serve a discernable ideological function by allegorically representing the proletariat and monopoly capital, respectively.[25] Drawing strongly on New Historical interpretive strategies, Judith Halberstam has influentially argued that Gothic anomalies like Dracula and Mr. Hyde should be understood allegorically as the Jew of anti–Semitism and as a negative reference for what passes as Englishness proper, thereby illustrating how Victorian Gothic fiction fixes horror elsewhere and serves the emerging dominant bourgeois xenophobic ideology.[26] Similarly, Stephen Arata has interpreted Mr. Hyde as a figure for the degeneracy and decadence that causes patriarchal anxiety; Burton Hatlen has figured Dracula as the sexual deviancy and licentiousness of the aristocracy that horrifies the Victorian middle class; and Christopher Craft has demonstrated how Dracula could be read as a figure for the breakdown and transformation of traditional gender roles occurring at the turn of the century.[27] From a postcolonial perspective, Kim Ian Michasiw and Stephanie Burley, in their own way, have read Charlotte Dacre's *Zofloya* as a critique of racial stereotypes about Africans; Massimiliano Demata has illustrated how William Beckford's *Vathek* can be understood as an anti–Orientalist allegory; and Renée Bergland has shown how early American Gothic fiction allegorically displays how American literature is terrorized by the haunting figure of the Native American.[28] From a cultural studies angle, there have also been numerous critical investigations illustrating the Gothic's dramatization of racial, gender and queer relations.[29]

Whether it is a corrupt Italian Catholic priest who cavorts with evil or the troglodytic, excessively hedonistic Mr. Hyde, the Gothic uncanny is often critically linked to an actual other that such novels bind to the perverse or the foreign. Gothic fiction, according to this type of allegoresis, is the most telling site in which to locate precisely what is not English and not native. The Gothic uncanny, by definition, then, is what cannot be imagined as fitting into the community. The Gothic's problem, it seems, is always that of the monster in our midst. From Catholic superstition and French Revolutionary terror in the early days of the Gothic novel to the Jew of anti–Semitism or the deviant sexualities of the Victorian Gothic, the sublime monstrous is thereby always fueling the fear of some actual historical other.

Most of these allegorical interpretations of Gothic repression and its uncanny return, focus on revealing the "true" locus of fear: the proletariat, monopoly capital, the Jew, the foreign, the racial other, the homosexual, etc. Within Moretti's allegorical account, for instance, this connection does not so much highlight the fact that we tend to desire what we fear, and vice versa, but rather the fact that we tend to desire and fear the same object. But since this emotional ambivalence is difficult to live with, we tend "to *repress*, unconsciously, one of the two affective states in conflict, the one that is socially more illicit."[30] Therefore, Moretti concludes, "from the repression arises fear."[31] In order to support this conclusion, he cites Freud as an authority: "'Every affect belonging to an emotional impulse, whatever its kind, is transformed, if it is repressed, into anxiety.'"[32] Then, Moretti draws a further conclusion: "And fear breaks out when — for whatever reason — this repressed impulse returns and thrusts itself upon the mind.... Fear, in other words, coincides with the 'return of the repressed.'"[33] Moretti might be correct in claiming that repression breeds fear, but he fails to acknowledge Freud's fundamental insight here: that what is repressed is not something fearful, but rather anxiety itself.[34] Fear is only a symptom of anxiety; it is what anxiety is transformed into when it is repressed. Fear, in other words, is always a fear of something, and therefore it is already a secondary formation, displacing anxiety as that which does not have a proper object. So, when Moretti and other allegorical critics provide a metaphorical object of fear (the proletariat, monopoly capital, etc.) as a substitute for the Gothic uncanny sublime, they tend to compromise the more foundational anxiety that is figured by Gothic narratives themselves.[35] In other words, when Moretti claims that "the repressed returns, ... but disguised as a monster" and then continues to tell us precisely what the monstrous is a figure for, he assumes that Gothic monstrosity, as a figure, has a specific content proper to it, one of which the novelist is more or less oblivious. Here he commits the same neoclassical crime as Mr. D'anvers: he flattens out the sublime dimension of the Gothic by ignoring the possibility that Gothic uncanniness may be a figure for that which can only be felt but never known (anxiety as a sentiment).[36] In *Seminar X*, Lacan claims that anxiety never deceives; it is real. Figures, on the other hand, are symbolic and are deceptive by nature. While discussing the intimate connection between the uncanny and anxiety, Lacan also argues that anxiety is the result of the lack of lack. If the lack necessary for the symbolic transmission of meaning, and, thereby, the space necessary for allegoresis, is itself lacking, one is confronted by the real claustrophobic feeling of anxiety.[37] Therefore, if a critic avoids allegorizing and allows Gothic figuration to pronounce its own failure in symbolizing, he or she will more readily bring to light the inherent failure of symbolism that broaches the aesthetic anxiety put in motion by the Gothic.

Since one could conceivably write a novel, or a political pamphlet for that matter, expressing fear of proletariat organization, fear of the monopolizing of capital, or fear of the foreigner without resorting to monstrous figuration, or since one can express these fears in a figure that is less monstrous, it might be more aesthetically honest to read the uncanny monstrosity of the Gothic as figuring the sublime — that which can only be articulated in a negative fashion, as that which makes all interpretation falter. When Moretti interprets Frankenstein's creature as a monstrous embodiment of the fear of the proletariat, he essentially testifies to the success of Shelley's metaphor. However, if read as a sublime figure, Shelley's monster can only function as a failed figure; it can only be read as a figure that demonstrates its own inability to express what it stands in for, displaying the very empty space of symbolic inscription that is responsible for the aesthetic anxiety that is evoked by the uncanny.

Towards the end of his analysis, Moretti claims that since the Gothic transforms the fear of the future proletariat and monopoly capital "into other fears, so that readers do not have to face up to what might really frighten them," the Gothic functions ideologically because "it distorts reality."[38] "It is," he adds, "a work of mystification."[39] Overemphasizing the contrived moral, happy endings of Gothic novels, Moretti criticizes both *Frankenstein* and *Dracula* because within their narratives, "the wound [of monstrous fear] is healed."[40] Ironically, this is precisely the crime that allegoresis' own metaphoric interpretations commit as they substitute a particular fearful object for the essentially contourless sublime object of anxiety. By allegorizing Gothic monstrosity, by spreading a symbolic understanding over the real dread of anxiety, critics essentially heal the wound opened by the Gothic sublime, transforming the allegorical drive of criticism into another form of mystification.[41] After all, the point of ideology — and the ideology of Gothic criticism appears guiltier than that of Gothic literature itself— is not to offer a point of escape from reality, but to offer an explanation or interpretation of reality as an escape from something more traumatic.[42]

Symptomatic of this critical displacement is Judith Halberstam's misreading of a passage from Freud. Halberstam offers the following claim made by Freud in *Studies on Hysteria*: "[trauma] acts like a foreign body which, long after its entry, must continue to be regarded as an agent that is still at work."[43] While correct in noticing the remarkable connection between trauma acting as a foreign body in hysteria and the role of the monstrous in the Gothic, Halberstam all too quickly substantiates actual foreigners out of, what for Freud is, a simile for an intimate inconsistency. Even though Freud is concerned with how this inherent foreignness surfaces as a sexual disturbance because we as humans are ontologically sexual, Halberstam reads this foreign-ness as a sexual outsider who surfaces in the Gothic as a racial pariah, a national outcast, or a class outlaw. Halberstam's error lies in literalizing Freud's figure, thereby assuming Freud is speaking somehow about actual foreigners. How-ever, Gothic novels are less concerned with what is properly English than they are concerned with the structure of subreption — where an idea that can never be experienced is falsely represented as if it were a possible object of experience. The uncanny monstrous manifestations that proliferate in Gothic fiction should be seen in this light. What is really foreign in the Gothic novel, I would argue, is that which is most intimate, the uncanny nature of the subject itself. To interpret the monstrous as the Jew of anti–Semitism, or the non–English national, is to remain on the level of fantastic projection and, thereby, remain oblivious to the formation and functioning of the fantasy surface itself.

One has to wonder whose desire is really being articulated in reading Dracula or Mr. Hyde as figures of the Jew of anti–Semitism or the disgusting foreigner. This particular mode of cultural criticism creates its own external Gothic monster, Stoker's or Stevenson's novel, as the locus of its own hidden desire. Why not, for instance, read Stoker's novel as a *critique* of the logic of anti–Semitism, as a sort of Gothic unveiling of the dirty underside of nation-alism? Is there any strong evidence in Stoker's novel that would preclude this alternative reading? This is precisely where the interest of the Gothic novel lies. Nowhere in *Frankenstein* is the creature explicitly marked as a figure of the nascent working class; nowhere in *Dracula* is the vampire specified as a Jew; and nowhere in *Dr. Jekyll and Mr. Hyde* is Hyde directly linked to deviant homosexuality. This is the first lesson of the power of literary discourse — especially sublime literary discourse: by seducing the reader to fill in the blanks of its indirect discourse, Gothic literature forces the reader to see his or her own desire presented on the pages right in front of him or her.[44] In the allegorical critics' insistence in locating the ideological meanings of the mon-strous manifestations in Gothic literature, in their insistence on reading alle-gorical meaning into what are otherwise monstrously sublime texts, they all too quickly turn the inherent aesthetic anxiety of these literary works into a fear that is easier to contain and criticize.[45] Ironically, allegoresis does to the Gothic novel what the critic claims the Gothic does to the foreigner.

In an essay by Slavoj Žižek that Judith Halberstam herself criticizes, Žižek offers the following uncanny insight about the role of the phantom from the *Phantom of the Opera*:

> The sexual relationship is, in itself, hindered, and the "phantom" qua object does nothing but materialize this "original" impossibility, this

inherent hindrance; the "perspective error" consists in conceiving him as a stumbling block to the emergence of the "full" sexual relationship as if, without this troublesome intruder, the sexual relationship would be possible in its intact fullness.[46]

This role of the phantasmic external hindrance is precisely the role of the Gothic villain in any of its forms, but it is a role that the Gothic unveils more than it promotes. Therefore, it is perhaps more correct to assume that the Jew of the anti–Semitic fantasy, for instance, is a typical Gothic villain than the reverse. The Gothic, as an agent exposing the hidden, reveals the buried psychic mechanism of xenophobia, the process of projecting an external hindrance to account for an inherent impossibility. The Gothic, it would seem, only promotes xenophobia to those that resist this exposure.

The strength of Žižek's essay lies in its unwillingness to succumb too rigidly to an allegorical accounting for the Gothic uncanny. He claims that the horrifying power of fascination that pertains to the sublime itself remains outside the formal symbolic moment and resists absorption into meaning. His aesthetic accounting shows how the uncanny manifests something in reality that has to remain incongruous with reality, so reality can maintain a semblance of coherence. But this thing that must remain structurally left out of any account of reality can only show up in the form of something otherworldly, leaving a stain on reality. And according to Žižek, this stain in the very heart of reality is ultimately the "objective correlate" of the subject itself: "By means of anamorphotic stains, 'reality' indexes the presence of the subject."[47] He continues by insisting that the emergence of this kind of stain — the uncanny sublime of Gothic fiction — emerges in the epoch when representations of reality can no longer bind the subject to that reality. And this severing of the subject from the symbolic meaning is, following Žižek, the constitutive gesture of the Enlightenment. The uncanny, as it appears in later Enlightenment literature, specifically in what is commonly referred to as the Gothic, is the mode by which the subject of the Enlightenment procures his or her "impossible positive existence."[48] When one substantiates this monstrous or uncanny stain by grafting a symbolic meaning onto it, then the place of its inscription disappears. The symbolic understanding promoted by materialist and historicist-minded allegoresis is an attempt, albeit an inevitably failed one, to fully account for a narrative structure whose very monstrous features are trying to prevent such totalization, and it is a means of keeping the uncanny at bay.[49] As Lacan would say, allegoresis is an attempt to colonize the field of *das Ding* with imaginary schemes.[50]

Further elucidating the relation of the external to the internal established by the uncanny sublime, Mladen Dolar claims that the uncanny actually blurs the distinction between interior and exterior by making them coincident. He agrees with Jacques-Alain Miller that the uncanny (what Miller calls "extimacy") is simultaneously the intimate kernel and the foreign body. Since extimacy is located where the most intimate interiority corresponds with the exterior in a manner that provokes horror and anxiety, it is *unheimlich*. Furthering Freud's analysis of the uncanny, Dolar illustrates how the uncanny "is the irruption of the real into 'homely,' commonly accepted reality."[51] The uncanny, therefore, is nothing other than the emergence within symbolization of what Lacan calls the real, which is why in Gothic fiction it assumes such a sublime force. This emergence puts the status of both the subject and objective reality into question. It marks the non-functioning function of *jouissance* within symbolic space.[52] Dolar points to the paradoxical nature of Freud's attempt to situate the uncanny as both a universal and as a particular historical rupture brought about by the Enlightenment. He notes that, with the rise of modernity and the removal of the realm of the sacred and transcendental, "the uncanny became unplaceable; it became uncanny in the strict sense."[53] Because popular culture is always extremely sensitive to historical shifts, Dolar claims that Gothic fiction uncannily gives one all the ghosts and undead which one might have expected to have been long since buried. Therefore, the uncanny is produced by the rise of modernity. What seems to be a "leftover" is actually a product of modernity, its underside. Without a transcendental realm, Gothic fiction, it seems, emerges in order to provide an aesthetic space to situate the uncanny.

Critical desire to project a meaningful content onto uncanny figures and the seductive interpretations this desire results in not only alleviate our immediate interpretive anxiety but also attempt to make the symbolic understanding consistent. Psychoanalysis, however, realizes that there is a fundamental schism between the object of knowledge and the object of terror. Therefore, no amount of knowledge about the sublime object, no amount of interpreting the uncanny, can completely tame it. According to Dolar, "the important thing from a Lacanian point of view ... is that while this content is indeed always present in the uncanny to a greater or lesser degree, it doesn't constitute it."[54] And ideology is thus what consists of a social attempt to integrate the uncanny, to make it not only conscious but also consistent with ideology's own conceptual symbolic space. Again, ideology does not offer us an escape from social reality; rather, it offers us the social reality itself as an escape from the distressing real. In other words, the desire to give metaphorical or allegorical meaning to the sublime, even as an attempt to expose the power relation underlying its formation, stays within the confines of the pleasure principle; however, the uncanny, just like *jouissance*, lies beyond the pleasure principle.[55] Reading the sublime figures of Gothic fiction as symbols for something that can also be presented literally — as is the case with most allegorical interpretations — treats the Gothic as symptomatic of its time and sometimes even as confirming the prevailing convictions of the culture that produces it. But Freud maintained that psychic drives emerge in two different manners: either indirectly through repression as symptoms or directly through sublimation. If read as symptoms, then the Gothic uncanny can be accurately read allegorically; Victor Frankenstein's creature can be arguably understood as a condensed figure for proletarian formation. However, if read as sublimations, then the Gothic uncanny can be read as figuring that which can only be viewed figuratively, as figuring that which has "no space within the given reality."[56] Therefore, from the allegorical/realist interpretive position, what the Gothic sublime represents appears as an element of symbolic reality that can be decoded since sublimity within the Gothic is considered a symptom. However, according to Slavoj Žižek, "'reality' is the field of symbolically structured representations, the outcome of symbolic 'gentrification' of the Real."[57] Therefore, from a psychoanalytic-interpretive position that takes the romance aspect of the Gothic seriously, the sublime does not symbolize as much as it represents the return of a non-symbolized, leaving a stain on its otherwise realistic depiction. In essence, the Gothic sublime functions as what Freud calls the *Vorstellung-Repräsentanz*. In his analysis of the dream of the burning child and Freud's nephew's *fort/da* game, Lacan essentially argues that the *Vorstellung-Repräsentanz* amounts to a paradoxical signifier that marks the real within the symbolic; it marks the primordially repressed as incongruent with the symbolic order.[58] Žižek further discusses the relation between the *Vorstellung-Repräsentanz* and sublimation:

> It is against this background that *Vorstellung-Repräsentanz* is to be conceived as an attempt to inscribe into the symbolic order the surplus that eludes the field of representation. The success of what we all "sublimation" relies on this reflexive reversal of the "lack of a signifier" into the "signifier of lack" — that is to say, on this primordial metaphor by means of which the stain — the brute enjoyment for which there is no signifier — is replaced by an empty signifier, a signifier which does not signify any reality — that is to say: a stand-in for a representation which is constitutively excluded from reality, which must fall out if "reality" is to retain its consistency.[59]

The Gothic sublime understood as sublimation, therefore, acknowledges what lies beyond the pleasure principle and what lies beyond our finite historic understanding (and understanding in general).

Consequently, psychoanalysis "doesn't provide a new and better interpretation of the uncanny; it maintains it as *a limit to interpretation*."[60] Even though psychoanalysis practices its own mode of allegoresis by providing a psychological account of the Gothic, it differs from other modes of allegorical interpretation by its insistence on the formal level of the uncanny over its content. So the Gothic novel of the eighteenth and nineteenth century, as a product of sublimation, can be read as an early literary attempt to point out the uncanny dimension pertaining to the very project of modernity, not in order to make it disappear, but in order to maintain it, to hold it open. Not attempting to move beyond the Enlightenment, the Gothic points to the Enlightenment's own internal limit, its own inherent inconsistency. While it is true that the Gothic sublime protects us from this inconsistency, it is, aesthetically, also what is responsible for introducing it in the first place. As Lacan points out, the sublime does colonize the field of the real with imaginary schemes, but it does so by representing emptiness as empty. It represents that which can only be represented by something else.[61]

While examining the "Preface" to the second edition of *The Castle of Otranto*, one can see that this divided nature of the critical appreciation of the Gothic novel — the division between the allegorical trend to tame the uncanny and the psychoanalytic attempt to recognize the truly uncanny nature of the Gothic — was built into the very structure of the text that founded the genre. When Horace Walpole acknowledges that his little translated medieval Italian tale is a sham, he simultaneously inaugurates the use of the term "Gothic" in the title of his novel. But, beyond this equation between things Gothic and things artificial, Walpole also inaugurates a new form of hybrid narrative — a combining of ancient improbability with modern realism:

> It was an attempt to blend the two kinds of romance, the ancient and the modern. In the former all was imagination and improbability: in the latter, nature is always intended to be, and sometimes has been, copied with success. Invention has not been wanting; but the great resources of fancy have been dammed up, by a strict adherence to common life. But if in the latter species Nature has cramped imagination, she did but take her revenge, having been totally excluded from old romances.[62]

In this famous statement from his Gothic manifesto, Walpole claims that Gothic literature, what he refers to as a "new route" in fiction, possesses a divided aesthetic: part novelistic probability and part a return to medieval romance (*O* 10). This divided nature of Walpole's "new species of romance" is, at least in part, responsible for the current division in the critical reception of the Gothic novel as either allegory or romance (*O* 14).

If one agrees with Northrop Frye, then all literature, from the perspective of critical commentary, is more or less allegorical. Fictional works written primarily for entertainment, however, lend themselves quite readily to allegory.[63] This is especially true of Gothic fiction because of its inherent hyperbolic outlandishness. Since allegory literally means "other speak"—to say one thing and mean another—critics who search for the deeper allegorical meaning of Gothic fiction treat the subliterary force as a form of encoded speech, a disguised means of dealing with social and political tensions.[64] The implicit symbolic meaning that critics excavate beneath the otherwise silly tales of Gothic exaggeration, by interpreting Hyde as a figure of repressed homosexuality, Dracula as Jew, Frankenstein's creature as the budding proletariat or any Gothic sublime excess as the fear of the day, invariably posits the true realist intention of the work and treats the Gothic from what amounts to a neo-classical perspective. While it is true that allegory does tend to possess a propagandistic function and does lend itself to polemical purposes, it is not necessarily true that Gothic fiction is through-and-through allegorical. It, of course, partially is, but when critics interpret the Gothic as allegorical, they tend to dismiss the real novel side of Walpole's divided aesthetic. The Gothic mode is indeed very seductive, but it is the critic's reading that is really responsible for creating allegorical meaning,[65] and this meaning is created by discounting the romance side of the Gothic and by interpretively damming up the great resources of fancy upon which the Gothic relies for its innovative vision.

Again, according to Walpole's often quoted "Preface," his literary experiment, his little "Gothic Story," as he refers to it in the second edition, "was an attempt to blend the two kinds of romance, the ancient and the modern" (*O* 9). Ancient romance is characterized by Walpole as filled with "imagination and improbability," whereas in modern romance, "nature is always intended to be, and sometimes has been, copied with success" (*O* 9). Walpole's Gothic romance, therefore, attempts to counteract the realist tendencies of the budding novel.[66] Realism is fine for providing an artistic view of everyday life, but a too strict adherence to it saps narrative plots of the, at times, hyperbolic imaginative force that characterized ancient romance. Walpole's new version of the novel, a mixture of the two, allows for an imaginative injection into the dull veins of the realistic modern novel while simultaneously providing probability control to any overly fanciful extremes. In essence, Walpole's blending of the two modes of narrative puts reality and its repressed (which, as repressed, gives reality its seeming coherence) on the same plane. This uncanny dimension of the Gothic novel—the reinvigoration of the new realist novel by allowing what had been supposedly long dead and buried to haunt the realist dimension—is precisely what is being tamed and subdued by the allegorical criticism that interprets the Gothic as an implicit or indirect realism by reading it as figuratively referring to some contemporary social reality. But

Walpole's Gothic strategy points to the fissure within reality, to that underside of reality that realism represses.[67]

The vast majority of eighteenth-century Gothic novels never explicitly labeled themselves Gothic, and most critics never called them by the term "Gothic novel." The term "Gothic novel" is really a literary-historical term, as the only noteworthy Gothic novels to use the appellation were the second edition of *The Castle of Otranto: A Gothic Story* and the second edition of Clara Reeve's *The Champion of Virtue*, which was re-titled *The Old English Baron: A Gothic Story*. Although a couple of other minor Gothic novels from the period may have used the term "Gothic" in their titles, the majority of works from the flourishing genre opted for the appellation "Romance," as in Ann Radcliffe's novels *A Sicilian Romance* and *The Romance of the Forest* or Matthew Lewis's *The Monk: A Romance*. According to E. J. Clery, in the eighteenth century critics also usually referred to these Gothic novels by the simple names "romances."[68] Because the allegorically-inclined critics tend to be more indebted to Horace's notion of believability than to Longinus's conception of sublimity, they also tend to dismiss and censure the Gothic novel because of its supernatural implausibility and because its reliance on the aesthetics of terror and horror take the genre too far away from the social concerns of realism. To echo Clery in a slightly different context, the problem allegorically-inclined critics have with Gothic literature revolves around romance's steadfast privileging of the pleasures of the imagination over moral instruction.[69]

As any reader of Walpole's inaugural Gothic romance knows, Walpole puts as much emphasis, if not more, on the pleasures of the imagination as on realistic representation. Although he explicitly states that he is constructing a balance between the two, terror is his admitted principle engine. With the rise of realism in the prose literature from the 1740s onward, the romance was increasingly viewed as an unworthy form of literature. Walpole obviously abhorred the growing resistance to the imaginative force of literature, but, in order to display his disapproval, he blended the pleasures of romance with the emerging taste for realism to create the Gothic. As Nicholas Royle has pointed out, the uncanny itself is based on this erasure of the distinction between the imagination and reality.[70] Therefore, this resurrected pleasure — an outmoded and archaic pleasure that should have remained long since dead and buried — returns within the confines of literary realism as an uncanny pleasure, an aesthetic approximation of the psychoanalytic concept of *jouissance* (a kind of pleasure beyond that demarcated by the reality principle).

Due to his antiquarian interests, Walpole utilized what Barbara Fuchs has identified as the metonymic association between romance and the Middle Ages to ironically breathe some new life into the budding novel.[71] Because his revival of romance is based on, to use Frye's terms, a misunderstanding of an earlier age that never existed,[72] it can be argued that he uses romance for symbolic purposes. Like allegory, romance is also a symbolic form. But, as I shall argue, where allegory represents indirectly, romance represents negatively. Frederic Jameson implies that realism's symbolic message is social, whereas romance's symbolism moves toward the metaphysical.[73] Therefore, the Gothic as inaugurated by Walpole — and as taken up by the "brighter talents" he mentions in his second preface — should be read as a mixture of the social and the metaphysical because it is a mixture of the allegorical and the romance. Where the allegorical side — housing the realist dimension of the Gothic — points indirectly to a meaning that can be uncovered, the romance side — the dimension that has been resurrected from the dismissal of realism — points to what can only be felt and is not reducible to the signifier and signification. It is, therefore, this latter side of the Gothic — the romance dimension — that houses the uncanny aspect of the Gothic, the aspect that always prevents the Gothic from being understood accurately through allegoresis.

Rather than arguing that allegorical interpretations of the Gothic novel read too much into Gothic uncanniness, it is more productive to argue that, since this type of reception favors a reading of the Gothic along the parameters of modern realism (one of the halves of Walpole's hybrid formula), it unavoidably reduces Gothic excess and uncanniness to a realist understanding and, thereby, dismisses what is aesthetically anxiety producing about the Gothic. Only a critical reception that interrogates how the spirit of romance (the other half of Walpole's formula) lies embedded in these narratives can achieve a truly aesthetic appreciation of the Gothic, without necessarily compromising a symbolic and literary appreciation. Taking seriously the claim made by most early Gothic novelists that their works were "romances" will inescapably reveal the essential uncanniness of the Gothic novel as figuring that which makes all realistic interpretation falter. Heeding the role of romance within Gothic narrative, the Gothic uncanny can also be read as a symbol that demonstrates its own inability to symbolize, its own inability to express what it stands for. Therefore, the crucial exploitation of the past in Gothic romance should be read as figuring a pre-symbolic mode of significance that pays homage to a fundamental anxiety that is warded off and covered over by strict allegorical interpretations, all too quickly succumbing to a logic and a demand to penetrate into the meaning of the uncanny. Read allegorically, Frankenstein's creature can accurately be read as a condensed figure for proletarian formation. But read as a romance, the Gothic uncanny can be read as figuring that which can only be viewed figuratively, as figuring that which has no space within a given realism.

Just as a Marxist or a New Historicist–influenced literary criticism is best to develop an appreciation of the allegorical dimension of the Gothic because of allegory's relation to social reality, a psychoanalytic-influenced literary criticism properly elucidates the importance of the romance dimension of the Gothic because of romance's relation to the metaphysical. But, more specifically, psychoanalytic criticism is better attuned for an appreciation of the romance dimension of the Gothic because, according to Jameson, in comparison to realism, romance "has older, more archaic origins and reflects some earlier, oral stage, some more passive symbiotic relationship with the mother."[74] While the allegorical interpretation of the Gothic might tell us something about the realities to which each Gothic romance responds, the romance potential recalls something more archaic, something more primitive, that the allegorical interpretation needs to repress in order to create a coherent understanding. Frye notes how the words "popular" and "primitive" have the same meaning, but he adds that this distinction has more to it than the distinction between class structure and historical periodization:

> If we define popular literature as what ignorant and vicious people read, the prejudice implied will make it impossible to understand what is going on in literature. Similarly, if we define the primitive only as the chronologically earlier, we create an illusion of literature gradually improving itself from naked savagery to the decent clothing of accepted cultural values. But actually the primitive is a quality in literature which emerges recurrently as an aspect of the popular.[75]

There is not, then, primitive literature that was eventually developed into modern sophisticated literature, but, rather, the primitive is an inherent aspect of literature that remains more or less latent in all literary works. The Greek romances may have been more primitive than Homer and Sophocles, science fiction may be more primitive than Joyce and Eliot, and the Gothic may be more primitive than Richardson and Austen, but popular literature is conventionally popular literature because it highlights the latent potential of the primitive in literature in general. From a developmental perspective, the emergence of the Gothic in the mid to late eighteenth century must appear as a step backward, as a reactionary development within British fiction, but viewed through Walpole's observations that romance was increasingly marginalized throughout the eighteenth century, the Gothic, by returning to the primitive, actually revives what is most literary about literature in the first place.

The romance dimension of the Gothic is also anti-realist in spirit because it maintains a persistent nostalgia for some other time that undermines the social ideals of the here and now. The allegorical dimension of the Gothic exploits medieval archaisms ultimately to reinforce the morality and manners of eighteenth or nineteenth-century British society. Conversely, the romance dimension exploits medieval archaisms ultimately to destabilize the morality and manners of eighteenth or nineteenth-century British society. This would explain why much current Gothic criticism is torn between understanding the Gothic novelists as either reactionary conservatives or as radical subversives. Nevertheless, Frye also claims that romance exists primarily to symbolize a contrast between two worlds, one above the level of ordinary experience and one below.[76] In other words, romance is less concerned with representing ordinary experience like the novel than it is with representing that which can only be imagined. Ultimately for Frye, "romance often deliberately descends into a world obviously related to the human unconscious."[77] While remaining highly adaptable to a particular historical and ideological context, romance in general, and especially the Gothic's use of romance, constantly harks back to a literary and cultural tradition as a means of intimating uncivilized primitive latencies in both literary convention and the human psyche. Gothic meaning is, therefore, partially allegorical and partially uncanny.

Only a psychoanalytic criticism is attuned to hear the uncanny importance of the Gothic use of romance. In her feminist analysis, Anne Williams likewise argues that "allegory and romance occupy the opposite ends of a spectrum in regard to meaning."[78] She claims that since, in allegory, the text conforms to a prior idea, it is the most patriarchal literary mode:

> In allegory, the reader is aware, conscious, of reading a text designed to embody, to incarnate, an abstraction (an idea, a concept, or even a theology or a history). The pleasure of the text in part lies in our perception of that "embodied" meaning. Allegory inherently affirms (and, in effect, enacts) the hierarchy of meaning inherent in the Law of the Father. The allegorist personifies the speaking subject as totalitarian overlord of language who directs and manipulates his world according to a priori thoughts.[79]

Ultimately, according to Williams, the allegorist creates a work long on soul and short on body.

Taking the allegory/romance distinction into Lacanian waters, Williams further claims that "romance is the opposite of allegory in its relation to the Symbolic."[80] By capitalizing the word "Symbolic," Williams puns on the relation between romance as a symbolic mode and romance's role in potentially suspending the Symbolic order. Romance suspends the Symbolic order because, "like the Freudian uncanny, the conventions of romance reinstate primitive, pre–Symbolic modes of significance."[81] In other words, unlike allegory, romance does not possess symbolic meaning; rather, it symbolizes the suspension of meaning. It does this by signifying emotionally, in a way that appeals to the unrealistic primitive feelings of childhood.[82] According to Williams, "the conventions of romance are thus literally 'unrealistic' because they ignore the principles that constitute 'reality.' In psychoanalytic terms, romance regresses us toward the moment at which the infant emerges from the pulsions of the Semiotic into its process as a speaking subject — the realm of the Kristevan 'poetic.'"[83]

On one level, then, the unrealistic hyperboles that run rampant in the majority of Gothic romances are used to appeal to the pleasures of the imagination of childhood that still persist latently in all readers. On another level, the unrealistic exaggerations of the Gothic symbolize the breakdown of reality, and of realism, that occurs with the return of the repressed that accompanies the uncanny. The allegorical strain running through the Gothic, therefore, hints at other meanings, meanings that can be uncovered by the sociologically-sensitive reader. But the romance strain cursing through the veins of the Gothic tradition hints at the other of meaning itself, something the Gothic sublime, since it is not attached to meaning, can only fail to reduce to the meaningful or recognizable. The allegorical understanding of the Gothic, therefore, restricts the pleasures of the Gothic within the confines of the reality principle by making its meaning reducible to an implicit form of realism, whereas the critical attention to the romance dimension of the Gothic opens up the possibility of envisioning how the Gothic intimates a space beyond a pleasure principle tied to the reality principle. Uncovering what the romance dimension of the Gothic reveals is best left to a psychoanalytic interpretation as strictly opposed to an allegorical hermeneutic. As Žižek informs us, psychoanalytic interpretation "involves the reduction of meaning to the signifier's nonsense, not the unearthing of secret meaning."[84]

Through this method of interpretation, ultimately, the romance dimension of the Gothic, by invoking an earlier time of maturation, can also be seen as invoking what Williams insists is the "inadequate and imperfect separation from the mother."[85] Although Williams insists that this receding of Symbolic civilization intimated by the Gothic obsession with nature reveals a feminist undermining of patriarchy, I would like to argue that the imperfect separation that is displayed by the Gothic, because it points toward the fragility of repression and the flimsy process of socialization, actually allows for the dramatization of the structures of psychopathology. The affinity between psychoanalysis and the Gothic romance is almost as old as Freud's claim in "Creative Writers and Day-Dreaming" that the less pretentious authors of romances, which have the widest and most eager circle of readers of both sexes, provide particularly fruitful objects for psychoanalytic analysis.[86] Writers of popular fiction like the Gothic touch a nerve that those writers with a more limited intended audience shy away from. The popularity of popular literature does not actually stem from the typically assumed superficiality associated with the production of entertainment goods. Rather, Gothic fiction's popularity stems from the powerful libidinal force with which romance affects character and reader alike. The typical Gothic romance always begins with the infiltration of some sort of mysterious libidinal force that throws the ordinary reality of the characters within the romance out of joint. Whether it is the gigantic helmet that falls from the sky in the opening pages of *The Castle of Otranto*, the return of the mother as figured by the personified castle moans in the early chapters of *The Sicilian Romance*, the demonic connivance of Mathilda early in *The Monk*, the death of Victor's mother in *Frankenstein*, or any hundred of other possibilities within Gothic fiction, this libidinal force creates an unnarrated mystery that also seduces and lures the reader. As soon as the sublime is introduced as an otherworldly mystery, a libidinal force unleashes anxiety upon the hero or heroine and captivates the reader.

As mentioned above, in "Instincts and Their Vicissitudes" Freud ultimately demonstrates that drive emerges either indirectly through repression or directly through sublimation.[87] While discussing the difference between repression and sublimation as two modalities of the drive in Freudian discourse, Mary Ann Doane claims that where symptoms, which are the product of repression, occupy "the level of the socially trivial," sublimation "has as its product the highest manifestations of human culture, that which constitutes, most exactly, the sublime."[88] Doane argues that the products of sublimation are sublime because they have a social aim and not a mere individual aim like the symptoms produced by repression. Sublimations have a social aim not because they attempt to represent the social in some form but because they attempt to represent what is constitutively lacking from social reality. In *Seminar VII*, Lacan, through a rather Delphic pronouncement, appears to anticipate Doane's claim concerning the aesthetics of the sublime. Shortly after his famous analysis of Sophocles's tragedy, while recognizing Antigone's sublime beauty during the moment of her burial, Lacan concludes:

> That, then, is what I wanted to remind you of today, so as to indicate to you the direction taken by our research on the subject of the beautiful and, I would add, the sublime. We haven't yet extracted from the Kantian definitions of the sublime all the substance we might. The conjunction of this term with that of sublimation is probably not simply an accident nor simply homonymic.[89]

Lacan here seems to profess that the sublime as an aesthetic affect is somehow connected to Freud's concept of sublimation.[90] Since Freud ultimately demonstrates that drive emerges either indirectly through repression or directly through sublimation, one can conclude that in repression drive is somehow hindered, whereas only with sublimation, which is not based on repression, does drive emerge in opposition to the reality principle, as somehow indicating that which is inaccessible to the existing reality principle and interpretations conforming to a realist aesthetic. Therefore, the sublime, as indicating the inaccessible negatively through the accessible, can serve a sublimatory aim.

To read the Gothic uncanny on its own terms, perhaps we ought to read its use of the sublime as a form of the latter manner of drive fulfillment, keeping in mind that aesthetic productions produce sublimations, not repression. Allegorical interpretations of the Gothic, which argue that there is latent meaning behind Gothic sublimity, treat Gothic fiction much like an analyst would treat the symptom formations of his or her analysand. To view Frankenstein's creature as symbolizing the repressed fear of organized labor or Mr. Hyde's presence as indirectly representing Victorian homophobia is to interpret Gothic sublimity as a symptom formation. But reading Gothic sublimity through the conventions of romance allows the critic to illustrate how Gothic sublimity renews primal affections that would be otherwise lost; it renews an animal power or muscular energy of infancy that appears oddly enough to resemble Freud's understanding of the drive. The Gothic sublime can therefore be understood as a form of sublimation because, not only is sublimation, according to Lacan, "also satisfaction of the drive,"[91] but through it the drive "aims at the past, at a time *before* the subject found itself where it now is, embedded in time and moving toward death,"[92] figured in the Gothic's obsession with the past. Joan Copjec argues that the prelapsarian past is mythic, but she also argues that sublimation provides "a small dose of surplus *jouissance* ... as a remainder of that past and, of course, its loss."[93] For my purpose, she further claims that "in contrast to the ordinary pleasure that everyday objects bring, *jouissance*, attached as it is to the memory of an originally lost object — *das Ding*—is a painful, immoderate pleasure."[94] The Gothic's use of the sublime can therefore be understood as representing negatively that which can only be represented, that which is not reducible to the signifier. And, by negatively signifying *das Ding* through the use of the sublime, the Gothic provides not just the pleasure of the imagination, but a sublimated enjoyment (*jouissance*) that is beyond the pleasure principle. But all this is only observable if we first take the uncanny dimension of the Gothic romance seriously.

2

Retrospective Fantasy and the Uncanny Structure of Gothic Romance

Michel Foucault claims that the latter half of the eighteenth century was haunted by "the fear of darkened spaces, of the pall and gloom which prevents the full visibility of things, men and truths."[1] The Enlightenment, in its endless endeavor to bring everything to the light of day, literally needed to eradicate the shadowy areas of society, demolish the unlit chambers where arbitrary political acts and monarchical whim gestated, and do away with the religious superstition which produced the illusions of ignorance. The enlightened age of universal freedom through knowledge could not begin until the dark superstitions of the past were illuminated and seen for what they were. Intentional fictionalization of the mysteriousness of the so-called Dark Ages was one of the primary forms this illumination took. According to Foucault, "Gothic novels develop a whole fantasy-world of stone walls, darkness, hideouts and dungeons which harbor, in significant complicity, brigands and aristocrats, monks and traitors."[2] Foucault situates these novels as the negative of the transparency and visibility that the Enlightenment endeavored to establish. In other words, through the fantastic representation of these archaic secret places, these darkened spaces and all the ignorance they embody are permanently located in a past era that is both prior to and distant from the Age of Enlightenment. The Age of Enlightenment willfully defines itself by setting itself off from the ignorance of the past, an ignorance that now belongs to the fantasy realm pertaining rightfully to fiction. This, according to Foucault's analysis, is the only way in which the Enlightenment can tolerate areas of darkness.

Elsewhere Foucault describes the Enlightenment as "the discontinuity of time: a break with tradition, a feeling of novelty, of vertigo in the face of the passing moment."[3] He says this while analyzing a short, emblematic text by Immanuel Kant on the Enlightenment. Kant's "What Is Enlightenment?" is itself emblematic of the Enlightenment not only because it was originally published in 1784 in one of the leading journals of the German Enlightenment, *Berlinische Monatsscrift*, but also because, true to modernity, Kant's essay is largely focused on its own contemporaneity. By all means, according to Foucault, it is not the first time that philosophical thought sought to reflect on its own present situation. In fact, this maneuver has basically taken three previous forms throughout the history of Western thought. In Plato, the present is represented as belonging to a certain era of the world; in St. Augustine, the present is interrogated in an attempt to read in it signs of a forthcoming event; in Vico, the present is analyzed as a point of transition toward the awakening of a new world. But with Kant's text something entirely novel takes place. Kant is less concerned with the present's role in any larger scheme than he is concerned with what Foucault calls the "question of contemporary reality alone."[4] Kant is not concerned, it would seem, with the present as a relative moment, a moment that would be best understood as belonging to a historically specific period — Kant is concerned with nothing less than universality itself. And he finds it in the Enlightenment.

Kant begins his essay with the line, "Enlightenment is man's release from his self-incurred tutelage."[5] Tutelage is further defined as man's inability to make use of his understanding without direction from another. In order to be enlightened, one needs to make a break; one needs to sever his or her relation of apprenticeship with the world and practice free use of his or her reason. Kant's motto for the Enlightenment is *Sapere aude!* — "have courage to use your own reason!" True to late eighteenth-century sentiment, Kant feels that laziness and cowardice are responsible for a greater portion of humanity remaining under lifelong tutelage: "It is so easy not to be of age."[6] Kant argues that we remain in a state of immaturity when a book takes the place of our understanding, when a spiritual director takes the place of our conscience, and when a doctor decides our diet for us.[7] Obviously, for Kant, enlightenment pertains to the free use of one's own reason.

But this does not mean that Kant suggests an enlightened world would be one wholly run by reason. Rather, he finds a contradiction at the heart of the Enlightenment: "Argue as much as you will, and about what you will, but obey!"[8] For Kant, reason cannot be free unless it is somehow limited. As has been noted by many, including Foucault, Kant reverses the realms where obedience and freedom lie. In the Age of Enlightenment, the free use of reason is to be found in the public realm, whereas obedience lies in the private realm: "The public use of one's reason must always be free, and it alone can bring about enlightenment among men. The private use of reason, on the other hand, may often be very narrowly restricted without particularly hindering the progress of enlightenment."[9] For instance, as a teacher one is compelled to do one's duty and follow the guidelines and protocols of the university. But as a scholar, to use Kant's term, one has free reign to argue against and criticize the general practices of pedagogy and the university. In one's private duty as a teacher, a duty in the interests of the community, one must, according to Kant, obey the rules of the post with which one has been entrusted. But, as far as one sees oneself as a member of the whole community or of society in general, one can certainly argue against such practices without hurting the affairs for which one is in part responsible for as a passive member. Therefore, what he sees as an inherent contradiction is less a strong split in society between what is public and what is private than a split between public and private at the heart of each member. The Age of Enlightenment harbors this inherent contradiction as far as each member is himself both an embodiment of this split and an embodiment of the Enlightenment itself. This split is the universal as far as it not only prevents each individual from being consistent to him or herself, but as far as it prevents the Age from also not living up to its own particularity. Kant even asks if we live in an *enlightened age*. His answer is a quick "no." But, he maintains, we do live in an *age of enlightenment*. For Kant, it seems, we are only enlightened to the extent that we harbor a contradiction, to the extent that we live in a split world. We are free because we have renounced the non-contradictory freedom that characterizes nature.

Mladen Dolar analyzes this inherent contradiction that Kant found at the heart of the Enlightenment through a brief reading of Kant's *Conflict of the Faculties*. The structure of the university, the topic of Kant's book, is itself a duplication of the structure of the Enlightenment. The university is divided into higher and lower faculties. The higher faculties (theology, law, and medicine) are higher in the sense that they are closer to power. In a sense, they run the system. They bring in the majority of the revenue and train those who will become the future social leaders. Philosophy, being the lower faculty, has no power. But, Kant insists, philosophy's power lies precisely in its renunciation of power. It is the faculty that follows only the autonomy of reason precisely because it is cut off from power. The power of the higher faculties lacks reason and the reason of the lower faculty lacks power. According to Dolar, the entire edifice is constructed on the basis of an underlying supposition that reason is powerless and that power is not based in reason: "The law is valid, but not true."[10] This sort of symbiotic relationship, this inherent split in the University structure, is what allows for the existence of academic freedom.[11] Whereas power allows itself to be scrutinized and criticized by reason, reason gives up all claim to power in order to exert its influence. Accordingly, Dolar argues, philosophy is situated at the very heart of the political: "It has radical implications precisely by virtue of its renunciation of any kind of political concerns."[12]

This structure parallels the structure that Kant sees as necessary for enlightenment. With the Enlightenment, the present appears for the first time as a philosophical event. It not only invents its own name, but, according to Dolar, it perceives itself as Enlightenment: "It defines itself as a privileged moment in history, as a way out of immaturity into adulthood, as Kant will put it, as a coming of age — an adulthood which implies the use of reason without any outside authority to rely on."[13] Enlightenment authority — the one, for instance, embodied in the higher faculties of the university — is inherent to its own structure. The Enlightenment and the enlightened individuals renounce any tethering to an external authority in favor of the freedom gained from the use of reason limited only by reason's own inherent limit.[14]

One can, I think, correctly draw a parallel between Kant's notion of enlightenment and Freud's notion of the Oedipus complex. Although not named until years later, the Oedipus complex first emerges in *The Interpretation of Dreams*.[15] Freud insists that if Sophocles's tragedy has the ability to move a modern audience no less than it did a contemporary Greek one, "there must be something which makes a voice within us ready to recognize the compelling force of destiny in the *Oedipus*."[16] Oedipus's destiny moves us only because it might have been ours. Through dream analysis, Freud is convinced that Oedipus lives out what for all of us is our first desire: to direct our first sexual impulse toward our mother and our first murderous rivalry toward our father. "King Oedipus, who slew Laius and married his mother Jocasta," Freud reasons, "merely shows us the fulfillment of our own childhood wishes."[17] What separates us by an imperceptible abyss from Oedipus is the fact that we have succeeded (success depending on our level of neurosis) in detaching our sexual impulses from our mother and our jealousy from our father. Oedipus, it would appear, is the only figure in history to have not accepted culture in return for this required renunciation of primal desire. This explains why he, in *Oedipus at Colonus*, hovers in a liminal state between nature and culture.

According to Freudian theory, the Oedipus complex determines how one is situated as a human being. Not long after the infant realizes that it is separate from its mother — usually when it realizes that nourishment comes from an external source — a third figure, the father, intervenes, upsetting the comforting and almost symbiotic relation the infant has with the mother. At this stage of development (which Freud locates between the ages of three and five), the existing object-to-object relation structuring the infant's experience morphs into a relation of relation-to-relation. When, for instance, the infant realizes that its privileged relation to its mother is no more privileged than the father's relation to the mother, it loses its initial direct connection with nature. Objects give way to relation itself. The child has two choices. To keep its fixation on its mother, it can create a rivalry with its father, or the child can throw its lot in with the father. If you can't beat him, join him. The father's "no" concerning the prohibition of incest forces the child to turn its jealousy into envy and enter into the world of language.[18] Symbolic reality is the return one gets for the renunciation of this primal desire.[19] Rather than being recorded in one's conscious memory, this primal scene only makes its appearance in oblique manners throughout one's life. As Freud concludes, "like Oedipus, we live in ignorance of these wishes, repugnant to morality, which have been forced upon us by Nature, and after their revelation we may all of us seek to close our eyes to the scenes of our childhood."[20] In *Totem and Taboo*, Freud notes that children lack the trace of arrogance that urges adult civilized men to draw a clear distinction between their own nature and that of all other animals.[21] But at a certain point, the child begins to separate from his relation to animals. Not infrequently, this rift manifests itself as some sort of animal phobia. And, of course, for Freud this animal phobia is a masked fear of castration. As anyone invested in psychoanalysis knows, fear of castration is already castration proper. Once this fears sets in, one has already, perhaps without knowing it, changed sides. In other words, the fear of an animal is a sure sign the child has already renounced what it thinks is its rightful claim to its mother, putting nature forever out of reach.

Freud feels that castration is the terminal point of the Oedipus complex, the point where instincts have been elevated to the level of drive, aligned, as Lacan would say, with the signifier. His overdetermined use of biology and anatomy aside, it is not difficult to see that for Freud castration is somehow connected to a maturation process. The initial desire for the mother and hostility toward the father are, through castration, relegated to some sort of long lost past out of reach to the newly-born subject. But the initial incestuous desire of the child was never known as such precisely because it is only now, with the advent of castration and the subject's entrance into the world of knowledge, that the subject acquires the means by which it can set itself off from its own experiences in order to know them. So the time of the initial incestuous and rivalrous desire actually exists in a sort of prehistory of the subject: a time, if you will, before record. Therefore, the maturation process as marked by castration and the renunciation required therewith retroactively posit this time before time. As with the prehistory of humans in general, it can never be known as such; it can only be mythologized. But it can be felt at the points and moments when the symbolic world that one receives in return for this initial renunciation shows its inconsistency. Kant's call for man's release from his self-incurred tutelage is basically a call for castration. It is a call, as is the Enlightenment in general, for a renunciation of our childish tethering to the parental figures embodied in anyone from the monarch to the clergy. And the late eighteenth century's growing obsession for its own past is itself a manifestation of the Enlightenment's own symptom, a sign of its own castration anxiety.

As early as 1712, in Joseph Addison's *Spectator* No. 419, one can already find early praise for the "kind of Writing, wherein the Poet quite loses sight of Nature."[22] Writers of this fabulous type of writing primarily entertain the reader's imagination by offering characters and actions that are most improbable. It appears the only limits imposed on the construction of events in this kind of writing are the ones the writers themselves impose. Although this "fairy way of writing,"[23] in accordance with eighteenth-century literary aesthetics regarding the rules of probability, is usually written off as childish and immature, Addison maintains that it is the most difficult form of writing — if only because these writers have no pattern to follow and are forced to work completely out of their own invention. At the same time, he adds that writers of fantasy must have a particular cast of fancy as well as an imagination naturally fruitful to superstition. Fairy writers cannot, in other words, construct an entirely foreign environment if they do not make their characters alien to contemporary sentiments. The ability of fairy writers to tap into current prejudices and to humor those notions that all readers have imbibed in infancy, for Addison, is the key to becoming an ideal writer of the fabulous. Fancy, it seems, is endemic to infancy. According to Addison, tales of the fabulous raise a paradoxical kind of pleasing horror in the mind of the reader by amusing the reader's imagination with a certain strange familiarity: "They bring up in our memory the stories we have heard in our childhood and favor those secret terrors and apprehensions to which the mind of man is naturally subject."[24] It appears that fabulous writing uses what was once so familiar to us, what properly belonged to us in our infancy, as the material to construct the utterly foreign for sophisticated readers. Addison notes that "men of cold fancies and philosophic dispositions" reject this type of literature on the grounds that its utter improbability hinders any effect on the imagination. But, Addison retorts, there are different laws and economies than those of mankind. The representations in fantastic stories must have their appeal because we have all heard "so many pleasing relations in favor of them."[25]

While noting that the ancients — whose aesthetics are emulated by the neoclassical forms of the eighteenth century — do not have much of this "fairy way of writing" among them, Addison concludes that the whole substance of this type of writing owes its debt to the "darkness and superstition" of the Middle Ages.[26] According to Addison's understanding, it was typically during the Middle Ages that people, not yet enlightened by philosophy and learning, looked on nature with more reverence and horror: "There was not a village in England that had not a ghost in it, the churchyards were all haunted, every large common had a circle of fairies belonging to it, and there was scarce a shepherd to be met with who had not seen a spirit."[27] Following general Enlightenment understanding, Addison cleverly connects the Middle Ages with a sort of infancy of the human race, turning these fantastic stories into what amount to archeological artifacts. But, in the next paragraph, while discussing how the English are the best suited to the fantastic, Addison maintains that the English are often disposed to the "gloominess and melancholy of temper" reflected in this type of writing.[28] The childish appeal inherent to the fairy way of writing is not wholly limited to either children or the Middle Ages. Once Addison moves from the Middle Ages to statements on the nature of being English, he arrives at the eighteenth-century world of universality. He further argues that writers of fantasy possess the ability to use imaginary beings and events in their writing as caricatures of human passions. Towards the end of "*Spectator*, No. 419," Addison intimates the metaphoric relation between the fictionally fabulous and the human passions by claiming that imaginative fiction "shows us persons who are not to be found in being, and represents even the faculties of the soul, with her several virtues and vices in a sensible shape and character."[29] Basically, according to Addison's conclusion, supernatural elements in fiction, especially as they will be utilized throughout the century, point less to something beyond the human realm than they point to that part of the human realm which cannot be viewed directly, that part of the inner life of the human that can only be portrayed through hyperbolic figuration.

It has been noted numerous times that the supernatural elements of medieval romance, which are indispensable to the Middle Ages, provided the inspiration for the first Gothic novels.[30] But, one must ask, what exactly is the role of the supernatural in the functioning of the realistic novel after its birth in the 1740s? How precisely is the rebirth of the supernatural within the eighteenth-century Enlightenment to be read? Before answering these questions, one needs to briefly examine the growth of interest in medieval romance that led to Horace Walpole's *The Castle of Otranto*.

The term "Gothic" in the eighteenth century signifies something slightly different than it does today. Today, of course, the term is applied almost exclusively to the Gothic revival of the latter part of the eighteenth century, whereas in the latter part of the eighteenth century, "Gothic" was used to refer to the barbaric and superstitious aspects of the Dark Ages.[31] According to Arthur Johnston, the period of English literature prior to the rise of the Gothic, the period of Dryden and Pope, was preoccupied with creating a literature in English that could stand beside the poetry of Augustan Rome. In the age of Dryden and Pope there was an intentional choice to ignore the present's own more immediate past in favor of a forced affinity with a literature that was considered more sophisticated and mature. In a sense, the neoclassical poets attempted "to disentangle themselves from what they felt to be the barbarisms and provincialisms that characterized the literature of their own immediate past."[32] And, of course, the classical model became the most effective means to craft such a clean break. But just as Dryden shunned Elizabethan literature in favor of a sort of antithetical poetry, by the second half of the eighteenth century writers were having a similar reaction to the neoclassical literary conventions. As Johnston maintains, "what had been a liberating influence on Dryden and his successors came to be regarded as a restraining force."[33] Just as Dryden and Pope sought a model for poetry in a distant past (Classical Greece and Rome), there was a growing tendency in the latter half of the eighteenth century to turn to the more recent past of the Gothic for a new and more imaginative paradigm.

The eighteenth-century antiquarians, who basically invented modern literary scholarship, were primarily literary writers who investigated medieval romances as a source of inspiration for the modern writer.[34] These scholars were concerned with capturing some of the imaginary potential which characterizes these old romances. The point of the historical research was, of course, not to go back into the glory of the past (it was not nostalgic at all), but to rejuvenate contemporary literary work by displaying to the current reading public the more audacious imaginativeness of these old writers. More than plot, character, or setting, fancy was being drawn out of the past as a source of inspiration. Since medieval romance was considered to be the most fictitious of all fiction, it came to be seen as possessing what was most proper to literature. The very reason the Gothic was ridiculed earlier in the century became the very reason it was emulated later in the century.[35]

According to Johnston, the unbelievable supernatural elements of the medieval romances were never considered as acceptable as those belonging to Homer and Virgil. While the marvelous aspects of the medieval romances were regarded as childish and superfluous, the literature of the ancients was more easily regarded as concerned with a deep understanding of human nature. Also, medieval romances were written in a more immature style, characterized by an "unpolished" English. Neoclassical scholarship considered medieval romances as infantile compared to the heroic epics of the Greeks and Romans. But as the century wore on these archaic romances became somewhat esteemed for their ability to recall images from childhood. Most writers of the eighteenth century were themselves nursed on these silly tales of knights, damsels, dragons, and fairies; it was as if many writers were retroactively touched by these old stories of excess. It even became generally accepted, according to Johnston, that the English people themselves had been nurtured on romance.[36] Not only were most English writers weaned on these childlike tales, but medieval romance was considered more and more as the first truly English literature. At one level, this latter consideration can be easily considered proto-nationalistic, but, on another level, it can be seen as critical of the neoclassical tendency of seeking English literary origins elsewhere.[37] So even though it may be correct to say that this new, burgeoning aesthetic was trying to solidify Englishness by closing off its literature from outside influence, it is just as important to see this growing trend of romanticizing and glorifying past English literature as a means of showing English literature's difference from itself.

Not only were medieval romances increasingly seen as part of a nostalgic memory of childhood, but the period when these overly imaginative romances were written was becoming increasingly considered a time when learning itself was in its infancy. As these romances were becoming considered more and more the primitive outpourings of the eighteenth century's own ancestors, these "ancestors" were, likewise, increasingly becoming seen as the eighteenth century's own infancy. As a reaction to the neoclassical rules of probability, a literature drawn from carefree, childlike imagination was increasingly emulated. It would be more accurate to say that the Gothic romances of the Middle Ages were idealized because of their barbarous and uncivilized elements than to say that the eighteenth-century Gothic revival sought to rescue everything Gothic from such contemptuous views. Gothic revival sought less to rescue what was Gothic from the stereotypes it lived under for so many years than it sought out the uncivilized aspect of this more imaginative fiction as a way of pointing to the infantile side of English literature, which neoclassical aesthetics seemed to have discarded.

Richard Hurd, more a popularizer than a learned scholar, played what is usually considered an extremely important role in reviving things Gothic just two years before the publication of *Otranto* with his 1762 *Letters on Chivalry and Romance*.[38] Although Hurd's *Letters* attempt to glorify the chivalric romances of the Gothic past, he never analyzes any actual medieval romances. Rather, he focuses more on widely read and famous writers whom he feels are, without ever really having been recognized as such, highly influenced by these old imaginative romances. His primary focus is on Spencer, and, to a lesser degree, Milton, Shakespeare, Tasso, and Ariosto. According to Hurd's reasoning, the medieval romantic influence on these writers' genius is not easily recognizable because it is not always direct. These writers are at their best when this influence shows itself in an oblique form:

> The greatest geniuses of our own and foreign countries, such as Ariosto and Tasso in Italy, and Spencer and Milton in England, were seduced by these barbarities of their forefathers; were even charmed by the Gothic Romances. Was this caprice and absurdity in them? Or, may there not be something in the Gothic Romance peculiarly suited to the views of a genius, and to the ends of poetry?[39]

More than the plot and all the marvelous characters and events that litter the pages of these Gothic romances, it was the imaginative spirit behind these literary gems that influenced these men of genius. The writer's ability to maintain the rules of unity in their fabulous works is more the mark of genius than any use of elves, fairies, dragons, armored knights, and damsels in distress. This ability is, according to Hurd, the richest gift of the Gothic romance and that aspect which the moderns have overlooked in their perpetual ridicule and contempt.

Hurd is not only credited with challenging the prejudices of neoclassical aesthetic taste, but also for beginning a process of literary reevaluation.[40] In order to be fully appreciated, Hurd insists that literary productions must be evaluated on their own terms rather than the universal terms of neoclassical aesthetic taste. If a critic were to look closely at Gothic romance, look without neoclassical blinders, "he would discover some latent cause of their production."[41] And, of course, for Hurd the latent cause of these literary productions is not necessarily consistent with the prevalent neoclassical forms. But, Hurd assures his reader, understanding the nature of this latent cause is the difficulty. It will require, as the reader will see, a reevaluation of literary criticism.

First off, Hurd recommends evaluating these works from their own vantage point — the Middle Ages. But, Hurd warns, this maneuver cannot simply rest with excusing poor writing by its environment. This is exactly what the common readings of medieval Gothic romances simply do when they equate these romances' uncivilized traits with their barbarous environment. What is really required for a complete understanding of these barbarous romances is a more complete evaluation of the very times and circumstances to which they are obviously a reaction. Barbarians have their own philosophy, such as it is, even if they are not enlightened by our reason.[42] Hurd is not an apologist for the barbarity of the Middle Ages; he feels that the strength of those dark times lies precisely in its barbarity. Rather, he demands the barbarity be recouped as an imaginative device for literary production. In fact, at times barbarity, for Hurd, becomes an almost relative thing. He contends that during the era of the great Greek epics, Greece itself, with an almost infinite number of petty independent states, was in a situation not dissimilar to feudal Europe. More implied than directly stated in Hurd's *Letters* is the idea that Ancient Greece, as a cultural entity of its own, was later mythologically solidified in and by Rome. Paralleling this ancient retroactive determination is the contemporary one where the Enlightenment itself is responsible for constructing the Middle Ages into something that can be conceptualized as a whole. In other words, the Middle Ages in general, and as specifically dark, is wholly an Enlightenment product. This is why the Gothic in general is impervious to neoclassical standards. It is not so much that the Gothic lies outside the parameters of eighteenth century aesthetics as it is that the Gothic is the ultimate result of these very Enlightenment standards. Hurd's entire text testifies to this. His *Letters*, if anything, is itself a part of the very construction of the so-called Dark Ages. In the end, it is this retroactive construction that may be the true sense and design of the Gothic. Hurd may not be aware of it himself, but through his participation in the retroactive production of the Gothic shines his own text's latent cause of production.

This is why Hurd feels the need to echo, albeit to a different judgment, the words commonly used by critics of Gothic that these romances are unnatural and absurd productions that "look more like the dreams of children than the manly inventions of poets."[43] As Freudian theory shows, dream reality less designates a different realm from waking reality than it designates the repressed underside of waking reality. The Enlightenment's manner of picturing itself as awakening from a long, dark sleep is based on the presupposition that reality can be divided into the two worlds of "actual reality" and the "world of sleeping." The Middle Ages, with all its superstition and marvelous literature, is marked as the dream world of illusions from which the eighteenth century awoke as if from a nightmare. But, using Lacanian language, one could say that this so-called dream world constitutes the real of the Enlightenment project. This retroactive displacement of the Enlightenment project's real event is the very fiction it constructs of the Middle Ages. And it is in the eighteenth-century rise of the Gothic novel where this displacement is most effectively displayed. The eighteenth-century Gothic revival, in effect, says not that the Middle Ages were a dream and now we are all enlightened, but rather that we are all barbarians who are actually dreaming that we are enlightened.[44]

Hurd echoes this sentiment when he contends that the Gothic "conceives the existence of such things as his reason tells him did not, and were never likely to exist."[45] Therefore, the Gothic aesthetic imagination is more important than experience because only the imagination can display those elements and events of our experience, like the Dark Ages, that never existed as such. Not only does Hurd see the imagination as "a young and credulous faculty," but he notices it "has no need to observe those cautious rules of credibility,"[46] for the Gothic imagination points to precisely what is repressed, conceived in the strict Freudian sense, by these very rules.[47] By the end of his *Letters*, Hurd actually reverses the polarity around which allegory is customarily conceived. Normally, allegory is viewed as a device that can indirectly bring to light something which otherwise should remain hidden. For instance, a novel like Walpole's *Otranto* can be read as an allegorical critique of the excessive power and presence of the nobility. The spectacular giant that inhabits the castle represents the claustrophobic omnipotence of the ruling classes. A direct critique of the nobility must remain veiled if it is to reach the light of day.[48] But, Hurd contends, Gothic writing uses allegory as a way to actually apologize for the literature's otherwise unseemly excessiveness. Allegory is a reasoned device that attempts to bring the fascinating in line with truth and reality. It is a mechanism that strives to make the literary function in line with neoclassical rules of taste. Under the disguise of allegory, Gothic literature, according to Hurd, was able to walk the world a while.[49] Here, and this is a truly marvelous step by Hurd, allegory less hides the true message of a literary work than it hides the fact that the literary work possess no message at all. Gothic literature appears to exude a kind of surplus.

This new literary model was imaginative in more than just one way. By the second half of the eighteenth century it became a commonly held belief that the neoclassical rules of probability, those rules supposedly governing the newly flourishing novel writing, sacrificed an imaginative outlet in favor of realistic portrayal. Naturally a growing interest in what was seen as the over-imaginative literature of the Middle Ages emerged as a reaction to the confining neoclassical aesthetics.[50] The romances of the Middle Ages appeared, at this time, as a perfect antidote to the everyday probability of current literary representations. Not only were medieval romances demeaned as childish by neoclassical scholars — thereby providing the impetus for a reactionary emulation — but, in general, these old romances were viewed as unrestrained and liberating. They, in turn, could be revived in order to rearrange the general direction of English letters. And here is where the other, less obvious, imaginative aspect of the Gothic lies. Northrop Frye, for instance, maintains that, as far as he knows, there has never been any period of Gothic English literature.[51] Every Gothic is, in a sense, always already a Gothic revival. It is always easy to view literary movements of the late nineteenth and late twentieth centuries as Gothic revivals, but when viewing the literary movement of the late eighteenth century more closely, the notion of revival seems less than adequate. Reading Horace Walpole, for instance, as a synecdoche for eighteenth-century early Gothic novelists, one encounters, paradoxically enough, at one and the same time the revival of the Gothic and its origin. The Gothic revival enacted in late eighteenth-century English literature less revives something that pre-exists itself than it revives something that never was as such. As any student of the Gothic will testify, Gothic romancers were hardly concerned, in their use of romance techniques, with anything remotely close to historical accuracy. They, in a sense, used the past — what was imagined as a particularly dark past — as a figure for the unseen, the underside, of the literature of their own age.

What is peculiar to the Gothic of the eighteenth century is that it arises in the very heart of the Enlightenment. After the advent of the Gothic, marvelous incidents become forever located in the realistic setting of neoclassical convention. Because of this, the sublime begins to play a much more psychological role than it had ever before. In other words, the supernatural element of the Gothic romance is much more figurative than it was in the Middle Ages. According to Margaret Carter, this distinction is even felt by the psuedo-medieval characters that inhabit the Gothic: "By the eighteenth century Gothic characters, in contrast to most of their medieval prototypes, tend to be preoccupied with questioning the ontological status of their 'supernatural' experiences."[52] By the second half of the eighteenth century, the supernatural becomes a paradoxically locatable element built into the very narrative. By locating the supernatural into the realistic setting of the novel, the eighteenth-century Gothic romance puts reality in suspense by calling attention to reality's suspended element. As David Punter points out, with the Gothic "the supernatural becomes a symbol of our past rising against us."[53] The Enlightenment may have done away with the supernatural superstitions once and for all, but the Gothic novel testifies that it can only do so by producing the uncanny in its place.

Let me, at this point, recall Freud's notion of the uncanny at some length. Although Freud frequently resorts to poetic writers for evidence of psychoanalytic concepts, only the topic of the uncanny seems to compel the psychoanalyst to directly investigate the subject of aesthetics. While recognizing *das Unheimlich* as undoubtedly related to what is frightening, to what arouses dread and horror, Freud asserts that the uncanny pertains to an affect much more specialized than what excites fear in general.[54] Freud, in all honesty to his topic, begins his paper by claiming a "special obtuseness" in his understanding of this highly specialized subspecies of the frightening. As the reader will see, this "special obtuseness" seems to be a prerequisite when it comes to any attempt to intellectually grasp the uncanny. Due to this lack of personal insight and due to a dearth of uncanny events from his own life, Freud turns to literature for help. Freud begins by offering a working definition: "the uncanny is that class of the frightening which leads back to what is known and long familiar."[55] He then adds the seemingly contradictory further stipulation that *unheimlich*, being the opposite of *heimlich* and, therefore, the opposite of what is homely and familiar, is frightening precisely because it is not known and is unfamiliar. It is, however, not enough to be novel to be uncanny; something has to be added to what is novel and unfamiliar in order to make it uncanny. In what might amount to be one of his most truly exploratory papers, Freud sets out to explore exactly what this something is.

As far as Freud is concerned, E. Jentsch's 1906 paper on the psychology of the uncanny is the only fruitful work on this subject. But Jentsch's equation of uncanny with "intellectual uncertainty" lacks, for Freud, the needed penetration. So Freud, playing the part of the etymologist, offers numerous definitions of *das Heimlich* from various languages in order to obtain a more penetrating understanding.[56] While proceeding through the variety of tedious dictionary definitions, Freud comes across a usage of the word *das Heimlich* that appears to coincide with its opposite.[57] *Heimlich*, which was originally defined to mean homeliness and familiarity, now, after some etymological research on Freud's part, starts to take on the opposite meaning of concealment. What is concealed by the canny, according to the usages Freud offers, is what is most intimate. For instance, one has canny meetings behind other's backs; one looks with canny pleasure at other's misfortunes. The canny appears so familiar that it seems to take an utterly singular nature. While Freud is offering definitions of "uncanny" as eerie, weird, and arousing gruesome fear, the above-mentioned coincidence of opposite meanings gets articulated. Usages like, "I had already long since felt an *unheimlich*, even gruesome feeling" and "the *unheimlich* fearful hours of night," point to a similar type of intimacy which the definitions of *das Heimlich* approach above. Finally, Freud hits on a definition that appears to contain this very contradiction that is harbored in *das Unheimlich*. The definition is Schelling's: "*Unheimlich is the name for everything that ought to have remained ... secret and hidden but has come to light.*"[58] As far as definitions go, the uncanny seems to be that which is most intimate to the subject but which appears as utterly strange. And harbored in this strange feeling is the uncanny feeling of something familiar. Freud finally notes that this coincidence of opposites locates the uncanny as a sub-species of the canny. Ultimately, it will be Freud's intention to show that the uncanny is a moment when the familiar itself takes on an utterly foreign aura.

Freud begins his illustration of this novel definition of the uncanny with a reading of E.T.A. Hoffman's famous tale "The Sandman," a tale he considers quite unparalleled in evoking the uncanny. Unlike most readings of Hoffman's tale, which locate the uncanny in the realistic appearance and movements of the automaton Olympia, Freud highlights the uncanny significance of the title character. The Sandman is the character — an even less real character than the automaton — who is "always re-introduced into the storyline at critical moments."[59] The story centers around young Nathaniel. Every night around nine o'clock Nathaniel's mother sends him with his siblings to bed with the warning that if they are not in bed when they become sleepy, the Sandman will not be able to put the sand in their eyes necessary for a good sound sleep. Even though Nathaniel is assured by his mother that the Sandman is only a figure of speech made up to explain the crud that accumulates in the corner of one's eyes while sleeping, he constantly becomes disturbed when he hears the tread of a nightly visitor enter his father's den. Unsatisfied with his mother's figurative explanation, Nathaniel questions the maid. She, being either somewhat devious and resentful or of the servant class and somewhat more inclined to the confusion of literal and figurative language associated with children, concocts a story for young Nathaniel about how the Sandman is a wicked man who comes when children refuse to go to bed and throws enough sand in their eyes to make them jump out bleeding from their sockets.[60]

Young Nathaniel's fear results from a common enough youthful confusion between the literal and the figurative, between imagination and reality. Later, while away at college, Nathaniel is re-frightened by the appearance at his apartment door of a spectacle salesman whose name closely resembles that of his father's old lawyer whom Nathaniel had originally mistaken for the evil Sandman. The Sandman wanted eyes; the optician deals in eyes of a figurative sort. The Sandman was named Coppelius; the optician is named Coppola. It is important to recall that the story of the history of Nathaniel's youth is being told from the present perspective of a more mature Nathaniel. The incident of the optician somehow makes Nathaniel recall the fantastic narrative regarding the Sandman's murdering of Nathaniel's father. A murder, incidentally, only young Nathaniel knows about and believes happened. But, Freud notes, Hoffman, to the narrative's benefit, leaves in doubt whether what we witness with regard to the primal scene of murder is the first delirium of the panic-stricken boy or a succession of events that are to be regarded as real.[61] Hoffman, or the writer in general, creates striking instances of uncanniness by maintaining a kind of uncertainty as to whether the supposed supernatural elements should be taken as part of the real world or as part of a purely fantastic world existing only in the mind of a certain character.[62] This is, as

I have been arguing, how the supernatural functions in an enlightened era that no longer supports a two-fold world hinged on superstition. Terry Castle perceptively notes that the primal scene in the story, where the Sandman supposedly murders Nathaniel's father, is based on the same illumination that figured in the Enlightenment discourse concerning itself. The uncanny "bringing to light" in the story, figured in the Sandman's attempt to blind young Nathaniel with the "bright glowing masses" of embers from the fire in Nathaniel's father's den, parallels the paradoxical "blinding illumination" of the Enlightenment itself.[63] Only Freud realizes that this primal murder is actually a sub-species of the type of murder known as patricide. But, of course, this patricide is an unconscious murder as a figure of castration. Just as Nathaniel's emergence in the world begins with a sort of patricide, the Enlightenment figures itself as beginning from a certain killing off of one's ancestors.[64] The "being alone in the world" and the responsibility that this type of maturation entails, which Kant emphasizes as necessary for the Enlightenment project, is the same situation Nathaniel finds himself in while away at university. Only his horrific experiences highlight the uncanny aspect of this illumination.

Freud maintains that we know from psychoanalytic experience that the fear of damaging or losing one's eyes is a terrible one — especially in children — a fear that often persists throughout maturity in various disguised forms. But the fear associated with losing one's eyes is itself a disguise for the more primordial fear of castration. The self-blinding of Oedipus, which occurred at the point of full acknowledgment of his hideous desire, pertains to castration as the fulfillment of the Oedipus complex. This is why, for Freud, the Sandman always appears at crucial moments in the tale. He marks the split inherent to Nathaniel himself. The Sandman separates the unfortunate Nathaniel from his betrothed and his best friend; he destroys the second object of his love, the automaton; and he drives Nathaniel to suicide the moment when he is reunited with his beloved Clara. Freud claims that elements like these appear meaningless as long as we deny the connection between fears about losing one's eyes and castration. Rather, the Sandman, the great castrator, must be seen as a substitute for the castrating threat embodied in Nathaniel's own father. Nathaniel's father and the Sandman represent the split inherent to the father. The one father threatens to blind young Nathaniel while the other, more benevolent father, intercedes for his sight. Nathaniel's death wish for his father is a reaction to the inadequacy of his father's intercession. Just like Freud's later reading of the seventeenth century case of demonic possession, the son is faced with a dual father, and it is the father perceived as enjoying which haunts the son through maturity.[65]

Freud concludes by positioning the uncanny effect of the Sandman in the anxiety belonging to the castration complex of childhood.[66] Castration — being born into the language that distinguishes between the figurative and the literal — blinds the subject to the time before castration when he or she possessed an immediate relation to what was most intimate to him or herself. With the maturation that accompanies castration, what was once part of one's intimate universe can only reemerge as what is most strange. The uncanny, for Freud, is "a harking-back to particular phases in the evolution of the self-regarding feeling, a regression to a time when the ego had not yet marked itself off sharply from the external world and from other people."[67] The uncanny is, for Freud, nothing new or alien, but something which is familiar and old established in the mind that has only become strange through the process of repression, the process of castration. Freud draws enough parallels between what is forever lost to us from childhood and what is forever lost to us from our own pre-history as a species to conclude that history repeats itself in every individual in the same manner as the Enlightenment takes place in every individual. The eighteenth century, with all its emphasis on maturity, transforms the supernatural and marvelous aspects of the past (a supernatural and a marvelous that was not wholly strange) into the uncanny element which points to the present's own inconsistency with itself. The uncanny, in effect, points to the Enlightenment's own repressed enjoyment.

Since what is canny is what is homely and since the uncanny is what is most familiar turned strange, Freud further directs his attention to what is known in German as *das unheimlich Haus*. He claims that this edifice, the haunted house, is the most striking example of the uncanny.[68] Basically, our views on death and the afterlife have not changed since our prehistorical days. Unconsciously, we believe we are immortal. Since, according to Freud, the primitive fear of the dead is still so strong within us, it is always ready to come to the surface with any provocation: "Most likely our fear still implies the old belief that the dead man becomes the enemy of his survivor and seeks to carry him off to share his new life with him."[69] But in our enlightened times when repression has distanced us from the direct beliefs of primitive man, it is only necessary that those primitive feelings, including those stemming from our own infancy, recur in the shape of the uncanny. This, for Freud, is what makes the uncanny a special type of the frightening. When one is frightened by something uncanny, one is frightened by something that is most intimate to oneself.[70] This is a consequence of the Enlightenment. Once any external realm is banished, up to and including the Enlightenment's transformation of its own past into part of itself, the supernatural finds its manifestation in the uncanny. In the Middle Ages maladies like madness and

epilepsy were understood as caused by the external force of demonic possession, but in the Enlightenment — and here psychoanalysis has to be conceived
of as an Enlightenment project — the cause is sought in the dimly lit corners
of our own being.

According to Freud, only English carries a term that closely approximates
the meaning housed in the German word *das Unheimlich*. French relies on
the not very reliable term *l'inquiétante étrangeté*. Mladen Dolar maintains that
the inadequacy of this term is illustrated by Lacan's invention of the neologism
extimité.[71] While sketching the parameters of his notion of *das Ding* in *Seminar
VII*, Lacan uses this newly-created word as a condensation of "intimate exteriority."[72] But earlier in the *Seminar*, while discussing the difficulty in representing the topology of *das Ding*, Lacan claims that *das Ding* is located at the
center only in the sense that it is excluded. In Lacan's words, "in reality *das
Ding* has to be posited as exterior, as the prehistoric Other that it is impossible
to forget — the Other whose primacy of position Freud affirms in the form of
something *entfremdet*, something strange to me, although it is at the heart of
me, something that on the level of the unconscious only a representation can
represent."[73] In Freud's words, that thing that is both strange to me and at
the heart of me is precisely what is familiar and old-established, that which
has become alienated through the process of repression — the uncanny.

Because of its injection of old romance into the modern realistic novel,
the eighteenth-century Gothic's use of the sublime conveys the immersion of
fantastic psychical reality into the realm of material reality.[74] What should
have remained hidden — psychical reality — comes to occupy the same topo-
logical space as material reality. What makes the Gothic novelist a different
kind of supernatural writer from any previous scribbler who dabbled in the
marvelous is this intrusion of the uncanny into the world of common reality.
Just as there is no uncanny in fairy tales because we readily accept their fantastic
elements as crucial to their existence, there is, likewise, nothing uncanny
concerning the marvelous elements in literature ranging from Homer to
Shakespeare. But once the realism proper to the novel form normalizes eighteenth-century literary prose, one can no longer go back to the fantastic literature of the Middle Ages. One can only reinvigorate the contemporary form
by creating a sort of pastiche. The old elements within the new form signify
differently. They are on the same plane as the more realistic elements; they
are merely a realistic depiction (for all realism is always a depiction) of psychical reality. So rather than viewing the Gothic novel as a reaction to the
realistic sentimental novels which preceded it, it should be viewed as the realistic sentimental novel brought to its extreme, or logical fulfillment. The key
element in this understanding of the uncanny is the idea that the uncanny is

produced by the rise of modernity. What seems to be a leftover is actually a product of modernity, its counterpart. The Gothic romance less attempts to move beyond the Enlightenment than it attempts to point to its own internal limit. As we shall see in the following chapters, the Gothic romance, through its use of this type of sublime uncanniness, allows the irrational drives of psychic reality to exist within the realist paradigm of its narrative structure.

3

~~~~~~❖~~~~~~

Horace Walpole and the Perverse Origins of the Gothic Romance

In perhaps the most often quoted passage from Horace Walpole's correspondence, at least as far as interest in *The Castle of Otranto* is concerned, one can find a reason why his romance bleeds, much like the statue of Alfonso within the narrative, for a psychoanalytic investigation. In a letter to his friend William Cole written in March 1765 from Strawberry Hill, Horace Walpole, interested in exposing himself as the author of the anonymous romance *The Castle of Otranto*, makes the following disclosure concerning the origin of his literary fantasy:

> Shall I even confess to you what was the origin of this romance? I waked one morning in the beginning of June from a dream, of which all I could recover was, that I had thought myself in an ancient castle (a very natural dream for a head filled like mine with Gothic story) and that on the uppermost bannister of a great staircase I saw a gigantic hand in armour. In the evening I sat down and began to write, without knowing in the least what I intended to say or relate. The work grew on my hands, and I grew fond of it — add that I was very glad to think of anything rather than politics — In short I was so engrossed with my tale, which I completed in less than two months, that one evening I wrote from the time I had drunk my tea, about six o'clock, till half an hour after one in the morning, when my hand and fingers were so weary, that I could not hold the pen to finish the sentence, but left Matilda and Isabella talking, in the middle of a paragraph. You will laugh at my earnestness, but if I have amused you by retracing with any fidelity the manners of ancient days, I am content, and give you leave to think me as idle as you please.[1]

The dream origin of *Otranto* invites the psychoanalytically-inclined reader not only to interpret the first Gothic romance as some type of literary rebus

50

harboring a latent psychological dimension but to also connect the Gothic in general to the seamy underbelly of the unconscious.

Critics have often debated the seriousness with which readers should take Walpole's claim. Reacting to the Surrealists' championing of the early Gothic romance as their precursor, and no doubt indirectly reacting to his fear of, and distaste over, an "official intimacy between Surrealism and Communism," Montague Summers, in his ground-breaking integrative text on the Gothic romance, discounts the over-determined reception that takes Walpole's dream too seriously. After quoting part of the above passage from Walpole's correspondence, Summers claims that "because a vague recollection of a dream suggested the romance of *Otranto* to Walpole it is hardly possible and certainly not reasonable to build up from this whole Nephelokokkugia of Freudian speculation."[2] In turn, criticizing Summers's "turgid" attempt to make the Gothic novel "an aristocrat of literature," Devendra Varma sees the Surrealists' inheritance claim as legitimate as any other branch of modern thought, including Summers's school of "Divine Right."[3] Attempting to justify the Surrealists' claim that *Otranto* is a part of their legacy, Varma focuses on two specific aspects in Walpole's letter to Cole concerning that nightmarish night when *Otranto* was supposedly born. Varma maintains that surrealism is nothing other than the bringing of dream reality onto the same plane as waking reality, basically making material reality coincide with psychical reality. Here, Varma makes the not necessarily obvious connection between dream processes and surrealist automatic writing. The latent dream content, hidden under and between the manifest content of the dream, can be tapped through free association because, like latent dream thoughts, free association gives free reign to the imagination. Therefore, the Surrealists, particularly Andre Breton, felt justified in making an analogy between the dream process and what they schematized as automatic writing. Automatic writing, much like the unconscious latent dream thought, produces very little rational, moral, or aesthetic censorship. From this perspective, Varma swiftly correlates Walpole's authorial claim that he "began to write, without knowing in the least of what [he] intended to say or relate" with free association.[4] Because in basic Freudian analysis one has to uncover the latent dream thought beneath the manifest dream thought, and because Walpole's reaction to his inspiring dream was a quasi-automatic writing, Varma recognizes the necessity of interpreting the plot of *Otranto* as a manifest content masking something psychical: "The part played by the 'unconscious' and the 'automatism of creative activity,' which Andre Breton has always made the criterion of a surrealist attitude in art, is apparent in the first Gothic novel."[5] So, as far as Varma is concerned, the Gothic romance originates not so much in the content of a dream, but in the

very dream process. In other words, *The Castle of Otranto* is less a representation of the mysterious content of Walpole's dream than it is a repetition of
the dream process itself.

The idea of specifically reading Horace Walpole's *Castle of Otranto* as a
manifestation of some latent content lurking beneath the far-fetched narrative
has spawned a number of interpretations of said latent content, which invariably revolve around figuring just how Walpole's dream-like narrative might
reflect his personal and social life. In his analysis of *Otranto*, Martin Kallich
feels justified in reading Walpole's chronicle as a dream precisely because, in
Walpole's often-cited letter to Cole, the author claims that the writing of the
literary work was spawned by a dream. Following Freud's basic interpretative
process for dream analysis, Kallich attempts to establish what current episode
in the author's life may have triggered this dream narrative. Once again, the
answer is implied in Walpole's letter to Cole. Since Walpole claims that, while
writing *Otranto*, he increasingly grew fond of the manuscript if only because
he "was very glad to think of anything rather than politics," Kallich locates
a potentially stressful situation behind the dream narrative. Two months before
Walpole wrote his letter to Cole, his closest friend and cousin, Henry Conway,
was "cut off by the king from his two sources of income as Groom of the Bed
chamber and as commander of a regiment of dragoons for voting against the
court on the issue of John Wilkes and General Warrants."[6] The specifics of
the parliamentary issue that Conway voted against is of less importance for
Walpole's psychic state than the fact that Walpole himself had strongly urged
his cousin to vote the way he did. Understandably enough, Walpole felt somewhat responsible for the action taken by the king against Conway. Following
this incident around his cousin's dismissal from both his civil and military
positions, Walpole persistently did whatever he could to restore both Conway's
name and stature. Kallich focuses on this complex incident as the triggering
source of the dream narrative and outlines the allegorical displacement of this
stressful situation at the heart of *Otranto*. According to Kallich, the manifest
plot of the romance, fueled by terrifying violence and conflict centered around
a ruthless tyrant, is a slight exaggeration, if an exaggeration at all, of the political intrigue in which Walpole as a member of Parliament found himself. So
even though Walpole had assured Cole that he was very glad to be away from
politics for a while if only when writing, it seems he did not psychically escape.

Nonetheless, there are two overlapping themes running through the manifest plot of *Otranto*, according to Kallich. On one level, the tyrant of the
story, Manfred, represents the very governmental powers that ruthlessly dis-
missed Conway from the positions he held. The conclusion of the novel, the
bringing down of the overzealous tyrant Manfred, accomplishes Walpole's

wish fulfillment to revenge a situation which he otherwise has little if any power to influence. The narrative thus reads as Walpole's desire to transform his impotence into a power guided by justice. But, following Kallich, the impotence theme runs further. On the second level of manifest content, Manfred, the character "in charge" throughout the novel, figures as Walpole's own father, Sir Robert Walpole. Since Robert Walpole was at one time a prime minister much in the king's favor and influence, *Otranto*'s narrative can be read as Walpole's desire to become a figure as powerful and influential as his father once was. In this manner, Walpole would easily be able to correct the wrong that he feels guilty for at least partially causing. In either case, Walpole must figure as the orphan character Theodore, the triumphant hero who rightfully assumes power by overcoming all potential despotism and protecting the virtuous.

Although this manifest allegorical meaning which Kallich puts forward sounds like the ultimate childish fantasy, it actually, according to a basic Freudian analysis, masks a more primordial infantile wish. In the *Interpretation of Dreams*, Freud writes:

> But in general, I think, a wish that has been left over unfulfilled from the previous day is insufficient to produce a dream in the case of an adult. I readily admit that a wishful impulse originating in the conscious will *contribute* to the instigation of a dream, but it will probably not do more than that. The dream would not materialize if the preconscious wish did not succeed in finding reinforcement from elsewhere. From the unconscious, in fact. *My supposition is that a conscious wish can only become a dream-instigator if it succeeds in awakening an unconscious wish with the same tenor and in obtaining reinforcement from it.* From indications derived from the psycho-analysis of the neuroses, I consider that these unconscious wishes are always on the alert, ready at any time to find their way to expression when an opportunity arises for allying themselves with an impulse from the conscious and for transferring their own great intensity on to the latter's lesser one. It will then *appear* as though the conscious wish alone had been realized in the dream; only some small peculiarity in the dream's configuration will serve as a finger-post to put us on the track of the powerful ally from the unconscious.... But these wishes, held under repression, are themselves of infantile origin, as we are taught by psychological research into the neuroses. I would propose, therefore, to set aside the assertion made just now, that the place of origin of dream-wishes is a matter of indifference and replace it by another one to the following effect: *a wish which is represented in a dream must be an infantile one.*[7]

Kallich's analysis adheres to the Freudian truth that the manifest content "represents the transvaluation of repressed dream thought and wishes."[8] The manifest level of meaning, the allegorical meaning already outlined by Kallich, is, for Kallich, a symbolic subterfuge and repression "used to evade psychic censorship."[9]

Kallich therefore begins with an interrogation of the narrative's opening paragraph in an attempt to reach the latent level of meaning. The novel begins:

> Manfred, prince of Otranto, had one son and one daughter: the latter, a most beautiful virgin, aged eighteen, was called Matilda. Conrad, the son, was three years younger, a homely youth, sickly, and of no promising disposition; yet he was the darling of his father, who never showed any symptoms of affection to Matilda. Manfred had contracted a marriage for his son with the Marquis of Vincenza's daughter, Isabella; and she had already been delivered by her guardians into the hands of Manfred, that he might celebrate the wedding as soon as Conrad's infirm state of health would permit. Manfred's impatience for this ceremonial was remarked by his family and neighbors. The former, indeed, apprehending the severity of their prince's disposition, did not dare to utter their surmises on this precipitation. Hippolita, his wife, an amiable lady, did sometimes venture to represent the danger of marrying their only son so early, considering his great youth, and greater infirmities; but she never received any other answer than reflections on her own sterility, who had given him but one heir. His tenants and subjects were less cautious in their discourses: They attributed this hasty wedding to the prince's dread of seeing accomplished an ancient prophesy, which was said to have pronounced, *That the castle and lordship of Otranto should pass from the present family, whenever the real owner should be grown too large to inhabit it.* It was difficult to make any sense of this prophesy; and still less easy to conceive what it had to do with the marriage in question. Yet these mysteries, or contradictions, did not make the populace adhere the less to their opinion [*O* 17–18; italics in original].

Analyzing the "prehistoric unconscious" of Walpole's narrative, Kallich claims, "the first sentence sets up the dual role for Walpole as both Matilda and Conrad."[10] The "sickly" Conrad refers to remarks made by Walpole when he was 70 recalling what he had heard said by others about himself as a child. "Sickly," therefore, points to Walpole's own impotent nature with regards to both his father's authority — as both father and as political leader — and to his impotence in challenging the political removal of Conway.[11] Kallich claims that Walpole has also crafted Matilda as a figure for himself in order to highlight his typically ambivalent attitude toward his father and to express his ambivalence: "Thus, by projecting his split ego into two different people, Walpole's unconscious self expressed contradictory attitudes of tenderness and hostility."[12] Accordingly, Manfred then represents Sir Robert, a man who instills both respect and fear, and Hippolita represents Lady Walpole, a woman maltreated by her husband but protective of her children. Finally, Manfred's eventual desire for a divorce from Hippolita and marriage to Isabella reflects Sir Robert's affair and second marriage to Maria Skerritt.

From this figuring of the latent cast of characters, Kallich proceeds to illustrate the infantile wish that, for some reason or another, was triggered by the political affair with Conway, resulting in the dream narrative. For Kallich, it is all too Oedipal. Walpole, through the character of Theodore, the rightful heir to Otranto, wants his father dead so he can have an uninterrupted sensual relationship with his mother: "The latent prehistoric theme of the dream is patricide, in association with the theme of incest."[13] But here Kallich's speculative biographical reading reaches a stumbling block. Since Walpole already possessed uninhibited access to his mother (as his father was always absent on governmental and extra-marital business), why would he need to indirectly dream a desire of ridding himself of his father? Being the youngest child by 11 years, Horace never received the attention of his father in any way similar to his siblings.[14] Why, one needs to ask, would Walpole unconsciously desire something he already had? Where's the fantasy in that?

On the contrary, but still based on Kallich's initial reading of the novel's manifest content, I would argue that Walpole's fantasy narrative less manifests a wish for the annihilation of his father than a desire to have his father's presence more strongly felt. Because of a lack of his father's presence, Horace perhaps never matured beyond a rivalrous relation with his father. Theodore's usurpation of Manfred's throne is less a desire to get rid of the father in some patricidal wish (Manfred is not even killed in the romance) than it is a fulfilled wish to surmount rivalry and mature to the father's level. According to the Oedipus complex, one acquires power, so to speak, not by killing the father, but by overcoming the very desire for patricide and becoming like one's father. Within Kallich's interpretation, *Otranto*, as a dream narrative, should be read as a desire for envy over jealousy — a level Walpole never supposedly matured to in his actual life.

Countering Kallich on an altogether different level, John Samson points to the limits of Kallich's psychoanalytic reading as "relying too little on historical details and too much on Freud's formulations."[15] He dismisses the all-too-easy belief by most critics that Walpole, in writing *Otranto*, really was satisfied to think of anything rather than politics. Not only does Samson maintain that there are political complications in *Otranto* to which even Walpole himself was most likely oblivious, he claims that the historical political elements of the narrative are vital for understanding *The Castle of Otranto* as a Gothic romance which illustrates the "'*perpetual spirals of power and pleasure*' that Michel Foucault sees characterizing Western discourse since the eighteenth century."[16] Samson perceptively picks up on Walpole's clue in the preface of the first edition of *Otranto* as a guide for reading this supposed fantasy of an escape from politics. In the first preface Walpole states, "If a catastrophe, at all resembling that which he [the fictive author, Onuphrio Muralto, who supposedly wrote the original Italian tale] describes, is believed to have given rise to this work, it will contribute to interest the reader, and will make *The Castle of Otranto* a still more moving picture" (*O* 8). Although one may be tempted to read this prefatorial statement made by Walpole as alluding to some catastrophe that happened when the supposed original Italian tale was written in the twelfth century, Samson wishes to read it as Walpole's own masking device. Uncovering this device allows the reader to see this "catastrophe" (especially with the second edition when Walpole exposes himself as the actual author) as the current political disaster involving Walpole's cousin, Conway. Samson sees in the novel "a startling infusion of the characters, events, and ideas in Walpole's political life in 1764."[17]

After George III's head minister, Grenville, had John Wilkes arrested for satirizing the royal family in his *North Briton*, Parliament spent the rest of 1763 and 1764 continuously debating the legality of general warrants. Walpole, as a MP, increasingly perceived Grenville as a tyrant and began involving himself in what he thought was an issue concerning freedom of expression. It is here that Walpole convinced his cousin Henry Conway to vote with him in opposition to general warrants, indirectly causing Conway's dismissal from both his public and military positions. Walpole, feeling dismayed by what happened to his best friend and cousin, attacked the administration in a fruitless attempt to restore Conway to his positions. According to Samson, Walpole had his famous dream and began to compose *Otranto* following the events of this political crisis.

Samson cleverly juxtaposes extracts from *Otranto* with various political writings taken from Walpole's *Memoirs* in order to convince the reader that *Otranto* is itself a thinly veiled reproduction of the Grenville/Conway affair. Because Walpole uses the terms "tyrant" and "despot" to describe both Manfred in his Gothic story and Grenville in the *Memoirs*, Samson feels there is more than coincidence guiding this linguistic connection. Since both Manfred and Grenville are viewed by Walpole as attempting, in their political intrigues, to cement their own political power, the former must be read as a figure for the latter. Furthermore, because Theodore from the novel is described as courteous, generous, noble, brave, honest, handsome, and virtuous (descriptions Walpole apparently only bestows on his favorite cousin), Samson concludes that Theodore is a figure for Conway. And, finally, Samson sees Father Jerome from the romance displaying the same virtuous opposition against all odds

that Walpole thought himself exhibiting against the tyranny of the administration. Through the general plot of the romance, Samson finds many convincing and intriguing parallels with the actual historical circumstances that
spawned Walple's text.[18]

According to Samson, the really imaginative aspect of Walpole's writing
begins with the scene of Theodore's near execution; this is the scene where
"the story and history diverge."[19] Where, in history, Walpole failed to have
Conway reinstated to his previous positions, Jerome, in the story, miraculously
succeeds in obtaining Theodore's pardon. And for Samson, of course, this
split between history and story exposes the depths of Walpole's emotional
state during the period when he so furiously drafted *Otranto*: "The Gothic
fantasy thus shows signs of Walpole's desire, perhaps subconscious, to rid
himself of responsibility or guilt by finding a successful solution to the Conway
incident."[20] But, Samson adds, Walpole's desire turns out to be prophetic
when, a year later, Grenville is ousted and Conway is promoted to leader of
the House of Commons. This reversal — Grenville becoming stripped of power
and Conway becoming reinstated to his rightful position of power — is nothing
other than the story contained in the second half of *Otranto*.

Samson further associates the inherent ambivalence of the character Manfred with Walpole's desire for a moral or even religious imperative in politics.
Manfred, as unrelenting tyrant, has lost all moral sanction for his authority.
Accordingly, Walpole demonstrates this strife between politics and morality
by setting all scenes in either the castle — the domain of politics — or the
monastery — the domain of morality. Because the monastery functions as a
place of sanctuary for those tyrannized by Manfred, Samson concludes, "Walpole reaffirms religion as a powerful counter force."[21] Therefore, the ending
of the romance, in which Manfred retires to the convent and the religious
Jerome and righteous Theodore gain the principality, displays a reconciliation
of moral and political authority.

The fantastic Gothic narrative, mixed with historical events, produces a
confused sort of political theory. Walpole sets the novel in the medieval past
"when religion was the integrating force in society and when politics was
dominated by its norms and not by the extremes of tyrannical authority."[22]
If I am reading Samson correctly, the Conway incident, together with
Grenville's tyrannical practices, caused Walpole to reflect on the contemporary
societal breakdown caused by a newly arisen rift between politics and morality.
Fiction allowed Walpole to set his reflections in a past where an external moral
authority still had some weight — thus, the heavy-handed role given to fate
and prophesy. Walpole, it seems, knows perfectly well that the loss of moral
authority is the cause of current political tyranny, but he seems only able to

offer a nostalgic solution. Walpole can tell us, at least indirectly, that politics has lost its governing morality, but, following Samson, he can only look to the past for a fantastic solution. But if placing religious and moral characters in the seat of political power demonstrates the reconciliation of moral and political authority as Samson assumes it does, why, precisely, does the political edifice itself— the castle — dissolve in ruins?[23] It seems the novel's conclusion points to something potentially more catastrophic than politic's loss of a moral support. Walpole's novel, more or less, suggests that the attempt to fuse politics with an external authority dissolves politics itself. If the medieval past was a time when religion was the integrating force that gave politics its productive norms, and if Walpole's romance is set in this medieval past, why would *Otranto* be a story about a political tyrant stripped of morality? Rather, it appears Walpole uses the past only as a way of marking the blind spot of his current historical situation — a blind spot, it would seem, no amount of historicizing could bring into the light. If one were to follow Samson's historical-political-biographical reading of *Otranto*, one would, I think, have to conclude that for Walplole, the only thing worse than eighteenth-century politics' loss of an external authority is politics possessing an external authority. Pushing Samson's allegorical account further, *Otranto* is about the confusion pertaining to an authority that no longer simply exists in a separate realm. One must keep in mind that within the novel — between the castle as the place of politics and the monastery as the place of morality — there exists the darkened subterranean passages where, apparently, confusion rules.

This other type of authority, this new type of authority, is further investigated in what is perhaps the most psychoanalytically interested study of Walpole. In *Horace Walpole and the Unconscious,* Betsy Harfst attempts to figure these darkened passages omitted in Samson's account as a link to the hidden side of the novel. From her all too brief reading of Freud's *Totem and Taboo*, Harfst accurately and insightfully draws the analogy between humankind's evolution from its earliest stages and a child's psychical growth.[24] Through this analogy, she indirectly points to the strategic use of the medieval past in Walpole's romance as a figuring of Walpole's own early psychical growth. Like Kallich, Harfst attempts to interpret Walpole's tale as a dream narrative after evaluating Walpole's now famous letter to Cole. In Walpole's particular case, the creative process, as in a dream, "temporarily loosened the censoring guards of the practical, conscious world and allowed his unconscious thoughts to become conscious."[25]

After briefly summarizing the general plot of the novel as a reconstructed dream, Harfst begins to illustrate how this manifest version represents the final transformation of the repressed wish fulfillment. Interpretation must begin with the realization that the narrative's coherent plot is a distorted displacement manufactured to evade psychic censorship. In fact, even though Harfst admits that the manifest content of the narrative shows obvious traces of the current political problems of 1764, she, at the same time, realizes that this surface meaning is valid only so far as this current political tension triggered the dream. It does not, however, penetrate beyond the obvious. Any political statement Walpole wished to make would not, out of necessity, need to take the form of a fantastic narrative. He does not need to disguise a political message by transcribing it into an indirect discourse. Harfst's claim that Walpole less needed to evade some external authority's censorship than his own internal censorship is, I think, quite consistent with eighteenth-century production of knowledge. For Harfst, the Conway affair triggered something more intimate in Walpole's life that surfaces through the indirect discourse of the dream narrative.

Through a study of Walpole's correspondence and a number of biographies, Harfst proceeds by taking a closer look at Walpole's early development in order to fully appreciate the latent content hidden in *Otranto*. She, therefore, begins by reading the parallel between the current political friction and something much more intimate that has bothered Walpole since his early years. Walpole's relations with his mother and cousin turn out to be the most striking and important parallel with the current political crisis Harfst finds for her reading of the romance. Basically, according to Harfst, after his mother died when Horace was around 20 years old, Conway became a substitute for his mother within the family romance. This is why the political incident with Conway triggered a dream that is, through Harfst's reading, essentially a wish fulfillment for the mother. Harfst's Freudian interpretation of *Otranto*, therefore, is more penetrating than Kallich's reading in one major way.[26] In order for Walpole's Oedipal desire (to kill his father and have a sensual relationship with his mother) to evade internal censorship, his dream narrative creates a surrogate group of characters who can obtain the satisfaction that Walpole desires. On one level, Manfred represents Sir Robert, Hippolita represents Lady Walpole, and Matilda/Conrad represent Horace.[27] But, in order for Walpole's unconscious wishes of patricide and incest to be carried out guilt-free and to even make it into the dream narrative, Sir Robert has to be displaced into Jerome, Lady Walpole into Isabella, and Horace into Theodore. This way Walpole can enjoy the fruits of his mother without committing incest and without the guilt that would be associated with patricide.

Although Harfst's reading of Walpole's romance as an acting out of an Oedipal wish appears viable and even somewhat convincing, one wonders how well these hidden Oedipal desires determine a narrative that is already extremely derivative of Sophocles's *Oedipus*. Walpole's Gothic story, at least its skeletal form, is nothing other than a re-telling of the tragedy of *Oedipus*. It is basically a story about a ruler who, in his very attempt to ward off a prophesy that predicts doom for his kingdom, only brings this doom to fruition. Even though the original crime was committed by Manfred's grandfather, making Manfred two generations removed, the story is still about a kingdom founded on illegal grounds. It would seem Walpole was all too aware of the potentially hidden impulses by which one, even two millennia removed from the source, is defined. The two generations Manfred is removed from his grandfather's crime represent the infinite gap between any present and its origin. At this point, where one notices Walpole's virtually intentional use of the Oedipus theme, one would have to admit that what Harfst found as the latent content of the dream narrative — Walpole's desire for incest and patricide — is actually the dream narrative's manifest content. One would still need, therefore, to investigate what precisely is the latent content of this dream narrative. Although Harfst's interpretation of *Otranto* appears oblivious to the romance's overdetermined use of the Oedipus myth, it indirectly opens up an alternative and wholly original psychoanalytic interpretation of the narrative's possible latent meaning, circulating around the structure of perversion.

Distinguishing between psychosis proper and perversion, Lacan, in his essay "On a Question Preliminary to Any Possible Treatment of Psychosis," states, "the whole problem of the perversions consists in conceiving how the child, in relation to the mother, a relation constituted in analysis not by his vital dependence on her, but by his dependence on her love, that is to say, by the desire for her desire, identifies himself with the imaginary object of this desire in so far as the mother herself symbolizes it in the phallus."[28] Under perversion, the child's separation from the mother is never completed. Perversion is structured by an incomplete castration. Because the Oedipus crisis is determinate in sexual maturation, an incomplete Oedipal phase in the subject's development results in a retarded development that "linger[s] over the immediate relations to the sexual object which should normally be traversed."[29] Castration remains incomplete if the paternal function is somehow not substantiated enough to separate the child from his bond with the mother. According to Lacan, "Freud reveals to us that it is thanks to the Name-of-the-Father that man does not remain bound to the sexual service of his mother, that aggression against the father is at the very heart of the law, and that the Law is in the service of the desire that law institutes through the prohibition of incest."[30] The Name-of-the-Father, as function, not person, allows the child to see there is more to the mother than the child and, therefore, more to the child than the mother. The child, *via* castration, becomes more than just an object of his mother's satisfaction. Perversion, as an interrupted castration, leaves the child as separate from the mother, but not separate enough to become elevated to the level of the father. Thereby, he remains his mother's little object.[31] Jacques-Alain Miller maintains that "we have the mother and the imaginary object, the phallus. The mother here is responsible for the perversion of the male child, but at the same time uses the child as an instrument of jouissance."[32] Miller continues by asking whether or not the first perverse couple was mother and child, referring obviously to Jocasta and Oedipus.

Perversion, as both a Freudian pathology and as a Lacanian structure, is distinguished from psychosis and neurosis by the operation of disavowal (*Verleugnung*). Due to the inadequacy of the paternal metaphor in his development, the pervert disavows castration. Since he has not properly been cast in a symbolic role, he believes he can directly become on an imaginary level the male organ he perceives his mother lacks. This is the famous "I know very well, but nevertheless" which characterizes disavowal.[33] In disavowal, the father's castration threat is put out of mind if only because it is never adequately introduced in the first place.

In Lacan's structuring of Freud's Oedipus complex and primary and secondary repression, he distinguishes two stages that the subject must go through: alienation and separation. The father's "no," the prohibition of a direct, unadulterated incestuous connection with the mother, inaugurates alienation.[34] Not only does the prohibition of incest alienate the child from the mother for the first time, but the prohibition is necessary for setting up the Lacanian imaginary order. In order to fully undergo castration, however, one must be further separated from the mother through the father's maintaining himself as that which the mother desires. Without showing that the mother has an interest in her life beyond the child, a desire of her own, the child cannot be fully separated from the mother to become a proper member of society. In other words, the child cannot realize his own lack unless he notices that his mother's lack is fundamental. The disavowal proper to perversion is characterized by alienation without the ensuing separation. The child recognizes himself as different from his mother and even that she is lacking in some sense, but, because separation never takes place, because the mother's (the Other's) desire is never substantiated by the Name-of-the-Father, the child becomes that which will fill the mother's lack, making her complete. I know very well that mother lacks the phallus dad has, but nevertheless I am going to act as if she doesn't by becoming for her that thing she lacks (the imaginary phallus). For Lacan, the paternal function is the key in his linguistic rewriting of the Oedipus complex. In psychosis, the paternal function is absent (foreclosure); in neurosis, it is fully established, but never fully trusted (repression); in perversion the paternal metaphor is symbolized to some extent, but not conclusively (disavowal). The pervert's actions, then, are always a staging of the paternal function. This is why Bruce Fink maintains that in perversion — where the Name-of-the-Father and, therefore, the law, is not adequately instilled — the pervert attempts to prop up the law so that limits can be set to *jouissance* (enjoyment).[35]

When the neurotic goes through separation (a phase the pervert disavows), he or she gives up one thing to gain another. One only sacrifices when there is a return. The neurotic gives up his imaginary phallus, which he is for his mother, in return for the symbolic phallus, the phallus as signifier — "the socially recognized signifier of value and desire."[36] He gives up the enjoyment associated with his mother, the supreme enjoyment, in the hope of gaining the symbolic equivalent of esteem, recognition, and approval. The pervert, on the other hand, refuses to give up that enjoyment associated with proximity to the mother. The pervert does not give up this primal enjoyment because the mother's lack, or desire, is never symbolized. And since it is never symbolized, since the symbolization as the necessary return for giving up this primal, suffocating enjoyment never takes place, the pervert believes he can be that which will fulfill his mother's lack. Her lack has to be named in order to be turned into desire, and desire has to be awakened for the child to properly separate from the mother.

Now, the actual reason why separation never takes place for the pervert usually revolves around the absence of the paternal function. This absence can be read as the actual absence of the father, but, since the paternal function is more symbolic than real, this absence really points to the absence of a naming of the mother's lack as desire. Without the mother's demand being articulated as a desire, the child becomes stuck at the level of that which satisfies the mother. According to Fink:

> To return to the question of why one boy might agree to give up pleasure while another might refuse, we see that in cases in which there is a very close bond between mother and son, a father — in order to bring about a separation — has to be quite forceful in his threats and/or quite convincing in his promises of esteem and recognition. But the very fact that such a close bond has been able to form suggests that the father either is incapable of fulfilling the paternal function or does not care to interfere (perhaps happy to be left alone by his wife, who is now preoccupied by her son). The father, while avoiding the rivalrous ferocity of certain psychotic's fathers, does not forcefully put himself in the position of symbolic separator (the one who says, "This is mine and that is yours"— in other words, the one who gives the child a symbolic space). And even if he tries

to do so, he may be undermined by the boy's mother, who, the moment
the father's back is turned, winks at the boy, letting him know that their
special relationship will secretly remain unperturbed.... In cases where
there is a strong mother-son bond and a weak or indifferent father, the
paternal function, though not altogether absent, may well stand in need
of a boost.[37]

Within perversion the child's disavowal of the mother's lack and his refusal
to give up the enjoyment he acquires in his relationship with his mother or
mother substitute results from the inadequacy of the paternal function. The
father's "no" enacts alienation, but since the Name-of-the-Father, as the naming of the mother's desire, is never adequately instilled, separation is thwarted.

As far as the pervert is concerned, the mother cannot technically be seen
as lacking because her lacking is never adequately pronounced as a longing
for something beyond the child. Her longing or desire has to be put into
words (usually by the father) in order for the child's elevation into the symbolic
order to take place. As Fink comments, "once it has been named, the weight
of her demands (her real, physically unavoidable demands regarding the child's
bodily functions, for example) lifts, and a space of desire opens up — a space
in which her desire is articulated and moves, and in which her child can model
his desire on hers."[38] If the mother's demand is not converted into desire by
being named, symbolized, the child is submerged in the mother (Other) and
cannot develop his own position within the economy of desire that wards off
the encroachment of enjoyment. According to Fink, "the child here is confronted with what we can refer to as a *lack of lack*. Only the mOther's demand
exists; she is lacking in nothing 'to speak of,' nothing that is symbolizable for
the child."[39] Not only can the pervert not ward off enjoyment (as a neurotic
devotes his or her life to doing), but he actually becomes the very object of
the mother's (Other's) enjoyment. This is why perverts do not go to analysis.
Their being is not structured by a lost object (the mother as lost upon inau-
guration of the paternal function); rather, perversion is characterized by the
object being too proximate to the point that the perverse subject is the object.[40]
Not only does the pervert have complete access to enjoyment (*jouissance*), but
he has little defense against enjoyment. But all three of the pathologies, as
has been pointed out by Fink, are themselves positions structured in relation
to enjoyment: "Jouissance is simply overrated. It is not so wonderful that
everyone really wants it, the pervert supposedly being the only one who refuses
to give it up and who is able to go out and get it.... The psychotic suffers due
to an uncontrollable invasion of jouissance in his or her body, and neurosis
is a strategy with respect to jouissance — above all, its avoidance. Perversion,
too, is a strategy with respect to jouissance: it attempts to set limits thereto."[41]

The pervert's actions always tend toward enacting the law that will then allow enjoyment to be limited. This enacting of the law peculiar to the pervert is, in turn, an attempt on the part of the pervert to enact some sort of symbolization that will produce the lack where enjoyment can be relegated.

Here one could reconstruct Harfst's psycho-biographical reading of Walpole's *Otranto* around the structure of perversion. Harfst actually begins her analysis of Walpole's life by pointing out how many critics throughout the years have agreed about the capricious nature of Walpole's character. In fact, his erratic, unpredictable, and impulsive personality and actions are manifested quite nicely in objects like *Otranto* and Strawberry Hill — his *faux* Gothic residence. Harfst recounts how Walpole's odd behavior toward keeping his cousin's image secure follows in this vein: "The fervent effort to keep Conway's image in this state of perfection became one of Walpole's major concerns."[42] Some of Walpole's correspondence, quoted by Harfst, significantly displays a structurally perverse side to Walpole's attitude toward his cousin. In his correspondence with Conway, Walpole states, "I am of no consequence; but at last it would give me some, to act invariably with you; and that I shall most certainly be ever ready to do," and "for I always think for you more than myself," and "I, who never did anything right or prudent myself..., am content with your being perfect, and with suggesting anything to you that may tend to keeping you so."[43] One can hear Walpole's desire to be the object of the Other's (here Conway's) satisfaction. Conway, in some perverse manner, becomes the cause of Walpole's existence. Walpole, it seems, will take it upon himself to fill in the gap that separates Conway from perfection. Harfst even concedes that Walpole's fanatical determination to defend Conway's character was the all-engrossing event that absorbed Walpole's energies just prior to the dream that *Otranto* supposedly recreates.

But (and Harfst is quite concerned with this "but") Walpole's intimate attachment to Conway — his over-proximate relation with his cousin in which difference becomes obliterated — must be seen as a substitution, on Walpole's part, of Conway for his late mother. Not only was Walpole the youngest of six children, but also he was born 11 years after the last of Sir Robert's other children. During young Horace's childhood, his father was manifestly absent, away on governmental business. Horace was entirely left in his mother's hands. Reflecting on his constant poor health as a child, Walpole states in his "Reminiscences," "the supposed necessary care of me so engrossed the attention of my mother, that compassion and tenderness soon became extreme fondness."[44] So, prior to making himself the object of his cousin's satisfaction, Walpole already appears to have become the object of his mother's enjoyment. One could speculate that Lady Walpole, finding herself dissatisfied with her husband, looked for satisfaction in her relationship with her son. Likewise, Sir Robert, supposedly engrossed in politics and his extra-marital affair, never presented himself enough for young Horace to be able to symbolize his mother's desire. For Harfst, it becomes evident that Sir Robert, by removing and alienating himself from the domestic scene, caused resentment. This resentment, of course, would be situated toward the father's "no." Without the second step, resentment turning into the envy necessary for Horace to separate from his mother's demand, Walpole remains suspended in the perverted space between alienation and separation. This may explain why, on the conscious level, Walpole maintained a marked hatred for any kind of authority throughout his life. Walpole apparently made it to the first level of castration, characterized by hatred of the father, but failed to succeed to the second level of the envy of the father necessary, according to Freud's reasoning, for the maturation into culture.[45]

Perhaps the reason why Walpole so hated authority was because it never served him in curtailing the onslaught of enjoyment proper to the pervert. This would be, it seems, the real reason behind the "deep underlying resentment" with which Harfst is so concerned. Claiming that the paternal withdrawal from family life would present both advantages and disadvantages for any little boy, Harfst erroneously places unrivaled possession of the mother on the side of advantage. She even claims that this "unrivaled possession of his mother's time and affection ... would, no doubt, be a very pleasurable situation."[46] But, I would have to counter, this unimpeded relationship with his mother could have been, for Walpole, a most horrifying thing — not very pleasurable but beyond pleasure. The resentment he had for his father, manifested in his hatred for authority in general, was more likely resentment for not being protected from this suffocating and limitless enjoyment.

Again, one has to wonder, according to Harfst's reading of *Otranto*, why Walpole would write a dream narrative about an unconscious wish to have full access to his mother when he already possessed this access in actuality. Harfst concludes that Walpole's effort to be a man was never completed, but she fails to observe that Walpole's narrative begs to be read as an unconscious desire to prop up the law, to substantiate the father function, to stage the completion of the Oedipus complex that was never fully established in his life. On the manifest level of *Otranto*'s narrative, Walpole may very well display a wish to continue procuring a certain enjoyment from his mother. On its latent level, however, the narrative should be read as a wish that she would develop some desire that does not concern him. The romance is about separation anxiety. According to Fink, the pervert's "separation anxiety reflects a wish to continue to 'coax' with his mother — in other words, to obtain certain pleasures with her — but a simultaneous wish for an end to be put to that 'coaxing,' to that jouissance, since the latter engulfs him and stops him from coming into being as a desiring subject. Thus, his 'separation anxiety' is actually indicative of a wish for separation — separation from his mother."[47] Following the logic of perversion, one can read *Otranto* as an attempt to stage precisely what Sir Robert failed to stage: the naming of the mother's (Other's) lack.

Freud maintained that the uncanny is a sort of harking back to a particular phase in the evolution of self-regarding feeling, "a regression to a time when the ego had not yet marked itself off sharply from the external world and from other people."[48] Not only does this earlier time reflect one's personal infantile history, a time before castration, but it also refers to an earlier age, an age less mature than the present one. Walpole's desire to "blend the two kinds of romance, the ancient and the modern," as he maintained in the novel's second preface, reflects the uncanny return of the past in the present. For, although this tactic of placing the modern novel in a fantastic past setting eventually became a commonplace of the Gothic romance, in *Otranto* it takes on a more peculiar role. Its peculiarity may very well revolve around the fact that this first experimental Gothic romance had yet no technical parameters, a reflection of the very unique situation of the perverse. Not only is the perverse subject's subjective space not articulated, but also the perverse subject uncannily exists only as an object. The point, therefore, is to move from the psycho-biographical account of reading *Otranto* as a perverted fantasy written by a pervert to using the structure of perversion as a way of understanding this rather bizarre and immature first Gothic romance.[49] This type of analysis can provide a fresh reading for the content of the romance itself, but it can also situate it within its rather unique space in eighteenth-century aesthetics. Just as Richard Hurd claimed that Gothic narratives need to be read on their own aesthetic terms in order to be fully appreciated, *Otranto*, in order to be given its due weight, requires to be read on its own perverted terms.

Horace Walpole's fetish for the Middle Ages, evidenced by his Strawberry Hill estate with all its Gothic memorabilia, spilled over into his romance. Perhaps riding on the successful confusion over Macpherson's *Ossian* poems, Walpole also attempted to write a novel disguised as a discovered ancient manuscript. The title page from the first edition (published on Christmas Eve in 1764) claims that *The Castle of Otranto* is an English translation by William Marshall of an original Italian text written by Onuphrio Muralto. The disguised fabrication fooled some and made others question its authenticity.[50] In the first preface, Walpole claims that the translated romance was found in the library of an "ancient Catholic family" in the north of England (*O* 5).

The translator claims that it was originally printed in Gothic script in Naples in 1529, even though he speculates it was most likely composed between the first and last crusade. After a feeble attempt to speculate on the authorial intentions behind such a text, the translator offers the following insight:

> The solution of the author's motives is however offered as a mere conjecture. Whatever his views were, or whatever effects the execution of them might have, his work can only be laid before the public at present as a matter of entertainment. Even as such, some apology for it is necessary. Miracles, visions, necromancy, dreams, and other preternatural events, are exploded now even from romances. That was not the case when our author wrote; much less when the story itself was supposed to have happened. Belief in every kind of prodigy was so established in those dark ages, that an author would not be faithful to the manners of the times, who should omit all mention of them. He is not bound to believe them himself, but he must represent his actors as believing them [O 6].

Not only does this tropological gesture of splitting himself into author and translator allow Walpole to make a meta-commentary on his own artistic work, it follows the movement of disavowal proper to perversion. While discussing the splitting of the ego in *An Outline of Psychoanalysis*, Freud insists that "the disavowal is always supplemented by an acknowledgment; two contrary and independent attitudes always arise and result in the situation of there being a splitting of the ego."[51] So on one level, Walpole can acknowledge that the type of fantastic narratives which more or less flourished during the Middle Ages have no room in the enlightened eighteenth century, while, on another level, he will nevertheless write one. *Otranto* can, at this point, almost be seen as following the dictates of disavowal: "I know very well, but nevertheless I will act as if I do not know." This, in fact, may be the truth that Walpole, speaking as translator, believes "that the groundwork of the story is founded on" (O 8).

In the second preface, with the exposing of the contemporary origins of the ancient tale, Walpole claims that his nostalgic little romance "was an attempt to blend the two kinds of romance, the ancient and the modern" (O 9). This now famous claim not only situates *Otranto* in the present, but its presence remains haunted by the past. Walpole seems to know very well that those old narratives written solely for enjoyment, as he characterizes *Otranto* in the first preface, no longer have a function in the contemporary age ruled by aesthetic realism. The only way he could write a romance with enjoyment as its primary purpose would be to disguise it as a relic from a long lost past ruled by ignorance. But in the second preface, when the cat is out of the bag,

Walpole provides what could be read as a feeble attempt to manufacture some didactic purpose behind this novel. He is trying, in a sense, to ward off its enjoyment. He explains its backwardness by claiming that it is a literary experiment, a blending of ancient and modern romance.[52] According to Walpole's reasoning, in the Middle Ages all was imagination and improbability, whereas modern writing always intends a natural representation of daily reality. Walpole's complaint against contemporary eighteenth-century aesthetic ideals centers around how "the strict adherence to common life" as the primary literary motive has dammed up the great resources of fancy (*O* 9). Following the parallel previously articulated between Kant's notion of enlightenment and Freud's notion of castration, Walpole's desire to blend the two types of romance can be understood as an attempt to construct a narrative where immature fancy has not been wholly warded off by the laws of proper composition. *Otranto* can be read as a literary work that is alienated enough from infancy to be written at all, but not sufficiently separated from the days of immaturity to give an accurate representation of reality. Walpole, in a sense, knows full well that contemporary laws of literary production dictate the more mature copying of nature, but he cannot help producing a work too strongly fixated on an earlier, more immature type of fantasy. At the same time as his refusal to wholly give up the enjoyment associated with this past type of literary fantasy, Walpole, in his perverse wish to prop up a law that would supplement an inadequately installed reason for his bizarre fictional experiment, refers to Shakespeare as the model and master to copy.[53] Whether or not Shakespeare operates as a sort of surrogate paternal function, his presence in the second preface illustrates that the narrative's will to improbability encounters a limit in a law of its own making. Also, if Walpole is somehow indirectly representing the perverse structure in a literary form, it would appear that the enjoyment peculiar to perversion, that enjoyment associated with a too proximate relation to the mother as a figure of the lost past, can only be presented through fantasy.

This inability of Walpole to fully escape the limitless enjoyment associated with perversion begins to explain the role of the uncanny in *Otranto*. First of all, the two prefaces indicate that Walpole's romance is structured by the uncanny, especially since the past medieval superstitious aesthetic they highlight should have remained hidden. Secondly, the content of the "Gothic story" is also concerned with this very uncanny existence of the past in the present.[54] Immediately following the prefaces and the particulars of the hastily assembled wedding ceremony between Manfred's son Conrad and Isabella, the narrator points out a possible anxiety-inducing prophecy befalling the House of Otranto. The ancient prophecy pronounces "that the castle and lordship of Otranto should pass from the present family, whenever the real owner should be grown too large to inhabit it" (*O* 17). Immediately following this pronouncement ensues the claim that "it was difficult to make any sense of this prophesy; and still less easy to conceive what it had to do with the marriage in question. Yet these mysteries, or contradictions, did not make the populace adhere the less to their opinions" (*O* 17–18). The only way for the characters, and probably the reader, to understand the prophecy — and these are the "opinions" they adhere to — is to regress to what Freud calls "the omnipotence of thought." Stated bluntly, the omnipotence of thought is the idea that thoughts in some way or another affect matter. According to Freud, this fantastic effect is easily produced when the distinction between imagination and reality is effaced. This effect of the omnipotence of thought occurs not only more frequently in literary works, it is a reflection more particular to psychical reality than to material reality.[55] The prophecy, at first only feared, becomes uncanny once the giant helmet falls from the sky, crushing Conrad. Add to this seemingly uncanny, if not absurd, event of the later witnessing of the armored giant by the servants Diego, Jaquez, Frederic, and Bianca, and the reader can observe the narrative's literalization of the figure "the real owner should be grown too large" from the prophecy necessary for the uncanny's emergence.[56]

In his reading of Hoffman's tale "The Sandman," Freud asserts that young Nathaniel's anxious encounter with the uncanny begins when he reads the Sandman as an actual being beyond his function as a figure of speech. From this point on, young Nathaniel becomes immersed in a suffocating world increasingly inhabited by that most uncanny figure: the literal.[57] For Freud, this type of phenomenalization of language is rooted in infancy. Because children live in a more imaginary world lacking the mutual hostility between words and things, the uncanny phenomenalization from the prophecy's "largeness" into a giant haunting the castle marks a return of the past into the present. On one level, Walpole's choice for a medieval setting of the novel functions as an appropriate time when the superstitious belief in the omnipotence of thought was a more likely commonplace. On another level, the medieval setting figures as that which, according to Freud's working definition of the uncanny, should have remained hidden in the past but has resurfaced as a symptom of the present. The medieval setting utilized by Walpole not only lends credence to the fantastic aspects of his story, but it allows him, however inadvertently, to point to the disavowal necessary for a realistic representation of nature. At the very least, *Otranto* states a truth that the idealization of realistic representation is the superstition of eighteenth-century aesthetics. The uncanny, as far as Freud is concerned, emerges because one's infancy, whether thought of as the individual's infancy or as the Middle Ages construed as the infancy of the Age of Enlightenment, has been supposedly surmounted. Walpole, however, creates a more perverse atmosphere in his romance by conflating the infantile onto the same plane of reality as the matured adult world.

Since *heimlich* signifies a space and feeling of comfort usually associated with the home, and since *unheimlich* marks the moment that this most comforting of places becomes strange, one can begin to see the prophecy's effect on the princedom of Otranto. The prophecy, in announcing that there is a real owner of Otranto, indicates to Manfred and his people that there is a mystery regarding the past history of Otranto, a mystery that would, once uncovered, reveal the meaning of this otherwise cryptic prophecy. Whether the giant specter lurking around the castle is a manifestation of some sort of retributive justice or an over-imaginative literalization of the prophetic metaphor is less important than the fact that it surreptitiously indicates that something is rotten in the state of Otranto. As the romance proceeds and one uncanny episode follows another, Manfred's sovereignty becomes undermined from within as the once familiar surroundings take on an eerie strangeness.

Concomitant with the various sightings of the uncanny giant is the arrival of the presumed peasant Theodore. Although it is not revealed until the end that Theodore is the rightful heir of Otranto, it is not difficult for the reader, observing the inconsistency between Theodore's supposed class and his noble virtue, to surmise this fact. Matilda instantly notices the uncanny similarity between the stranger, Theodore, and the armored statue of Alfonso, the original ruler of Otranto. This similarity becomes more uncanny when Manfred sees Theodore donned in a suit of armor and perceives the vengeful return of Alfonso: "Is this ghastly phantom sent to me alone — to me, who did not.... What, is not that Alfonso? Cried Manfred: dost thou not see him? Can it be my brain's delirium?... He has unhinged the soul of Manfred" (*O* 83). Others may notice the similarity of Theodore and the old statue of Alfonso, but only the one who harbors the guilt of the illegal usurpation of Otranto sees Theodore as an uncanny spectral appearance. This distortion of reality has to be viewed less as coming from an external source like Theodore than it must be read as the inherent inconsistency of Manfred's sovereignty. Earlier in the novel when Manfred is faced with the inevitability of returning Isabella to her father and thereby losing his chance to produce the heir needed to maintain possession of his princedom, he tells Frederic about the origin of his family's rule in Otranto: "You must know, your lord knows, that I enjoy the principality of Otranto from my father Don Manuel, as he received it from his father Don Ricardo. Alfonso, their predecessor, dying childless in the Holy Land, bequeathed his estates to my grandfather Don Ricardo, in consideration of his faithful services" (*O* 67). At this point in Manfred's narrative, Frederic, the addressee of Manfred's little tale of deception, is said to have shaken his head, tipping off the reader to the potentially fabricated aspect of Manfred's history. And it is the fact of fabrication that should remain secret as long as Manfred can maintain his line (family line as well as story line). As the secret of Manfred's illegal usurpation of the sovereignty of Otranto boils to the surface, the uncanny occurrences increasingly conflate with the homey reality around the castle. Manfred's home, that which is most intimate to him, takes on an increasingly alien form.

The end of the romance reveals the secret of the illegal grounds upon which Manfred's authority rests, leading to a catastrophic climax. Manfred, faced with the bitterness of mistakenly killing his daughter in what would appear a foolhardy attempt to save his sovereignty, is forced to divulge the perpetration of his family's crime: "I would draw a veil over my ancestor's crimes — but it is in vain: Alfonso died by poison. A fictitious will declared Ricardo his heir. His crimes pursued him — yet he lost no Conrad, no Matilda! I pay the price of usurpation for all!" (*O* 113). At the moment of this revealing through the uncovering of the veil of mystery, "the walls of the castle behind Manfred were thrown down with a mighty force, and the form of Alfonso, dilated to an immense magnitude, appeared in the centre of the ruins. Behold in Theodore, the true air of Alfonso! Said the vision: and having pronounced these words, accompanied by a clap of thunder, it ascended solemnly towards heaven" (*O* 112–13). By the time that the truth, which should have remained secret and hidden, has come to light, Manfred's authority and sovereignty lies both figuratively and literally in ruins. That which used to be the place of absolute familiarity has, through the uncanny revelation of the hidden truth, metamorphosed into an utterly unrecognizable scene.

The fact that the fully assembled giant specter of Alfonso — the completed literalization of the prophetic metaphor of "too large" — bursts forth in his destructive fury from within the castle provides a clue to the true motive behind Manfred's actions throughout the narrative. Uncannily, throughout the novel, Manfred, in his desperate attempt to frustrate the prophetic threat to his authority, only seems to work on behalf of the prophecy's implementation. Everything Manfred does to thwart the prophecy only appears to fuel the fruition of the fate it pronounces. One is lead to believe that it is Manfred alone, without any external assistance, who wreaks the havoc wrought. This catastrophe should not be read as a result of Manfred's inherited guilt since this only obeys the medieval superstitious belief in some divine redistributive justice. Rather, Manfred must be read as taking an active pursuit in bringing the prophecy to fruition. From the very beginning, when Manfred imprisons Theodore for some bogus crime associated with necromancy, the narrative mentions how "he sought a subject on which to vent the tempest within" (*O* 21). Theodore, in a futile attempt to maintain his innocence, even claims that he is not answerable for Manfred's thoughts (*O* 31). Manfred's various actions aimed at saving his authority — ranging from divorcing his wife and marrying Isabella, attempting to behead Theodore, suggesting he and Frederic switch daughters, up to and, especially, including his reliance on ancient prophecy — only seem to raise the very confusion and curiosity that eventually will cause his downfall.

But why, on the other hand, would Manfred wish to bring about his own downfall? The answer is that he doesn't, or, at least, he is unconscious of the fact that he wishes this. Manfred's quest is not unlike that of Oedipus. Oedipus, too, without recognizing what he was doing in his obsessive desire to find out who killed Laius, only brought about the downfall of his own authority. Even though Manfred's actions appear by all narrative accounts to be directed at the desire to save his princedom, they are uncannily revealed as doing just the opposite. What, then, is Manfred's true desire? The only conclusion one can draw concerning the motives behind Manfred's actions is that, unbeknownst to himself, Manfred wants to bring about his own ruin. Since, in psychoanalytic theory, the perverse subject is the subject where drive is most clearly manifested, and since Manfred's authority is constantly undercut in the romance by an oozing of supernatural enjoyment, one can accurately read Manfred as a perverse character of pure drive.[58]

In his brief text, "On Freud's '*Trieb*' and the Psychoanalyst's Desire," where he begins a linguistic restructuring of Freud's notion of drive, Lacan insists, through his distinction between desire and drive, that "desire comes from the Other, and jouissance is on the side of the Thing."[59] Desire needs the Other, as the mother's desire symbolized, in order to function. Without this naming of the mother's desire, as in perversion, one becomes suffocated by the mother's enjoyment. This is why Lacan concludes that drive is more directly visible in the perverted subject. Under castration, the subject, *via* the prohibition of incest, loses access to that supreme enjoyment, *das Ding*. But since the perverted subject disavows, for whatever reason, the incest prohibition, enjoyment is not relegated in the manner it would be for the neurotic. Desire is by definition unsatisfied, precisely because the lost object desired can never be re-found along the axis of a symbolic space. This is the basic cause of neurosis. Drive, on the other hand, has no problem succeeding in its aim for satisfaction. And this is the dilemma of the pervert. Since the prohi-

bition of incest is never adequately instilled for the pervert, nothing is prohibited. Castration designates a lack of enjoyment, so what is essential for
desire is its impasse. Drive, however, never comes to an impasse. According
to Miller, "what Freud calls the drive is an activity that always comes off. It
leads to sure success, whereas desire leads to a sure unconscious formation,
namely, a bungled action or slip: 'I missed my turn,' 'I forgot my keys,' etc.
That is desire. The drive, on the contrary, always has its keys in hand."[60] In
fact, desire's constitutive failure is nothing other than drive's success. Drive,
if it does anything, makes desire constantly fail.

Since desire is based on not having, and since there is no lack in the
structure of perversion, the drive is highlighted in perversion. In Manfred's
desire to prevent the collapse of his sovereignty, he fails. But this failure
demands to be seen for what it is. It belies the success of his drive. All the
strenuous efforts aimed at warding off the prophecy are, in turn, driving at
bringing it to completion. One could even say that Manfred's inadvertent
murder of his daughter Matilda, as his last desperate attempt to bar the
prophecy's realization, was, at the level of drive, not a mistake at all. Not only
was the murder not a mistake, it was the ultimate act that proved the
prophecy's success. If one reads Manfred as a character of desire, as an everyday
neurotic subject, then one can conclude that he simply screwed up. But if one
reads him as a caricature of drive, as perverse as it takes a figure of authority
to be, one can begin to appreciate *Otranto* as a realistic romance about psychical reality.

This notion of perversion can also clarify *Otranto*'s place in the history
of the Gothic. There is growing debate today concerning the validity of considering Walpole's *Otranto* as the first Gothic novel. While it cannot be argued
that he labeled *Otranto* "A Gothic Story" for its second edition, it is debated
whether his nonsensical and immature novel has any remote relation to the
much more poetically sophisticated Gothic novels that flourished in the 1790s.
After all, much time elapsed between *Otranto* and the first novel that it supposedly inspired: Clara Reeve's *The Old English Baron*.[61] Ronald Paulson, who
insists that the Gothic is a "metaphor with which some such contemporaries
in England tried to come to terms with what was happening across the channel
in the 1790s," actually situates *Otranto* as a mere fable of the *ancien regime*.[62]
Perhaps Reeve could even be considered the founder of this new and fairly
successful genre. Perhaps it was her talent and technique in adapting elements
of Walpole's writing that only retroactively determined Walpole as the founder
of the modern Gothic. Anne Williams has focused on literary history's ability
to create its own myths of origin as a way to debunk the "patriarchal principles
of order" that necessarily lead to putting a male writer at the origin. After

quoting an extensive publisher's blurb from the jacket of an *Otranto* paperback claiming Walpole as the originator of a new fiction that eventually utterly transformed English letters, Williams claims that "Walpole's claim to be the Gothic creator *ex nihilo* is as dubious as Manfred's to the throne of Otranto."[63] This official story of Walpole as the father of the Gothic romance, according to Williams, effaces the mother as that less prosaic side of Gothic writing.[64] But, I would argue, by analyzing Walpole's *Otranto* as both immature and perverse, one cannot only account for the role of the mother in the origin of the Gothic novel, but one can move beyond the debate about whether *Otranto* really is the origin of the Gothic.

Paradoxically, *The Castle of Otranto* is often seen as a novel that is both an immature Gothic and the one Gothic that possesses all the gadgets and machinery that will sustain the genre for another 60 years. Just a cursory look at the many supernatural and uncanny occurrences within the bindings of this smallest of Gothic romances shows that Walpole's imagination captured the genre's entire gamut of effects. With Isabella mistaking Theodore's voice in the subterranean passageway between the castle and monastery as the ghost of Conrad (*O* 29) along with the pent-up vapors of sexual tension becoming displaced as a haunted castle's groan (*O* 74), Walpole designs the "explained supernatural" that will have to await the terrifying arrival of Ann Radcliffe's poetic mastery to become fully matured. With scenes like the bleeding statue of Alfonso (*O* 97) and the final destruction of the castle (*O* 102), Walpole has given the reader the actual supernatural that Matthew Lewis will perfect and use to horrify and titillate the reading public in 30 odd years. And lastly, Walpole even offers the reader the potentially, but not definitely, supernatural swaying of the helmet's plumes (*O* 25–6) and the portrait coming to life (*O* 26, 35). This debated first Gothic romance appears to have it all. But what makes *Otranto* unique is that all this Gothic sublime machinery lacks any anchoring point. It exists in a huge mass of confusion; enjoyment, in a sense, runs rampant. Contrary to Williams's claim that *Otranto*'s legacy is secured by some patriarchal principle, Walpole's novel suffers from and enjoys an utter lack of a paternal guarantee. Not only does *Otranto* not efface the mother, it cannot separate itself enough to not become the object of enjoyment. Without any firm idea of what he was writing, without that firm paternal anchoring point, Walpole's romance remains an immature bric-a-brac of all the future Gothic symbols; symbols that yet do not symbolize. *Otranto* is, in a sense, constituted by that "polymorphous perversity" with which Freud characterizes the immature sexuality of the pre-genital phase.[65] What makes *Otranto* different from all the following Gothic novels is its utter lack of any relegation of enjoyment. Because Walpole's writing and behavior can be seen as creating a sense of embarrassment and dismay in others, he can, perhaps, accurately be labeled the *enfant terrible* of eighteenth-century English letters.

As far as Walpole and myth-making go, I think it would be more accurate to situate Walpole's *Otranto* alongside Aristophanes's myth of the double-sexed being articulated in Plato's *Symposium*: the mythic figure *par excellence* of Freud's notion of the polymorphously perverse. In Aristophanes's comic myth of origins there exists a third sex: the union of the two.[66] This figure marks not only a time before sexual difference, but a structural stage prior to sexual difference. While Walpole's *Otranto* contains all the elements of the Gothic machinery, they remain in an undeveloped stage because of the narrative's perverse structure. Like Aristophanes's figure, *Otranto* exists in a sort of historical vacuum. Only when the Gothic romance becomes something of itself, only when it matures through castration, does one get the splitting between terror and horror narratives that defines the mature Gothic romance of the 1790s. Since Lacan observes that the pre-genital stages, or pre–Oedipal stages, are ordered only in the retroaction of the Oedipal complex,[67] it should be pointed out that those mature Gothic romances, those that have developed adequately through the Oedipus complex, those more neurotic novels of Radcliffe and Lewis, retroactively determine *Otranto* as their own lost origin. Consequently, *Otranto* should be considered more the poetic offspring of Radcliffe and Lewis than the reverse. Only after the Gothic romance has relegated its supernatural and sublime elements of enjoyment, only after it has become an enlightened literature, can it divide into the neurotic antinomical relation between terror and horror rooted in sexual difference.

4

⚜

Sexual Difference and
the Gothic Sublime

Horace Walpole's indignant reaction to Clara Reeve's corrective imitation of *The Castle of Otranto* is well known and acknowledged.[1] Less documented, however, is Walpole's much more jubilant reaction to the fragmented imitation attempted by Miss Aikin, a figure who has virtually vanished from the pages of Gothic history.[2] Appended to (and meant as a reader's guide to) Aikin's *Sir Bertrand, a Fragment* is the little essay "On the Pleasure Derived from Objects of Terror." In this essay, Aikin opposes Reeve's critical assessment that Walpole's text suffers from the confused role the supernatural plays in his romance. In fact, Aikin creatively praises the dynamic distinction of *Otranto*'s sublime machinery.

From the beginning of her text, Aikin distinguishes between two objects of terror: natural and artificial. The former object, even though it causes painful sensations, is attended by "virtuous sympathy." Instead of causing disgust and horror, this natural object of terror actually offers a sense of "exquisite and refined pleasure."[3] This pleasure, it seems, stems from the satisfaction of one's benevolent feelings. The other object of terror, what Aikin calls the "object of pure terror" because it fails to solicit our moral feelings in any way, is "much more difficult of a solution." This "artificial" object of terror, characterized by the marvelous, provides amazement more than pain and misery. When Aikin raises the question of how we are to account for the pleasure derived from these latter objects, she admits that she has "often been led to imagine that there is a deception in these cases."[4] In fact, the curiosity which attends this so-called object of "artificial" terror is not, for Aikin, "proof of our receiving real pleasure."[5] Naturally, the pain of suspense, inaugurated by an object of "natural" terror, produces "the irresistible desire of satisfying curiosity."[6] Aikin, therefore, points out the inevitability of substituting an artificial object of amazement to replace the suspended feeling provided by

76

the natural object of terror: "we rather chuse to suffer the smart pang of a violent emotion than the uneasy craving of an unsatisfied desire."[7] At this point where an "artificial" terror is substituted for a "natural" terror, passion and fancy co-operate in elevating the soul to its highest pitch, and "the pain of terror is lost in amazement."[8] "Natural" terror excites in us something so unfathomably primordial that causes us, in avoidance, to transfer the accompanying implacable pain onto some sort of marvelous object of "artificial" terror. Hence, "the more wild, fanciful, and extraordinary are the circumstances of a scene of horror, the more pleasure we receive from it; and where they are too near common nature, though violently born by curiosity through the adventure, we cannot repeat it or reflect on it, without an over-balance of pain."[9]

Aikin is one of the first to recognize the two types of sublime fear which have, in our day, become commonplace. On one side is the "natural" object of terror that produces the pain of suspense, and on the other side lies the "artificial" object of terror that amazes with its unrealistic appearance. Not only is she one of the first to notice this nuanced distinction, but she notices it within the narrative of *Otranto*. Because Aikin is not possessed of an unimaginative, literal mind like Reeve, she is able to locate what will eventually become the all-important Gothic sublime distinction within Walpole's otherwise perverse narrative. She sees *The Castle of Otranto* as a very spirited modern attempt to mix the two types of terror. And, in order to back up her theory of the two distinct types of literary sublime affect, Aikin supplies her own Gothic fragment "in which both these manners are attempted to be in some degree united."[10]

Although published within a year of Jacques Cazotte's *Diable Amoureux*, Aikin's fragment bears more than a passing resemblance to this better-known French novella. And, coincidentally enough, it is precisely where the resemblance between "Sir Bertrand" and Cozette's text begins that the reader can note the shift from one form of terror to the other. Aikin's fragment begins in progress with Sir Bertrand fleeing one adventure only to find himself imperiled in another. Lost in the darkness of the moor, the knight is beckoned by the ringing bells of a large antique mansion. In the following seven pages of this ten-page adventure, Sir Bertrand is confronted with two distinct instances of supernatural terror. Upon approaching the ruinous, abandoned mansion, Bertrand, suddenly witnessing a light appear and disappear at virtually the same moment in one of the upper windows, is seized with a terror that stops his fearful heart. The terror the knight feels, as described by the narrator, impels him to proceed into the abandoned building. In the midst of near darkness, a cold hand is described as firmly grasping Bertrand's hand and leading him through the confines of the structure's interior. Describing Bertrand's state, the narrator maintains that "he followed in silent horror."[11] From here the narrative spins a less suspenseful and more marvelous tale in accord with Cazotte's style. The fragment continues with Bertrand's rescue of a veiled lady from the confines of a coffin, leads to a sumptuous banquet complete with a troop of gay nymphs, and completes with the entire edifice's crumbling asunder with a horrible crash, à la the ending of *Otranto*.

By transmogrifying Bertrand's terror without object into the horror of the dead, cold hand grasping his arm, Aikin offers the reader a narrative on the distinction between two types of terror. And it is, perhaps, not accidental that this shift coincides with the narrative's shift from the term "terror" to that of "horror." Although, as argued in the last chapter, *Otranto* possessed both of these forms of supernatural fear in a sort of nondescript embryonic form, Aikin is able to utilize them in an experimentally aborted fragment to give life to the very distinction. She is able to see what is only latent in Walpole's Gothic story and to enact the separation process that will then be perfected in the 1790s.[12]

This distinction is further illustrated to the advantage of terror in the works of Ann Radcliffe. In *The Mysteries of Udolpho*, for instance, the narrative insists that "daylight dispelled from Emily's mind the glooms of superstition, but not those of apprehension."[13] By "glooms of superstition," Radcliffe denotes those fears that arise from some supernatural object that has been substituted for uncertainty and obscurity. This is what she will later refer to as "positive horror." "Glooms of apprehension," on the other hand, refers to those fears of an evil that itself is not manifest. These are fears primarily brought on by a limited perspective. Apprehension simply outruns comprehension, and the difference creates an anxiety-producing uncertainty. Later in *Udolpho*, when Emily is described as "relieved by [a] conversation from some of the terrors of superstition, but those of reason increased,"[14] the narrative suggests that the positive terror, which may have produced an original fear, once removed, only ignites an anxiety without any external locus.

In her posthumous essay "On the Supernatural in Poetry," Radcliffe draws a helpful distinction between these two types of fear. Through a dialogue between Mr. S and W., she maintains that writers "with whom certainty is more terrible than surmise ... must be men of very cold imaginations."[15] Where horror narratives offer a positive object of fear (a ghost, Satan, a corpse, murder, rape), terror narratives create only an anxiety-producing atmosphere where uncertainty and suspense rule. Radcliffe writes:

> Terror and horror are so far opposite, that the first expands the soul, and awakens the faculties to a high degree of life; the other contracts, freezes

and nearly annihilates them. I apprehend, that neither Shakespeare nor Milton by their fictions, nor Mr. Burke by his reasoning, anywhere looked to positive horror as a source of the sublime, though they all agree that terror is a very high one; and where lies the great difference between horror and terror, but in the uncertainty and obscurity, that accompany the first, respecting the dreaded evil?[16]

She also points out that even though Milton uses the term "horror," he actually engages in the aesthetics of terror precisely because the supposed horror is only seen through glimpses of obscurity and great outlines. Because Milton does not distinctly picture forth his scenes of horror, he opens up a space of wonder in the reader's imagination. In fact, Radcliffe further argues that an escape from the anxiety that accompanies the obscurity of terror can be provided when one can actually discover the fear-producing object. In other words, by externalizing the uncertainty that accompanies the dreadful feeling associated with terror, one brings this apprehension within the more comforting realm of comprehension. In the end, Radcliffe appears to be suggesting that horror narrative is a compromise formation.[17]

The Marquis De Sade more forcefully implies that this distinction between terror and horror narratives within the Gothic tradition is marked by sexual difference. In the 1800 essay "Reflections on the Novel," while focusing his analysis on the "new novels in which sorcery and phantasmagoria constitute practically the entire merit," Sade places Matthew Lewis's *The Monk* meritoriously ahead of the "strange flights of Mrs. Radcliffe's brilliant imagination."[18] Sade's infamous statement that writers, in order to create fictional works of an interest that could rival the attention paid to the devastating effects of the French Revolution, "had to call upon the aid of hell itself" suggests that the revolution had a direct impact on the history of the novel.[19] The revolution, in Sade's imagination, created a sort of castrating effect on narrative fiction, making it virtually impossible for the novel to return the realm "of man's daily life" that constituted the works of the *ancien regime.*[20] The Gothic novel of the 1790s, in a sense, matured from its origin by being utterly separated from it. Sade maintains that there are two possible directions a novel writer can take: "either one resorts increasingly to wizardry — in which case the reader's interest soon flags — or one maintains a veil of secrecy, which leads to a frightful lack of verisimilitude."[21] Sade associates Lewis with the former novel of "increasing wizardry," while he characterizes the poetics of Radcliffe as steeped in "veiled secrecy." Sade maintains that this emerging style of writing — the one that seems to have split into opposing schools — is doomed unless it can produce the virtually impossible work which does not "flounder upon one or the other of these two reefs."[22] But a work of this type, steeped in plentitude, it appears, can only exist in a realm of truly Sadean perversity. And it was already written in that lost past of 1764.

The terror/horror distinction that plays itself out within the eighteenth-century Gothic romance has been vastly commented on and developed in contemporary criticism. Fred Botting suggests that "while terror and horror are often used synonymously, distinctions can be made between them as countervailing aspects of Gothic's emotional ambivalence."[23] Echoing Radcliffe, Botting claims that terror leads to an imaginative expansion of one's sense of self, while horror, the other side of the Gothic supernatural dynamic, provokes the movement of contraction and recoil. And, following Sade, Botting sees the movement between terror and horror as part of a dynamic "whose poles chart the extent and different directions of Gothic projects."[24] Botting diagrams the difference between terror and horror through the distinction between the externalization and internalization of objects of fear and anxiety, and, again following Sade, he reads this difference around gendered lines. According to Botting, Radcliffe's work differs significantly from previous Gothic tales due to its more fully developed terrifying and mysterious scenes. Radcliffe skillfully utilizes darkened atmospheres set in unchartered realms of ruins, castles, and forests in order to add a terrifying sublime aura to a scene actually bereft of the supernatural. The imagined supernatural terrors that haunt the characters in Radcliffe's novels, in the end, turn out to be displacements of "mysteries that lie closer to home and reality."[25] Because the supernatural elements are eventually explained away by rational causes, Radcliffe's narratives, according to Botting's analysis, "bring readers and characters back to eighteenth-century conventions of realism."[26] By means of terror, the threatening object is escaped, paving the way for a return to patterns of sentimental fiction. Of course, Botting's logic presupposes that the "object" of terror is something present in the first place. Horror narratives, on the other hand, present their characters with threatening objects that cannot be recuperated within an otherwise realistic setting. Botting, reiterating the typical developmental overview of the Gothic, sees Lewis's narrative style as a direct reaction to the "explained supernatural" narrative inaugurated by Radcliffe. By describing "in lurid detail the spectres that Gothic fiction had previously left to the superstitious imagination," Lewis (and his so-called followers) turns terror into horror.[27] Rather than titillating the reader with the possibility of the supernatural, Lewis gives it directly in all its presence. Because of this dramatic move, Botting is led to believe that horror narratives move beyond and radicalize traditional narrative forms. But, precisely because Lewis shows the supernatural in all its being, because he reveals it, one would have to argue that the supernatural is no longer a possibility. Paradoxically enough, by giving the reader the supernatural on the narrative plane, Lewis systematically eradicates the narrative's supernatural potential. And this is precisely what Botting persecutes Radcliffe for doing.[28]

The relation between terror and horror narratives within the eighteenth-century Gothic romance, however, is hardly reducible to Botting's straightforward externalization/internalization schema. Even though Lewis brings the supernatural within the narrative boundaries of his novel, this very practice makes the supernatural object external to the characters of the story. And conversely, since Radcliffe expunges the supernatural from the interior of her narrative, it only seems to occupy a space within the imagination of her characters. Radcliffe's externalization of the supernatural becomes an uncanny sort of internalization, and Lewis's internalization of the supernatural, likewise, becomes an uncanny sort of externalization.

Frederick Frank suggests that prior to the 1790s, the decade when the Gothic romance flourished, "terror had been quite compatible with horror in the same works."[29] But with the two responses to the work of Walpole carried out by Radcliffe and Lewis, the sublime splits into two antithetical aesthetics: "The Gothic breaks down into two mutually disharmonious types and redefines itself along the lines of sex, ethicality, and aesthetic goals."[30] Frank sees Radcliffe's Gothic as a feminized myth of escape from the world of sexual danger. Her protagonists are invariably female, and the victory that her romances dramatize occurs when these maidens acquire their freedom from the so-called evil forces that confine them. Since the supernatural primarily figures as a marker of the general anxiety the heroine suffers upon maturation, Radcliffe's romances never directly display actual supernatural forces. The reasonable explanations given at the end of her narratives seem to certify a certain amount of disillusionment suffered by the heroine.[31] The terror offered by Radcliffe is offered to expand the range of the narrative into realms where narratives cannot directly go. Lewis, on the other hand, offers a masculinized version of the same "myth of deliverance from the lower world of sexual passion."[32] But, because Lewis does not stop short at suggestion, he creates a narrative universe where characters' and readers' imaginations are deflated. Without fully spelling it out, Frank maintains that this antithesis between Radcliffe's and Lewis's utilization of the sublime appears more like a contradiction than an opposition. For some unsaid reason, these two agents of the sublime do not, in any way, form a complementary set. Terror and horror, as two separate and distinguishable Gothic narrative devices, constitute more of an antinomic than an antithetic relation.

In order to understand how this distinction between terror and horror, developed from Walpole by Radcliffe and Lewis, delineates more of an antinomic relation around the contours of sexual difference, a lengthy detour through the eighteenth-century culmination of the theory of the sublime is needed.

Until the eighteenth-century, aesthetics had always been content and preoccupied with the notion of the beautiful. But eighteenth-century aesthetics is irreducibly marked by Boileau's seventeenth-century rediscovery and translation of Longinus's monumentally complex text on the sublime, *Peri Hupsous*. Edmund Burke is, of course, the most notable and influential British theoretician of the sublime in the eighteenth century. But, because Burke remains within a fundamentally empirical epistemology, his *Enquiry*, at least in part, must maintain that the beautiful and the sublime are characteristics that inhere in objects. The terror associated with the sublime is, in a sense, caused by the obscurity associated with certain objects. Since sensuous experience plays such a primary role in Burke's epistemology, he concludes that "the sublime ... always dwells on great objects, and terrible; the latter [beauty] on small ones."[33] That the cause of sublime feelings is reduced to the senses is obvious by a warning Burke offers in relation to searching for bodily causes beyond the realm of the senses: "When we go but one step beyond the immediately sensible qualities of things, we go out of our depth. All we do after, is but a faint struggle, that shews we are in an element which does not belong to us."[34] Because Burke aligns the sublime with the passions of self-preservation, he leaves open the possibility that there is indeed something objectively missing with regard to the sublime. Without quite putting his finger on it, Burke appears to notice something self-referential with regard to the solitude particularly associated with feelings of the sublime. And, one could argue, it is this something that then becomes the very thematic object in the Gothic novelist's innovative rewriting of the Burkean sublime.

Although Burke — being British, accessible, and proximate to the early rise of the Gothic — is traditionally viewed as having the most profound influence on the Gothic writers of the sublime, certain recent critics have shifted their belief from merely viewing Gothic romances as literary attempts to illustrate Burke's notion of the sublime to viewing these novels as implicit critiques of Burke. David B. Morris's brief, but influential, study of Gothic sublimity examines the manner in which "the Gothic novel participates in a significant revision of the eighteenth-century sublime."[35] Morris disassociates himself from the typically instrumental viewpoint that sees the role of the sublime in the Gothic novel as "merely an incidental, ornamental, scenic prop."[36] He attempts further to illustrate how sublimity is a "vital, integral part of the Gothic novel."[37] For Morris, the Gothic romance moves beyond Burke precisely at the point where it attempts to examine a terror and darkness irreducible to sensuous experience. Echoing Walpole, one could even say that the Gothic romance's utilization of the supernatural is necessary to frighten us out of our senses. Also against Burke's concern with a largely empirical account of terror, Vijay Mishra concludes that the Gothic romance appears more concerned with the idea of conflicting instinctual impulses irreducible to direct representation: "Gothic sublimity articulates that which cannot be articulated, or named, and in the process transforms the experience into something like a primal scream."[38]

This something "beyond experience," which the Gothic sublime attempts to highlight negatively, seems to anticipate what Samuel Monk called the unconscious goal of eighteenth-century aesthetics: Kant's Third Critique.[39] Unlike Burke's empiricist-oriented notion of the sublime, which is only able to account for improbable possibilities, Kant's idealist analysis of the sublime exposes the limits of the empirical. Although Kant sees Burke as "the foremost author in a merely empirical exposition of the sublime," he feels that Burke's analysis of the imagination and the representations of understanding remain, in the end, wholly corporeal.[40] Kant's main complaint with Burke's empirical analysis of the beautiful and sublime revolves around establishing a principle of judgment. Under an empirical framework, how can a universal aesthetic agreement be reached since, under such conditions, each person rightly consults his or her own personal feelings alone?[41] In order to maintain that there exists a fundamental universal judgment of taste occurring in everyone, the focus of attention must be on taste itself rather than on a series of particular examples. In other words, the judgment of taste must be based upon some *a priori* principle.[42] Kant's complaint, of course, is that the adding up of all empirical evidence can never get one to the unconditioned condition of universal taste. Burke, therefore, stands in a sort of perverse space between Hume and Kant. He seems to be beyond Hume's basic skepticism without yet realizing that this is the case. Kant, on the other hand, realizes that no amount of prying into the empirical laws can succeed in establishing an *a priori* principle of judgment. Empirical laws can only yield knowledge of how we judge, but they cannot command us as to how we ought to judge. In place of Burke's flawed empiricism, Kant offers a transcendental examination of the faculty of judgment itself. Kant contends that if the sublime is as terrifying as Burke claims, it needs to be viewed in relation to the absolute as a transcendental experience rather than in relation to any particular or relative experience.

Kant begins his analytic of the sublime by simply stating the difference between the sublime and the beautiful. For Kant, the beautiful is always a question of the form of a delimited object. The sublime, however, relates to an object devoid of form. The very limitlessness of the sublime determines its object as fundamentally indeterminate. Because the sublime object is devoid of form, it provokes a representation of limitlessness with a super-added thought toward its totality: "The beautiful seems to be regarded as a presentation of an indeterminate concept of understanding, the sublime as a presentation of an indeterminate concept of reason."[43] This distinction illustrates the different delights associated with both objects. The beautiful is directly attended with a feeling of the furtherance of life compatible with the playfulness of the imagination. The sublime, however, arising only indirectly, is brought about by a feeling of the momentary check to the vital forces. The beautiful, in this analysis, offers a positive pleasure, and the sublime offers only a negative pleasure. Where the beautiful is evoked by the power of the imagination's presentation, the sublime is evoked by the imagination's very inability to represent: "The sublime, in the strict sense of the word, cannot be contained in any sensuous form, but rather concerns ideas of reason, which, although no adequate presentation of them is possible, may be excited and called into the mind by that very inadequacy itself which does admit of sensuous presentation."[44] The sublime, therefore, is precisely what provokes the mind to abandon sensibility and employ itself upon ideas of a higher faculty. According to Kant, unlike the feeling of the beautiful, the sublime gives, on the whole, no indication of anything final in nature except where nature reflects back onto us a feeling of our own finality, independent of nature: "For the beautiful in nature we must seek a ground external to ourselves, but for the sublime one merely in ourselves."[45] Kant, therefore, articulates the distinction between the beautiful as representing the successful representation of the imagination and the sublime as pointing to imagination's inherent failure.

Therefore, for Kant, the greatness of the sublime lies not in the phenomena of nature — the field of phenomena — but in our own ideas. Since the sublime is evoked when our ideas outstrip our sensibility, it awakens the feeling of the supersensible faculty within us. Keeping in line with Kant's first two Critiques, one could assert that the sublime re-opens the space of transcendental apperception (First Critique) underlining the limits of any pathological content (Second Critique). In fact, at the end of Paragraph 25, Kant gives the following precise definition of the sublime: "The sublime is that, the mere capacity of thinking which evidences a faculty of mind transcending every standard of sense."[46] Magnitude summons the sublime precisely because it defeats the end that forms its concept. Magnitude, in Kant's estimate of the sublime, is not something found in external objects; it is to be sought in the mind of the judging subject. In a sense, the sublime object points to what is in the object more than the object: the very limitlessness marking the subject. Because the sublime fails as a representation, Slavoj Žižek argues, "it evokes its beyond by the very failure of its symbolic representation."[47] For

Kant, the sublime "is an object (of nature) the representation of which determines the mind to regard the elevation of nature beyond our reach as equivalent to a presentation of ideas."[48] Thus, ideas are represented at the point where the mind cannot find a purpose to some object of nature. The subject's confrontation with, and inability to incorporate into the field of knowledge, some senseless aspect of nature confronts the subject with its own supersensible realm. Since the sublime represents nature in its purposelessness, it shows nature expending its forces in a manner that does not serve any purpose. This is precisely Lacan's definition of enjoyment from *Encore*: "What is jouissance? Here it amounts to no more than a negative instance. Jouissance is what serves no purpose."[49] And, according to Žižek, "in the Sublime, nature does not know — and where 'it doesn't know,' *it enjoys*."[50] Since Kant views beauty as "purposiveness without a purpose," Alenka Zupančič has observed that the beautiful is the place where *nature* knows. Likewise, she concludes that the sublime is the place where *nature* enjoys. Because the sublime is explicitly a senseless and strictly non-empirical form, it appears as pure excess, as "the eruption of '*jouissance*,' as pure waste."[51] But, as Zupančič is careful to add, the sentiment of the sublime, while indicating the proximity of *das Ding* (as threatening the subject), provides a way of aesthetically avoiding the encounter with *das Ding*.[52]

This exposure to the Thing, or the *Ding-an-Sich*, in Kant's terms,[53] has to be thought of more as an encounter with the limit of sensible intuition, the limit of the phenomenal field, than as a confrontation with some actual thing beyond the domain of possible phenomena. While it is without doubt that the Kantian sublime exposes the subject to the unfathomable, it does not necessarily follow that there is something situated in the realm of the unfathomable to which one is exposed.[54] Since, according to Kant's analysis, the sublime has the potential to expose the subject to the non-phenomenal moral law within, one has to bear in mind Kant's reflection from the *Critique of Practical Reason* where he maintains that an essential uncertainty regarding pathological motivation is necessary to sustain the dimension of ethical universality. Precisely because the moral subject can never be 100 percent certain whether his or her ethical decision is completely free of any pathological stain — whether there is, in the end, not some narcissistic motivation, however slight, behind his or her act — the universal remains irreducible to the particular. If one knew that one's ethical act was wholly free of any pathological dimension, if one was sure that one's act wholly coincided with duty, one would surely be perverse. This is why Lacan articulated Sade as the truth of the Kantian categorical imperative.[55] Because Kant maintains that the subject can never know the moral law to the letter, the moral law, as that thing beyond our phenomenal field, can never itself become substantiated. When the sublime aesthetically exposes the subject to the noumenal realm of the moral law within, it exposes the subject to what is in him more than him, which can only be objectified *via* a fantasy screen. This is why, for Kant, the sublime is a wholly negative judgment.

Although the Gothic romancers of the 1790s were not particularly concerned with the ideas of reason in the Kantian sense, their use of the supernatural as sublime object should be understood as attempting to uncannily make the suprasensible coincide with the sensible, allowing the reader to perceive the inaccessible through the accessible.[56] The supernatural techniques of the Gothic novelists serve a sublime function: the function of functionlessness.[57] To read the supernatural experiences within Gothic narratives as sublime occurrences is to realize that they represent precisely what is unrepresentable, what is in the narrative more than the narrative. If these minor literary works have any worth within the aesthetics of the eighteenth-century, the sublime effects produced by these Gothic romances must be read as the narratives' acknowledged inability to represent everything. The sublime in these novels is, then, a materialization of a structural inability, a marker of enjoyment within the narrative. And just how this enjoyment is regulated, as in Kant, depends on whether the narrative aligns itself on the side of terror or horror.

Within Burke's analysis of the sublime, this Gothic distinction between the terror and horror modes of supernatural narrative would, obviously enough, play itself out in the opposition between the beautiful and the sublime. In Kant's estimation of the beautiful, however, the imagination and the understanding organize the object in conformity with its form, but with the sublime, where imagination is in collaboration with reason, there is no finality of the form of the object. Imagination simply cannot conform to reason's demand for totality. Imagination can only succeed in exposing us to reason's unreasonable demand by showing its own inadequacy in meeting this demand. Reason's supersensible demand can only be made intuitively evident by the inadequacy of the faculty of imagination. So, viewed through Kant's transcendental analysis, this Gothic distinction between terror and horror marks an inherent split within the sublime itself. If the sublime feeling is evoked in us when every standard of sensibility falls short of the ideas of reason, exposing us to the supersensible as the limit of experience, Kant insists that this "falling short" occurs in two asymmetrical ways. Within Kant's analytic of the sublime, he distinguishes between two separate modes: the mathematically sublime and the dynamically sublime. While the former modality deals with magnitude, the latter deals with might.

Kant begins his analysis of the mathematical sublime by distinguishing between a mathematical and an aesthetic estimation of magnitude. Mathematical estimation works logically through numerical concepts: "Now we can only get definite concepts of *how great* anything is by having recourse to numbers (or, at any rate, by getting approximate measurements by means of numerical series progressing *ad infinitum*)."[58] The numerical counting of magnitude is an objective determination. But since the series of numbers can logically proceed to infinity, something outside the range of intuition's comprehension, a wholly subjective aesthetic estimation of magnitude, pertaining to what meets the eye, limits the infinite mathematical counting. In other words, no purely mathematical estimation of magnitude by numbers alone can evoke the sublime. The evocation of the sublime occurs when aesthetic estimation of magnitude forces the numerically infinite to conform to what the subject can take in intuitively by creating an "absolute measure beyond which no greater is possible subjectively."[59] These two estimations of magnitude are simply apprehension and comprehension. Apprehension proceeds mathematically and can be carried on to infinity. Comprehension, on the other hand, reaches a limit to where it can no longer take in everything apprehended, and it soon attains its maximum. One can read every word of *War and Peace*, but surely one can never construct an interpretation of the novel that would include everything; the deed would indeed seem sublime.

The sublime feeling is roused in us because of the inadequacy of our imagination to keep up with the infinity of mathematical estimation of magnitude. The imagination of the aesthetic estimation simply cannot represent for us the totality that can be counted by numbers. Since numbers can continue to infinity, this totality simply does not exist. The sublime feeling occurs when "our faculty of imagination breaks down in presenting the concept of a magnitude."[60] The infinite progression of numbers is simply incongruous with a single intuition of a totality. Kant puts it: "The mathematical estimation *by means of numerical concepts* ... can never be completely thought."[61] This is why, in *Encore*, Lacan insists on reading Don Juan as a feminine myth. Don Juan simply takes women one by one.[62] But, for all that, he never takes them as a totality. This is why the women in Moliere's play are not the characters who become enraged at Don Juan. Rather, it is the men (the brothers, husbands, and fathers) who actively seek revenge on Don Juan for his revelation that these women, who can only be seen one by one and not as a totality, are irreducible to the signifier of mother, daughter, sister, or wife.[63] The myth of Don Juan illustrates in the mathematical sublime what Lacan calls the "non-all" character of the totality. Don Juan can make a list of all women, but for all that, the list could never amount to a totality. The mathematical sublime, then, occurs when the imagination, in progressive counting, proves inadequate to the idea of magnitude as totality.[64] The feeling of the sublime, according to Kant, is at once a feeling of displeasure, arising from the inadequacy of imagination in the aesthetic estimation of magnitude to attain to its estimation by reason (comprehension's inability to keep up with apprehension), and a simultaneous awakening of pleasure, arising from reaching the ultimate limit of the greatest faculty of sense.[65] And is this paradoxical pleasure in displeasure that Kant associates with the sublime not the very definition of Lacanian enjoyment?

But this is only half of the sublime story. There is another manner in which this enjoyment is produced and regulated. The object of the mathematical sublime, as illustrated above, marks the inherent limit of the phenomenal field, illustrating how the phenomena are inadequate to the thing-in-itself. The sublime feeling associated with the mathematical modality derives from what Kant calls the "objective impossibility" of the object of the phenomenal realm to adequately represent the Thing.[66] The sublime feeling, thus, arises by means of this very failure of representation. But, as will be seen, the dynamically sublime appears to overcome this hindrance of sensibility.

Kant begins his delimitation of the dynamically sublime through the concept of might. Almost immediately, the reader begins to see a distinction in the dynamical sublime from the impossibility associated with the mathematical. The very limit of reason, determining the indeterminacy of the supersensible, which Kant carefully articulates in paragraphs 26 and 27 on the mathematical sublime, is here transformed into a determined reason of limit. In other words, the very limit of reason, invoking the supersensible negatively in the mathematical sublime, is converted into a positively constructed object of the supersensible in the dynamically sublime. What was previously viewed as the limit of reason now becomes viewed as produced by the very limits of reason:

> In the immeasurableness of nature and the incompetence of our faculty for adopting a standard proportionate to the aesthetic estimation of the magnitude of its realm, we found our own limitation. But with this we also found in our rational faculty another nonsensuous standard, one which has that infinity itself under it as unit, and in comparison with which everything in nature is small, and so found in our minds a preeminence over nature even in its immeasurableness.[67]

Kant's strategy of starting with the mathematical attests to the fact that he views the dynamically sublime as secondary — a secondary type of resolution to the fundamental impasse articulated by the mathematical side of the sublime. The very limitlessness associated with the sublime in the former articulation metamorphoses into the condition of reason itself. When one is confronted with an object that outstrips one's concept (mathematical), it becomes equivalent to the very presentation of ideas. At first the sublime displays the inherent impossibility of phenomena from ever attaining the truth of the thing–in–itself, and then this impossibility becomes, oddly enough, the thing–in–itself. What was first the very limit of representation now becomes what is unrepresentable — a sort of positivization of a negative judgment.

Kant maintains that at a certain point the terror evoked in us by the sublime, intimating the helplessness of our nature, reveals a faculty of estimating ourselves as independent of nature. This revelation leads to the eventual discovery in us of a pre–eminence above nature that is the foundation of a self–preservation of a different order from that which may be assailed and threatened by external nature. In this way, external nature, for Kant, is not estimated in our aesthetic judgment as sublime insofar as it excites fear, but rather because it forces our non–natural power to "regard small those things which we are want to be solicitous (worldly goods, health, and life), and hence its might as exercising over us and our personality no such rude dominion that we should bow down before it."[68] Kant suggests that this sublime might, associated with the dynamical sublime, provokes us to view things from a more elevated point of view. There is, therefore, a moment when something has an effect on us to the point where we realize that everything pathological we live for is worthless in comparison. We are willing to give up everything we hold dear — up to and including our life and well–being — precisely because this "giving up" is itself already an overcoming of the might and power that the sublime provokes in us.[69] In this manner, according to Kant, we gain an extension and might greater than that which we sacrifice. So, where on the mathematical side of the antinomy the sublime appears to point to an inherent impossibility of our judgment, on the dynamical side this impossibility is transformed into the might (of the mind itself) to overcome any hindrance of sensibility.

The idea of linking the enjoyment evoked by the sublime to sexuality might seem permissible on the level of affect but would probably strike most as obscene on a more logical level. But it is precisely by way of logic that one can best demonstrate such a link. Joan Copjec has argued that sex itself, being a non–discursive entity and, therefore, a thing–in–itself, coincides with the impossibility of articulating it. Rather than viewing sex as a pre–discursive entity — something that pre–dates castration — Copjec argues that sex is a logical effect, an outgrowth of the cut made on the body by language acquisition. Sex remains fundamentally enigmatic not because its meaning is incomplete or unstable, but because it is the impossibility of completing meaning: "The point is that sex is the structural incompleteness of language, not that sex is itself incomplete."[70] Once one becomes a subject by way of castration, one is alienated and separated forever from direct access to being. In return for this sacrifice of being, one acquires the knowledge produced by language. Therefore, the feeling of the sublime exposes the limit of the knowledgeable, or phenomenal, world. The sublime — just like sex in Copjec's argument — serves no other function than to limit understanding, to mark the fundamental incompleteness of the Oedipus complex, to remove the subject from the realm of possible experience or pure understanding. Not only is the sublime opposed to our senses, but it is opposed to any meaningful sense. In this vein, it would not be incorrect to assert that the feeling of the sublime exposes us to sexuality. The castrated subject surrenders enjoyment upon entering language, forcing enjoyment to show up only as an impasse in language. Since the sublime is evoked by the impasse of language, and since this impasse exposes the subject to a negative experience, the sublime can be read as the negative experience of enjoyment. In Lacanian terms, the sublime is less a signifying material, less a symbol, than it is an emergence of the real within the symbolic, or a symbolization of the real. Since language is a differential system, differences are inscribed in the symbolic. Sexual difference, however, is not. Only the failure of sexual difference's inscription is marked in the symbolic. And this failure is itself productive of sublime feeling. Therefore, there are two different modalities of the sublime in Kant precisely because of sexual difference.

Even though Copjec, in her analysis of sexual difference, focuses on the antinomies of pure reason from Kant's First Critique, she claims a parallel between the mathematical and dynamic antinomies of the *Critique of Pure Reason* with the mathematical and dynamic modalities of the sublime in the *Critique of Judgment*. Following Kant's analysis of the antinomies of pure reason, Copjec maintains that if language — or reason — had only one mode of misfire, the subject would in fact be neuter. But since language or reason — that which we acquire upon castration as the completion of the Oedipus complex — may fail in one of two different ways in Kant's philosophical critique, Copjec writes that "Kant was the first to theorize, by means of this distinction, the difference that founds psychoanalysis's division of all subjects into two mutually exclusive classes: male and female."[71] Copjec then proceeds to ingeniously align Kant's antinomies of reason with psychoanalysis's sexuation of the subject. She convinces the reader this can be done in all honesty because, in *Encore*, Lacan reiterates the position of psychoanalysis with regard to sexual difference through a logical field. According to Lacan, our sexed being is not a biological phenomenon; it does not pass through the body, but results from the logical demands of speech.[72] Words, in a sense, fail. But, as Lacan insists, they fail — just as they do with the sexual relation — in two ways: in the male manner and in the female way.[73]

Copjec's analysis draws on Kant's antinomies of pure reason as an explanation for the two different manners in which reason fails. The mathematical and the dynamic antinomies of reason are the two mutually exclusive ways in which reason fails to conceptualize the universe as a whole totality. The mathematical antinomy comes about when reason attempts to think the totality of the universe by way of "the mathematical total of all phenomena and the totality of their synthesis."[74] This antinomy is constituted by a thesis that claims the world has a beginning in time and is limited in space, and it is further constituted by an antithesis which maintains that the world is infinite with regard to space and time. Kant's point is that this antinomy is one of contraries. Both statements, the thesis and the antithesis, may be simultaneously false. The falseness of one does not verify the truth of the other. On the other side, the dynamical antinomy is characterized by a thesis and antithesis which are both true. The thesis that declares that the laws of nature are accompanied by freedom as the causality of all phenomena in the world appears, at first sight, to be contradicted by the antithesis which maintains that there is no such thing as freedom because everything in the world happens according to the laws of nature. But on closer scrutiny, one not tethered to Aristotelian logic, even if everything in the phenomenal field is indeed caused by the laws of nature this does not necessarily negate the existence of another realm caused by freedom. The field of phenomena can be totally accounted for as long as there is something exempted from this field. According to Copjec, "where thesis and antithesis of the mathematical antinomies were both deemed to be false because both illegitimately asserted the existence of the world, the thesis and antithesis of the dynamical antinomies are both deemed by Kant to be true."[75]

Copjec perceptively draws a correspondence between these two antinomies of reason as outlined by Kant in the *Critique of Pure Reason* and Lacan's formulas of sexuation outlined in Seminar XX: *Encore*:

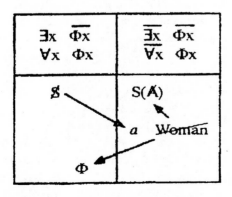

Figure 1. Lacan's Graph of Sexuation.

The above symbols read as logical structures. On the left is listed the male side of sexual difference expressed in the parameters of the dynamical antinomy, and on the right is listed the feminine side of sexual difference expressed in the parameters of the mathematical antinomy. Lacan maintains that "every speaking being situates itself on one side or the other."[76] On the lower left, $\forall$ x stipulates that all x's (men) are subject to Φ (the phallic function, or castration). After all, to be a speaking being means to be castrated. The top left further indicates that there is at least one x (father function) that is not subject to Φ (castration; the bar over Φx indicates negation). "$\forall$x Φx indicates that it is through the phallic function that man as a whole acquires his inscription, with the proviso that this function is limited due to the existence of an x by which the function Φx is negated. That is known as the father function."[77] The totality of men can be inscribed with the proviso that one man, in this case the primal father, is exempt from castration. One can add up all men and come up with man in general, but only when one man is exempted from the whole does the field change from men in general to man in its universality (Man as notion). Everything, therefore, is inscribable for man except that which has been exempted from the field.

However, the other side of sexuation, according to Lacan, "will not allow for any universality."[78] At the top right, the formula, since both elements are negated, stipulates that there is not one x (woman) that is not subject to Φ (castration) with the proviso below that not all x (woman) is subject to Φ (castration). Since the feminine side lacks the one exception that constitutes the male side, it does not constitute a universal set. This is why Lacan insists that woman cannot be written with an upper case W (he puts a bar across Woman). This also explains Lacan's famous insistence that Woman does not exist. Woman, for Lacan, does not exist as a universalized field since there is not one x not subject to castration. The feminine side of sexuation's insistence that there is not one x not subject to castration comes with the further proviso that woman is non-all to castration. This, of course, is the famous non-all (*pas tout*) of feminine sexuality, implying that femininity is based on the recognition that the Φ (phallus) is only a filler covering the lacking foundation of the symbolic order. For Man there appears to be something beyond the Φ, but for woman, there is only appearance.

The bottom half of the graph illustrates the sexual subject's relation to the object. The masculine subject is barred ($\math$) because his subjectivity is based on an exemption. This subject aims toward woman as his object of desire, but only comes up with *objet a*—the object cause of desire. As Lacan points out, "he is unable to attain his sexual partner, who is Other, except inasmuch as his partner is the cause of his desire."[79] He, therefore, is caught up in Lacan's matheme for fantasy: $\mathcal{S}<>a$ (the barred subject in relation to his object cause of desire). The feminine side has not just one, but two possible forms of *jouissance* open to it. One, which parallels hysteric desire and is phallic in nature, is articulated as barred Woman→Φ (woman barred in relation to phallic enjoyment). This should be read as the hysteric's desire: woman desires the desire of the Other. But because the field of women, as illustrated by Don Juan, is non-all in relation to the phallic function — the signifier is inadequate with respect to woman — there is the possibility of an Other *jouissance* on this side of sexual difference. A *jouissance*, Lacan insists, of which even women have no knowledge. The matheme barred Woman→S($\mathbf{A}$) designates the non-all aspect of woman as the full subject in relation to the inconsistency of the field of the Other.[80] "Woman [barred] is related to the signifier of A insofar as it is barred."[81] The enjoyment articulated by Lacan as the Other *jouissance* is limitless and brought about through the realization of the fundamental incompleteness of the field of the Other, a fact covered up on the masculine side of sexual difference by Φ and the subsequent fantasy brought about by prohibition.

Copjec, perceiving the overriding privilege of the feminine side of sexual difference in Lacan's analysis, begins her fusing of Kant and Lacan by situating the mathematical antinomy into Lacan's logical paradigm. In Copjec's fusion, the top right symbols state that there is no phenomenon that is not an object of possible experience. The bottom symbols of the mathematical antinomy, listed below with a negation over the first symbol, states that not-all phenomena are a possible object of experience. Therefore, according to Copjec, the status of the world is not infinite but indeterminate.[82] Since the mathematical antinomy deals exclusively with sensible intuition, it is limited by its ability to encompass the whole of phenomena all at once. When it comes to the mathematical antinomy, the feminine side of sexual difference, Kant and Lacan are articulating an indefinite judgment. The totality of phenomena, of woman, can neither be confirmed nor contradicted by reason. In an indefinite judgment, the thing-in-itself is excluded from the domain of sensible phenomena, the domain of sense, without being posited as an object beyond sensible intuition. One is left with an inconsistency within the field of phenomena itself. Since there is then no meta-phenomenon, it is impossible to move from phenomena to a judgment about existence: "The symbolic fails to constitute ... the existence of woman."[83] If the Other is, by definition, that which guarantees our consistency, and if, as Lacan's graph makes explicit, the Other is inconsistent with respect to the field of woman, then "there is no guarantee where the woman is concerned. She, or the symbolic that constructs her, is fraught with inconsistencies. We are thus led to the conclusion that the woman is a product of a 'symbolic without an Other.'"[84] She, in other words, is not wholly susceptible to the "no" of castration. And it is my contention, as expressed throughout this chapter, that one experiences the feeling associated with the mathematical sublime when one is exposed to this internal inconsistency at the heart of the Other, the symbolic order.

The mathematical side is constituted by an impossibility and the dynamical side is constituted by a prohibition. The mathematical side, and the failure appropriate to it, centers around an inherent impossibility in constructing a totality of the phenomenal field. The absolute totality of an endless progression is inconceivable. Because no phenomena are excluded, the conception of a universe of phenomenon, of woman, is impossible to delineate. Kant, in fact, states this as the reason for the mathematical sublime: "In the case of the logical estimation of magnitude the *impossibility* of ever arriving at absolute totality by the progressive measurement of things of the sensible world in time and space was cognized as an objective *impossibility*."[85] Kant continues by adding that the feeling of "unboundedness" that characterizes this impossibility "is received as sublime with a pleasure that is only possible through the mediation of displeasure."[86] The dynamical side, on the other hand, constructs a totality only at the expense of something that is exempted from the phenomenal field. In other words, the dynamical sublime is evoked not by way of the unboundedness of the phenomenal field; rather, it is evoked by way of an object not of the phenomenal field. The field of phenomena can be closed and totalized as long as the impossibility to totalize the field, which is characteristic of the mathematical side, is incorporated into the field as an element beyond sense — a nonsensible element. This movement from the mathematical to the dynamical can be characterized as a movement from a lack of a signifier that would totalize the field to a signifier of lack. The field can be totalized as long as one thing is exempt from the field. Kant, therefore, maintains that the feeling of the dynamical sublime is produced by the feeling "that there is *something forbidden* to sensibility."[87] According to Copjec, Lacan defines man as the prohibition against constructing a universe and woman as the impossibility of doing so: "The sexual relation fails for two reasons: it is impossible and it is prohibited."[88]

Likewise, the mathematical and dynamical sublime delineate the two modalities of the imagination's failure to accomplish its synthetic activity. On one side, the imagination's synthetic activity is impossible, and, on the other side, its activity is prohibited. And these two different modes of the sublime, these two asymmetrical ways in which the imagination's failure is felt, produce two different sublime feelings. In the mathematical modality, the sublime feeling is evoked through the imbalance between apprehension and comprehension when the imagination fails to totalize the finite phenomenal field. Within this modality of the imagination's failure, the subject is exposed to a finite field without limits, to nature as the totality of phenomena that eludes our finite experience. The utter impossibility of a finite subject's transcendental imagination to schematize the finite field of phenomena in its totality produces the dizziness associated with the obscurity of the mathematical sublime. The dynamical sublime, however, evokes a feeling of awe by transforming the mathematical impasse of impossibility into the exposure of another realm: the supersensible as the domain of the moral law. If there is something our finite imagination cannot grasp, there must be something, a noumenal realm, beyond the finite field of phenomena. In this manner, the dynamical modality transforms the feeling evoked by the impossibility of the mathematical sublime into an awe-inspiring prohibition. The phenomenal field becomes totalized because what was barring its totalization (the impossibility of doing so) is simply prohibited from entering the field — it is elevated to an external realm. Where the mathematical sublime summons a feeling of obscurity because it exposes the subject to the inherent inconsistency of the phenomenal field (the feminine field of the "non-all"), the dynamic sublime, in its endeavor to totalize the field of phenomena, produces a larger-than-life, awe-inspiring object existing in a realm beyond the phenomenal playing field (the masculine field of the exception-based universal).

Both the obscurity produced by the mathematical sublime and the awe created by the dynamical sublime are the residual effects/affects of the imagination's failure to schematize. Since the subject feels the imagination's failure more than it knows about it, these two residual affects of the imagination's failure are the paradoxical pleasure (enjoyment) derived out of the pain of failure. Even though the imagination's failure produces pain, it simultaneously, according to Kant, opens the subject up to the space of the thing-in-itself as either the internal inconsistency of the phenomenal realm or as the noumenal realm beyond. Consequently, the Kantian *Ding-an-Sich* exists only negatively as either the contours of an invisible void (mathematical/feminine) or as the moral law as sublime thing (dynamical/masculine). Paradoxically, the sublime not only exposes the subject to *das Ding*, but it does so only by regulating the enjoyment this exposure evokes. The sublime opens the space of "beyond the pleasure principle" only temporarily; it must be understood as simultaneously the evocator and the defense.[89] Therefore, the sublime enjoyment associated with the feminine Gothic and that linked to the male Gothic remains asymmetrical.

Although the differentiation between the "Craft of Terror" and "Chamber of Horror" schools of Gothic writing became a bit of a commonplace in 1790s criticism, it is only with the recent advent of Gothic studies that any serious kind of gendered distinction of the Gothic sublime gets theorized. Maggie Kilgour maintains that these two gendered positions show up not only in character representation but in narrative structure itself. The male Gothic narrative centers around an "individual as a satanic revolutionary superman, who is so extremely alienated that he cannot be integrated into society."[90] The female narrative, on the other hand, plots out the return the female heroine safely into the social order. Because Kilgour sees the male plot as one of a teleological development toward detachment and the female plot as one of repetition and continuity, she concludes, at least for appearance's sake, that "the male Gothic follows a revolutionary aesthetic," while "the female, inversely, suggests a bourgeois aesthetic."[91] Although Kilgour reduces sexual difference as articulated in the Gothic romance to "the modern redefinition of sexual relations, based on the idea of separate spheres," as if sex were consistent with the signifier, she insightfully recognizes a productive difference between Radcliffe and Lewis. She asserts that Radcliffe's narratives bring the reader into the story while Lewis keeps the reader outside, making us marvel at his authorial powers.[92] Because Kilgour privileges politics over sexual difference (Wollstonecraft and Godwin are the radical counterparts to the conservative Radcliffe and Lewis), she ignores the role of desire in the narratives of Radcliffe and Lewis. Radcliffe, I would argue, pulls the reader into her plot much in the same way Freud's analysand Dora did: she questions the desire of the Other. In a similar way, Lewis keeps the reader outside precisely because his narrative, much like the Rat Man's, wants to ward off the desire of the Other. Even though both writers utilize a traditional third person narrative, Radcliffe's narrative voice, much less omniscient than Lewis's, relinquishes any pretense toward a totalitarian control of the storyline. Because Radcliffe's objective narrative is strongly subjectivist, it aesthetically illustrates that there is more to its story than it can account for. Therefore, the sublime occurrences in Radcliffe's narratives result directly from and convey the narrative's own internal limit. The supernatural caricatures in Lewis's novel, however, result from the narrative's desire not to abdicate control over its own production. Since terror is a fright with unknown origin, and since the affect associated with it arises from an obscurity one feels internally, it is more conducive to Radcliffe's narratives of feminine bewilderment. And since horror, on the other hand, is produced by an external threat, Lewis exploits its effects to describe in lurid detail what the terror narratives of Radcliffe leave to the imagination. His narrative utilizes horror in order to exile internal inconsistencies and bewilderment to the realm of the actual supernatural.[93]

Anne Williams has taken this distinction between terror/horror narratives a step further by analyzing how terror and horror concern two complimentary modes of the "unspeakable": "In defamiliarizing the Symbolic, Gothic narrative and plot devices bring us to its 'edge,' [back] ... to the pre–Oedipal otherland of infancy, the borderland where language starts to show stress, of the pressures exerted by the unconscious energies ordinarily repressed."[94] Therefore, according to Williams, terror and horror, traditionally considered the most potent affects of Gothic narrative, may also be identified "with early 'symbolization'— the infant's gradual acquisition of language, the constitution of the self as 'speaking subject.'"[95] The affects of terror and horror, therefore, not only mark a return to a pre-subjective time when order lacked full reign, but they display, according to Williams, "a smuggling into the Symbolic of the repressed maternal."[96] In other words, Williams praises the Gothic romance, at least in its "female" form, for countering the hegemony of the paternal symbolic order. The Gothic shows that something else, something the patriarchal order is repulsed by, lurks at its own "edges," waiting to call into question its authority. Noting also that the sublime "is less a matter of external phenomena than the function of structures that order subjectivity itself," Williams makes the correct leap in assuming that the sublime has something to do with the subject's experience with "the *nom du père* as theorized by Lacan."[97] Unfortunately, however, she believes that the *material prima*, which was discarded with the subject's emergence into the symbolic space, can be recouped as the maternal in the Kristevian semiotic in an effort to make the entire patriarchal symbolic order seem strange.[98] But in order for the maternal to return, the subject must never have separated from it to begin with. And, as we have seen, Walpole's narrative illustrates precisely the potentially catastrophic results of this lack of separation. Williams might be correct in assuming that men and women, as reflected in the difference between the male and female Gothic, experience the advent of the name-of-the-father differently, but she is incorrect in assuming that this experience is complete, that the Oedipal complex possesses a terminal point. Following feminist critics who have pointed out how Freud was blind to the ways in which patriarchal social arrangements are cultural rather than natural, she argues that "mothers and daughters are not easily accommodated as subjects (rather than as objects of a male perspective) in his system."[99] And because she feels that Freud's notion of castration makes the female, by definition, defective and lacking, she not only fails to see that lack is the constitutive attribute of the subject, but that the subject has a desired role in being "cut off" from many sources of enjoyment.[100]

There is no complimentary relation between the two modes of the "unspeakable," between terror and horror. Adding these two together, contrary to what Williams suggests, will never produce a whole. There is a fundamental asymmetry between these two modes of pointing out the Oedipal complex's inevitable incompleteness because the Oedipal complex fails in two different ways. Castration, therefore, has to be assumed by the subject not only in order to take up the sexual position of a man or a woman, but to reach a level of psychic normalcy. According to Freud, all pathologies stem from defensive reactions toward castration and malfunctions in the Oedipus complex. In psychosis, the name-of-the-father is foreclosed; in perversion (as we saw in the case of Walpole), it is disavowed; in neurosis, it is repressed. Since it is impossible to accept castration completely, since an utterly "normal" position can never be achieved, neurosis is the closest thing to normalcy. Even though neurosis is characterized by the assumption of the *nom-du-père*, the awareness of castration remains repressed. Since Freud argued that neurosis was achieved only at the genital stage, sexual difference is manifested only in the neurotic structure. In other words, Lacan's formulas of sexuation only concern speaking subjects. Since the symbolic is foreclosed in psychosis, and since the pervert is the object of the Other's enjoyment, sexual difference only concerns neurotic subjects. Bruce Fink maintains that "masculinity and femininity are defined as different kinds of relations to the symbolic order, different ways of being split by language."[101] Men and women differ from each other by the way they are alienated within the symbolic order.

    Freud also maintains that castration, as the culmination of the Oedipal complex, is the movement when the polymorphously perverse partial drives become unified under the primacy of the genital organs. In other words, castration, as the subject's emergence in the symbolic order, regulates the free flow of *jouissance*. The pleasure principle emerges in the symbolic as a phenomenon that relegates enjoyment within the limits of the reality principle. It creates a barrier where any encounter "beyond" produces a painful pleasure. Therefore, Lacan asserts that "jouissance is forbidden to him who speaks as such."[102] Lacan, however, ends his "Subversion of the Subject" essay with a rather cryptic claim: "Castration means that jouissance must be refused, so that it can be reached on the inverted ladder of the Law of desire."[103] Where the pervert does not give up access to enjoyment, and the psychotic cannot, the neurotic subject, the subject who is alienated and separated, must renounce his or her claim to enjoyment in order to function in any normative manner. The neurotic, however, does not fully give up his or her perverse sexuality. Rather, the perversity of the neurotic's sexuality remains repressed, emerging only in dreams and fantasy. In other words, there is an outlet for *jouissance* within neurosis. It does not simply disappear, rather it is "reached on the inverted ladder of the Law of desire." Castration at once bars the subject's access to his or her own enjoyment and prevents the symbolic order from ever closing precisely because the relinquished enjoyment is still floating out there somewhere. Unlike the pervert, who has no trouble locating enjoyment, the neurotic defends him or herself from the onslaught of enjoyment, an anxiety-producing onslaught that would compromise the integrity of the symbolic order. But, because of this defense, the neurotic is eternally unsatisfied precisely because he or she is barred from direct access to enjoyment and only receives a surplus *jouissance*.

This difference between the neurotic structure's relegation of enjoyment and the pervert's lack of relegation explains the different modes that the sublime materialization of enjoyment takes within Gothic narratives. I argued earlier that Walpole's use of sublime machinery was chaotic and unmanageable precisely because his narrative displayed a perverse structure. Radcliffe's and Lewis's more strategic use of terror and horror, however, belies a much more regulated and less disruptive use of the sublime, as the materialization of that which is incongruous with the patterns of realism. These later writers of the Gothic create narratives that are more marginally exposed than Walpole's to those very phenomena that have to be relinquished in favor of a more realistic story line. Where the sublime enjoyment appeared to run rampant in Walpole's perverse Gothic narrative, the presentation of enjoyment in Radcliffe's and Lewis's narratives functions in a more regulated fashion. However, the mode that the relegation of enjoyment takes in Radcliffe's terror narratives is far from the way it plays out in Lewis's text. If Radcliffe's works are to be considered a type of feminine Gothic relying on terror as its vehicle for introducing enjoyment into the narrative and if Lewis's romance is to be considered a masculine Gothic relying on horror, one must take the question of sexual difference seriously.

According to psychoanalysis, men and woman do not possess either the same or a symmetrical relation to the symbolic. They may both be castrated, but, as Freud always knew, castration is different for the two sexes. Initially Freud postulated that castration had differing effects on boys and girls. In any child's Oedipus complex, the desired parent is of the opposite sex while the rivaled one is of the same sex. The boy, however, fears that his penis will be cut off by the father, while the girl views herself as already castrated, already without a penis. Since the fear of castration is already castration proper (the fear of castration is what turns one's rivalry into emulation), Freud postulated castration as the terminal crisis of the Oedipus complex. Fear of castration forces the boy to renounce (repress) his desire for his mother in return for his opportunity to become a "man of the world." The girl, on the other hand, is less threatened by the fear of castration because she, in a sense, has nothing to fear. According to Freud, she is able to maintain a desire for her father out of some sort of resentment for her mother. Therefore, the Oedipus complex, in the case of the girl, lacks the determinable terminal crisis analogous to the boy's case.[104] Freud, however, admits that his "insight into the developmental process in girls is unsatisfactory, incomplete and vague."[105]

Regardless, Freud concludes that the movement out of the anal stage (stage of demand) into the genital stage (stage of desire) causes the child to forget this initial drama. This forgetting, of course, is nothing other than repression. Lacan, revising Freud, maintains that both the male and female child originally fixate on the mother. Even before the arrival of the father, through the "mirror stage," the child's relation to the mother is already mediated by the imaginary phallus which designates the mother as lacking. The child simply tries to become what the mother lacks. This is analogous to the structure of Walpole's narrative. With the arrival of the father, as the completion of the Oedipus complex, the child's relation to the imaginary phallus, for Lacan, is elevated to the symbolic phallus. In other words, the phallus, as the marker of relation, is now mediated through language by the signifier. Each sex, therefore, is defined differently with respect to a third term. Sexual difference stems from divergent relations to the signifier.[106]

Because of this divergence, Lacan felt that the Oedipal myth utilized by Freud to explain castration was insufficient, that it was strictly unusable for an understanding of hysteria.[107] In *Seminar XVII*, Lacan constructs another myth to help explain castration as embodied by the feminine subject. The Oedipal myth makes perfect sense as far as man is concerned. The boy desires the mother until the father comes around and articulates the *nom-du-père*.[108] The father's prohibition of incest and his naming of the mother's desire cuts the son off from enjoyment and forces him to desire along the path of the pleasure principle ("you can have any good but that one"). This narrative fits in line with Lacan's formulation of the male side of sexuation from *Seminar XX*. One has access to anything as long as one thing (enjoyment) is excluded from the whole. Enjoyment, for the male, is localized beyond the prohibition.[109] This one thing — the mother as object of incestuous enjoyment — is, however, not barred to the father. The primal father, therefore, is the one, according to the formula, who is not subject to castration. He is the exception that sets up the universality of man. The masculine subject is not wholly subject to the symbolic precisely because of the exception, because the father is not subject at all. Lacan notices through the primal father's lack of castration, through his total freedom, a slight connection to the lack associated with a woman's castration. The primal father's prohibition, which subjects the boy to the symbolic order, has a different effect on the girl.[110] The myth of the primal horde in *Totem and Taboo* reveals something new concerning castration, and the experience of the hysteric, according to Lacan, that should have guided Freud beyond the Oedipus myth.[111] The prohibition of the primal father ("I get all the women") is less articulated by the father than it is the result of the horde's murderous action. In other words, the prohibition is only set up by the guilt arising from killing the father. Where the myth of Oedipus allows the son to believe that beyond the prohibition he can enjoy his mother, the primal horde, just like Oedipus, believes it can have access to enjoyment if only it murders the father. But in the myth of *Totem and Taboo*, the elimination of the father only reveals the inaccessibility of the mother — that she is just a fantasy projection onto the empty space of the phallus. Castration, articulated through the myth of *Totem and Taboo*, determines the real as impossible.[112] The Oedipal myth establishes the prohibition of *jouissance* associated with the male side of sexual difference, whereas the myth of *Totem and Taboo* reveals the impossibility of enjoying the mother associated with the feminine side of sexual difference.[113]

Since *Totem and Taboo* reveals both the primal father as a myth and the impossibility of enjoying the mother, Lacan feels that this other Freudian myth is more closely associated with woman's castration. Because no woman is exempt from castration, there is no exempted realm that could house the unlimited enjoyment that needs prohibiting, as on the masculine side of sexual difference.[114] Although the feminine is also cut off from enjoyment, she is only cut off from something that is already impossible. The primal father's lack of castration, his total freedom with regard to enjoyment, points out something different to the feminine subject. Because the master signifier, the name-of-the-father, is just a signifier covering lack, it displays the lack of a limit to woman. Lacan recognizes a certain connection between the primal father's unlimited enjoyment and the feminine's lack of a limit. He claims that the dead father as enjoyment "presents itself to us as the sign of the impossible itself."[115] Because the father is the one x not subject to the phallic function, he is technically psychotic. In a similar fashion, the woman with a bar through "Woman" is wholly subject to the phallic function with the stipulation that since there is no exception, she undermines the universality of the symbolic order. She is the inversion of the father and not psychotic like the primal father, for she has access to the same type of phallic enjoyment as the male.[116] But she also has access to the Other *jouissance*, the one incongruous with the symbolic order, the one that is impossible to signify. In the woman's case, the master signifier not only does not set a limit to her enjoyment, but it points to the impossibility of setting a limit to her enjoyment. Her enjoyment, however, should not be thought of as unlimited like the primal father's; rather, it should be seen as lacking an articulated limit. On the feminine side of the division, the Φ simply gives body to the inconsistency of the symbolic order.[117]

Because of sexual difference, Bruce Fink argues that there is a difference between masculine and feminine sublimation. Masculine sublimation is characterized as "symbolizing the real object," and feminine sublimation is characterized as "realizing the signifier."[118] In other words, when the masculine subject encounters the sublime, he confronts the prohibited object that has been excepted from the phenomenal field. As articulated in the Kantian dynamical sublime, he encounters the noumena as that which is beyond the phenomenal field — the symbolic order. When the feminine subject approaches the sublime, since she is wholly integrated in the symbolic order, she encounters the signifier that designates the symbolic order's inability to say it all. As articulated in the Kantian mathematical sublime, she encounters the impossibility inherent to any totalization of the phenomenal field — its own inconsistency. The sublime, therefore, articulates the zero sum of castration, the incompleteness of the Oedipus complex. Within the split in the mature Gothic novel between masculine and feminine, "horror" should be read as the exposure of phallic enjoyment, while "terror" should be read as the exposure of the Other *jouissance*.

In psychoanalytic theory, enjoyment expresses the paradoxical satisfaction the subject derives from his or her symptom, the suffering derived from the subject's own satisfaction. Where the pervert devotes himself to being the object that the Other gets off on, neurosis, according to Fink, should also be regarded as a strategy regarding enjoyment. The neurotic's strategy, however, is to keep the Other's enjoyment at bay. The neurotic refuses to be the cause of the Other's enjoyment.[119] The difference between Walpole's Gothic and that of Radcliffe and Lewis, when articulated around these lines, becomes striking. Walpole's narrative is overcome with supernatural sublime events to the precise extent that his novel only exists for the purpose of displaying supernatural elements. The sublime in Walpole's writing lacks any ordered and meaningful purpose. The supernatural sublime in Radcliffe's and Lewis's writing, as we shall see, manifests itself instead as if it functions within the economy of the story line. At one level, its use appears domesticated, but at another level, it still disrupts the realistic trajectory of the narrative. Radcliffe's and Lewis's narratives may appear to have tamed the enjoyment associated with the sublime, but its very presence points to something unsatisfactory in the narrative, something the narrative is producing that is not perfectly adjusted to its realistic story line. Since enjoyment expresses the suffering the subject derives from its own satisfaction, Radcliffe's and Lewis's narratives can be viewed as neurotic narratives, as indicated by this maladjustment of story line. But since their narratives are asymmetrical within the Gothic aesthetic, they verbalize different neuroses. Radcliffe's narratives, because of the way they communicate indirectly that there is nothing beyond the master signifier, express the structure of hysteria. In Lewis's romance the obsession with prohibition and transgression expresses the structure of obsessional neurosis. So, where terror is the Gothic's literary depiction of the enjoyment associated with the feminine side of sexual difference, horror is the Gothic's portrayal of the enjoyment particular to the masculine side of sexual difference.

Although I plan to examine the specific details of hysteria and obsessional neurosis as well as the differences in feminine and masculine sublimation in my individual chapters on Radcliffe and Lewis, it is still necessary to say a few words here about the two distinct psychopathologies and the two forms of aesthetic sublimation. According to Freud, hysteria and obsessional neurosis develop as a defense against an incompatible idea, against that which was repressed upon entry into the symbolic.[120] This incompatible idea, of course, is associated by Freud with sexual enjoyment. The point here is not that neurotics try to avoid sexual thoughts or pleasures; the point, rather, is that sexuality — because it is of the real — is immune to the neurotic's symbolizing apparatus. This is why Freud regards the sexual experience of childhood as the cause of hysteria and obsession. Neurosis, as developed by Freud, is basically a defensive reaction to an incompatible idea. As mentioned above, this incompatible idea is not only associated with sexuality, it is incompatible with the signifying chain. But the specific defensive structure the subject sets up in reaction to this incompatibility determines whether the subject is a hysteric or an obsessional neurotic. According to Colette Soler, the incompatibility between sexuality and the signifying chain is divided into two component parts: the "representation" (signifier) and the affect (*jouissance*) of sexuality.[121] Freud makes it clear that in hysteria the return of the repressed shows up on the body while in obsessional neurosis, it shows up in the mind.[122] Because in obsessional neurosis sex can be signified in a signifier that is incompatible with the signifying chain (the repressed term shows up in the signifying chain itself), and because man is not wholly subject to the symbolic, obsessional neurosis largely tends to be the defensive mechanism developed by men. Enjoyment for the obsessional shows up on the symbolic level as something incompatible. Since no idea (or signifier) of the symbolic is compatible with sex, on the other hand, and since woman is "non-all" in relation to the symbolic, hysteria tends to be adopted by women as a defense mechanism. Enjoyment for the hysteric shows up as the inconsistency of the symbolic itself.

Both neurotic structures are a defense against the *jouissance* of the Other articulated through desire. The obsessional repudiates the Other's desire, choosing fantasy ($\$<>a$) so his desire is not the desire of the Other. The hysteric, likewise, tries to become the object of the Other's desire so she can control it and not become the object of the Other's enjoyment. Unlike the pervert, both neurotics defend themselves from becoming the object which the Other gets off on. The obsessional partakes in irrational ritualistic behavior as a means of maintaining a semblance of order in the world to prevent catastrophe. This is why the obsessional is characterized by guilt. The hysteric prevents the Other from enjoying her by always questioning the Other, never allowing the Other the potency necessary for enjoyment. This, then, is why the hysteric is characterized by repulsion.

Unlike the pervert who has perfect knowledge of where enjoyment comes from, the neurotic's position is always riddled by doubt, by a question. According to Lacan, the obsessional's fundamental question is "Am I alive or dead?" and the hysteric's question is "What is it to be a woman?"[123] Because the obsessional fears what's beyond the symbolic, his question is geared toward a doubt about existence in a signifying world. And since the hysteric cannot find a signifier adequate to woman, she doubts her gender since it does not register in the symbolic. In both cases, however, neurosis emphasizes in desire the dimension of defense against enjoyment. But this enjoyment, which never simply goes away, manages to return in unrecognizable forms through the breakdown of defense. For the neurotic, enjoyment is embodied in the symptom, which results from the failure of defense.

Aesthetic sublimation, as put into play by the early Gothic romance, attempts to elevate or condescend (depending on the writer) the repressed enjoyment in the symptom by forcing it directly into the signifier. Lacan himself formulates two modes of sublimation "that attract our attention to the possibility of formulating, in the form of a question, a different criterion of another, or even the same, morality, in opposition to the reality principle."[124] One of these modes of sublimation is characterized by the activity that most readers of Lacan's *Seminar VII* are familiar with: "[sublimation] raises an object ... to the dignity of the Thing."[125] As Zupančič has pointed out, and I am borrowing loosely from her throughout the following analysis, this mode of sublimation is based on an ascending movement; the object is raised up or elevated to a higher level.[126] This mode of sublimation, of course, seems to come very close to the traditional definition of the sublime, an elevation above the limit. Further in *Seminar VII*, Lacan in fact recognizes this affinity between sublimation and the Kantian notion of the sublime.[127] The other modality of sublimation is mentioned by Lacan three years later in his unpublished seminar on anxiety, where he offers the aphorism that only sublimation-love allows *jouissance* to condescend to desire.[128] Within the Lacanian psychoanalytic schema, *jouissance* (enjoyment) is Lacan's rewriting of Freud's notion of libido and not only points to what is beyond the pleasure principle but also, like the sublime sentiment itself, expresses the paradoxical satisfaction that one derives from suffering. Just as the sentiment of the sublime absurdly provides a degree of pleasure through terror or horror, the term *jouissance* expresses the pleasure derived from a painful or traumatic experience. This second mode of sublimation, which Lacan formulated after the first, is based on a movement in the opposite direction. Rather than the object ascending to a higher level, *jouissance* (enjoyment) *descends* to a lower level. Etymologically, *sub-limin* can actually mean both *above the limit* or *below the threshold*. In current usage we tend to differentiate between *sublime* and *subliminal*, but it seems the Romans had one word that meant both *up* and *down, above* and *below*.[129] In the first mode of sublimation — that of elevating the object to the level of the Thing — the sublime Thing points to something beyond it, above it, that the object can only fail to point to because, as in the dynamical sublime and the masculine horror Gothic, it is prohibited from directly representing something from the higher realm. In the second mode of sublimation — that of condescending — the sublime object is revealed, as in the mathematical sublime and the feminine terror Gothic, as just an object maintaining the illusion that there is something or some higher realm beyond it. The sublime object is revealed as a deception. In the end, it would seem that the first modality of sublimation is more akin to a masculine form of idealization because it sets up an inaccessible object. The second mode, however, appears more like a form of de-idealization because it exposes the fantasy behind the idealizing process. Where the dynamical sublime produces a mode of perceiving an object that is beyond our experience because it belongs to the noumenal realm, the mathematical sublime appears to produce the possibility of perceiving something that is also not an object of experience, without being the Thing in itself. Where the former points to the Thing beyond the pleasure principle, the latter simply points to, or reconfigures, the Thing as the very inconsistency of the pleasure and reality principles themselves. Unlike the masculine Gothic sublime that locates the real beyond reality, the feminine Gothic sublime illustrates how the real is nothing other than reality's own stumbling block, that which prevents it from ever coinciding with itself.

In my reading of the Gothic, since the masculine use of sublime horror brings the reader and characters too close to the Kantian Thing through the use, or overuse, of the actual supernatural, it points to another realm beyond the phenomenal and, therefore, it artistically performs the first mode of sublimation outlined above. On the other hand, the feminine sublime — as seen in Radcliffe's and her imitators' use of anticipated terror instead of anything directly otherworldly — functions as a form of desublimation, revealing the Kantian Thing, the sublime object, as that which is immanent to our symbolic universe and accessible, indicating that the Kantian Thing as otherworldly is only the product of a fantasy. The explained supernatural, on which the feminine Gothic plot notoriously relies, is the artistic device by which this breed of the Gothic illustrates the illusory nature of the sublime object. The feminine Gothic, as will be shown in the next chapter, relies heavily on a love story structure because it attempts to give value to love as that single passion that makes the sublime appear as something we can relate to, not as some extreme feeling from an ideal realm beyond.[130]

5

Ann Radcliffe and the
Gothic Terror of Hysteria

The Gothic romance as a tale of terror emerged at a significant time in the eighteenth-century understanding of psychology in general and of hysteria specifically. In 1764, the year that saw the publication of Walpole's originating Gothic romance *The Castle of Otranto*, the Scottish physician Robert Whytt argued that the etiology of nervous disorders lies in sensitive nerves, thus dispelling any lingering believe in a vaporous cause. Walpole's overuse of the supernatural to affect both his characters and his readers worked well with Whytt's theory that sensitive nerves could be violently affected by "moving stories, horrible and unexpected sights, great grief, anger, terror, and other passions."[1] Furthermore, in 1777, the year that saw the publication of Clara Reeve's *The Old English Baron* (originally entitled *The Champion of Virtue*), the English physician William Cullen coined the term "neurosis."[2] Even though Cullen's understanding of his newly coined term bares little resemblance to our modern understanding of neurosis, his insistence on a physical etiology for hysteria is likewise paralleled by Reeve's solitary physical supernatural entity as the primary cause of terror in her Gothic novel. However, in 1798, the year after the publication of the last Ann Radcliffe Gothic romance published during her lifetime, a huge theoretical advance was made in the understanding of hysteria with the French physician Philippe Pinel's *Nosographie*. In his text, Pinel argued that the neuroses were a product of "mental alienation" and did not necessarily originate from an actual physical cause.[3] Looking for another parallel in the emerging Gothic romance, one can successfully argue that Pinel's psychosomatic explanation for hysteria and the other neuroses is envisioned, anticipated, and even dramatized by the Gothic romances that Ann Radcliffe penned in the seven years leading up to Pinel's groundbreaking theory.

The mental alienation that was theorized by Pinel changed the etiology of hysteria from a physical to an imaginary cause much the same way Radcliffe utilized her Gothic "explained supernatural" to indicate that the terror both her characters and her readers feel likewise rested on an imaginary ground. Radcliffe utilizes this new Gothic "terror" as the cause of hysteria in order to illustrate a psycho-social conflict that many contemporary women faced in an era where love, more than the law, connected desiring women to the symbolic order.[4] Her strategic use of the "explained supernatural" and her dramatizing of hysteria in her romances anticipates the psychoneurotic findings that Pinel developed during the same decade in the same hospital where Freud would later attend Jean-Martin Charcot's famous hysteria sessions a century later. If one takes this anticipation of Pinel seriously and, even more so, the possibility that Radcliffe's romances foresee Freud's own understanding of hysteria, then one can gauge a more precise understanding of feminine desire as it plays itself out in Radcliffe's Gothic universe.

In his essay "Family Romances," Freud insists that, as the child grows up, the liberation from the authority of his parents is a necessary result of development. It is also, however, one of the most painful results. So painful, in fact, that there is, for Freud, a class of neurotics whose condition is recognizably determined by their having failed in this task.[5] As a child develops, it naturally becomes dissatisfied with and critical of its parents. As the child loses its initial and comfortable relation, it concocts a "family romance" as a supplement. On one level, the family romance — a fantasy about coming from a more important and ideal family — gives the child something in return for what it is losing. On another level, the family romance acts as a defense mechanism against this loss. Like all romantic myths, the family romance makes visible what is not there. But, as with all fantasy, it does not just make visible what is no longer there — it makes visible what was never there in the first place. Feeling discontent, a child exchanges what now appears as insufficient parents for ideal parents. The ideal parents, in turn, represent for the neurotic what it supposedly lost. The romance, then, acts as a psychical correction to a discontent felt in actual life. Freud, however, is quick to point out that "if we examine in detail the commonest of these imaginative romances, the replacement of both parents or of the father alone by grander people, we find that these new and aristocratic parents are equipped with attributes that are derived entirely from real recollections of the actual and humble ones."[6] Even though it appears that the neurotic is attempting to get rid of his or her parents, he or she is actually exalting them. Replacing the actual father by a superior one is only, according to Freud, an expression of the child's longing for the "happy, vanished days when his father seemed to him the noblest and strongest of men and his mother the dearest and loveliest of women."[7] The obsessional neurotic, as opposed to the hysteric, will view the insufficiency at the heart of his family — an insufficiency that requires the supplement of the family romance — as a loss of something precious. Therefore, he will, through fantasy, go out and re-find it in the quest that is his life. The hysteric, on the other hand, will have a tendency, through fantasy, to become the one who can make up for the insufficiency.[8]

Freud's notion of "family romance" is essentially the structure of the standard Gothic romance. Heroines in the feminine Gothic (epitomized in the works of Ann Radcliffe) and heroes in the masculine Gothic (epitomized in the works of Matthew Lewis and Charles Maturin) are customarily displayed as actual or metaphoric orphans whose whole story is a sort of neurotic quest for that supposed lost ideal family. This is remarkably staged in Radcliffe's Gothic romances. The heroine, abandoned by her family, is represented through a narrative that stages her fantasy and search for an ideal family. Julia de Mazzini, Adeline de Montalt, Emily Saint Aubert, and Ellena di Rosalba are all faced with the insufficiency of the paternal function to give them a proper place in the symbolic economy free from discontent. Their narratives are a displaced psychic reality displaying this content. In other words, their narratives are fantastic to the precise extent that they are the fantasy supplement correlate to the heroines' discontent. This is why each of these characters, in her own way, actualizes what Freud refers to as the "nothing can happen to me" attitude typical of fantasy. Each one of these Radcliffean heroines can be ruthlessly pursued and threatened, but, in the end, they all inevitably emerge somehow untouched and unscathed. Even in the critically neglected early Radcliffe Gothic *A Sicilian Romance*, it is possible to see how the Freudian family romance hysterically provides this supplemental fantasy for the heroine Julia de Mazzini.

The romance begins with the conventional Gothic editorial introduction. The authorial voice, while recounting travels to Sicily, describes in an almost dreamlike narrative an old ruined castle met with on the northern shore. This decadent castle has an air of ancient grandeur forcing on the present misery an image of ideal past glory, of hospitality, and of festive magnificence. Only when the narrator's heart swells in this reflection of a long-lost golden age does she encounter a nearby friar who tells of the lost luxury and forgotten vice of these ruins. The superior of a nearby monastery further presents the narrator with the manuscript containing the history of this long-ruined monument. As these reflections occur, the solitude of the narrator is quickly supplemented with a nostalgic longing for a "better time," a sort of lost prelapsarian time when things were more ideal. But the supplemental manuscript containing the story of this long-lost ideal time appears insufficient.

For the manuscript itself— as the history of a time before the present lonely solitude suffered by our narrator — needs some particulars added by the narrator before it can become *A Sicilian Romance*: "I was permitted to take the abstracts of the history before me, which with some further particulars obtained in conversation with the abate, *I* have arranged in the following pages."[9] The narrator's own additions to the manuscript are evidenced by the numerous gross mistakes regarding the actual practices of Catholicism made throughout the romance (especially putting an abbot in charge of a nunnery), mistakes an abbot would never make. The inadequacy of the fragmented paternal manuscript provided by the father of the convent demands a supplement that both defends the heroine from and exposes her to the terrors of this inadequacy. Radcliffe's Gothic romance illustrates precisely this aspect of the fantastic psychic reality of hysteria. The erotic object of the hysteric is not so much that lost object that forms her fantasy as it is the inconsistency of the symbolic economy itself. In her Gothic romances in general and in *A Sicilian Romance* in particular, Radcliffe offers the reader a textual trauma as a displacement of a sexual trauma — the trauma of locating an adequate erotic object. Radcliffe's overused textual devices of aborted, fragmented, and partial narratives in conjunction with her use of concealed doors, narrow towers, labyrinthine corridors, rusty missing keys, and winding hidden stairwells all conspire to illustrate the textual inadequacy in accounting for the sexual. These half-revealing narrative devices, including the abbot's insufficient and incomplete manuscript, point not to something beyond the narrative, but to the narrative's own inherent insufficiency — the insufficiency to which the hysteric bears witness.

Although it would be quite legitimate to read *Civilization and Its Discontents* or *The Interpretation of Dreams* as Freud's attempt to write a Gothic novel, it is Freud's case study *Dora*, with its mystery concerning the essence of femininity, that convincingly reveals the truth of the feminine Gothic of Ann Radcliffe.[10] Much like any heroine of an eighteenth-century Gothic romance, Dora finds herself, within Freud's reconstructed case study, caught up in an apparently disheartening family romance. During his analysis Freud figures out that Dora's hysterical ailment is symptomatic of her feeling used by her father. Not only has Dora surmised that her father is having some sort of affair with a certain Frau K., but she feels she is being bartered over to Frau K.'s husband, Herr K., in a mutual exchange of women as goods. Freud presumes, much like Dora's father, that Dora's ailment stems from a certain discontent she suffers due to her particular position in this family intrigue. Because Dora was her father's favorite, because she "was most tenderly attached to him," she "took all the more offence at many of his actions and peculiarities."[11]

Through the brief analysis and reconstruction of two of Dora's dreams, Freud eventually concludes that Dora's ailment stems primarily from a conflict between her outward role as a victim within this family romance and the unacknowledged investment she has in this role. In other words, to maintain a certain amount of social respectability, even toward herself, Dora feels she must view herself as a helpless pawn in a game where only her father wins. Her hysteria thus arises because she consciously refuses to accept her own interest in this little game of sexual exchange. Even though Dora's various somatic symptoms — ranging from aphonia and migraine headaches to chronic shortness of breath — circulate around the unwanted advances of Herr K., the man to whom Dora has been traded by her father, they arise only due to a conflict in Dora's psyche. In other words, if Dora was merely repulsed by the advances of Herr K., she would simply feel common disgust with both Herr K. and her father. But Freud surmises that she develops particular somatic symptoms in reaction to an unconscious conflicted feeling of love for Herr K. She complains about being a pawn in her father's game of betrayal, but, at the same time, she hysterically revels in her role as pawn and victim. Being a victim does not give her as much satisfaction as complaining about being a victim does; this allows her to maintain a certain substitute enjoyment in her neurosis. Her hysterical formation illustrates for Freud Dora's own personal investment in her father's deceptive game. Even though Dora feels embittered that she has been handed over to Herr K. as the price of his tolerating the relations between her father and his wife, Freud notices how Dora herself lends more than a helping hand in arranging the clandestine meetings between her father and Frau K. She, in fact, looks after the K.s' children so that Frau K. can spare the time needed for her secret rendezvous with Dora's father. Even the symptoms that Dora develops as a repulsive response to Herr K.'s advances are read by Freud as partially desirable. In other words, Dora desires to be the object of Herr K.'s desire, but she is repulsed about being the object of Herr K.'s enjoyment. Like a true hysteric, Dora simply desires to keep desire unsatisfied. This is why Freud reads Dora's loss of voice as a tribute to Herr K.'s absence: "Dora's aphonia, then, allowed the following symbolic interpretation. When the person she loved [Herr K.] was away she gave up speaking; speech had lost its value since she could not speak to him."[12]

In the "Postscript" to his case study, Freud slightly changes his conclusion concerning the ultimate aetiology of Dora's hysteria: "The longer the interval of time that separates me from the end of this analysis, the more probable it seems to me that the fault in my technique lay in this omission: I failed to discover in time and to inform the patient that her homosexual (gynaecophilic) love for Frau K. was the strongest unconscious current in her mental life."[13]

Frau K. becomes, within the aftermath of Freud's analysis, not only the object of Dora's desire, but also the source of Dora's knowledge concerning sexual matters. With this new conclusion, the slap that Dora gives Herr K. at the scene by the lake can no longer be directly attributed to Dora's attitude of repulsion toward Herr K.'s advances. Rather, Dora slaps Herr K. because he refers to his wife as "nothing." Dora's slap is a reaction to Herr K.'s calling her love object "nothing." Freud feels that this homosexual side to Dora's hysteria explains, despite all her protests, why she does her best to maintain the structure of exchange within which she is caught. Dora complains of being a victim in the exchange of objects, but, at the same time, she finds a certain libidinal satisfaction in her position. Since she cannot desire Frau K. directly, she relishes her indirect relation to Frau K. (her assistance in Frau K.'s secret rendezvous) as it gets played out in this family romance.

Although Freud is correct in his retrospective insight, his whole theory of homosexual desire needs, as it were, another turn of the screw. Dora did not love Frau K. homosexually as much as she emulated Frau K. for being the answer to the riddle of femininity. If the question one needed to ask a hysteric in order to get at the bottom of her pathological structure were simply "What is your object of desire?" then the understanding that posits Frau K. as the homosexual object of Dora's desire would be accurate. But since the interrogating question in regard to the hysteric's position is "Where does she desire from?" or, more accurately, "Who is the other person through whom she is organizing her desire?"[14] Dora's hysteric desire is irreducible to an object.

In order to illustrate the complexity inherent in the way women in general, and hysterics specifically, desire, Darian Leader draws a simple anecdote around a chance sighting at a sidewalk cafe: "A man is sitting in a cafe," Leader begins, "and sees a couple walk past." If the man finds the woman attractive he will watch her. A woman, however, in the same situation will act differently: "She may be attracted to the man, but will nonetheless spend more time looking at the woman who is with him."[15] The woman is less interested in the man or the woman than the relation between the couple itself. If the woman is attracted to this coupled man, she will wonder what this woman possesses that allowed her to attain an intimate relation with him. This anecdote aptly illustrates how women are much more attuned to relation where men are more attuned to objects. This is precisely why, within the Gothic tradition, the masculine horror of Lewis's narrative derives from actual external supernatural objects, whereas Radcliffe's feminine terror is bereft of any objective physical support. Regardless, this other woman whom the woman in the cafe watches is watched precisely because she supposedly (a neurotic supposition if there ever were one) holds "the secret to the mystery of what it is that traps the desire of the man."[16] Leader maintains that his little scenario exemplifies the difference between man's and woman's relation to desire. The man will want to obliterate his rival in order to obtain his prized object, but the woman's desire is directed less at the object than at the other woman's desire. The hysteric's desire is always the desire of the Other.[17] This scenario not only explains the different results between boys' and girls' Oedipal complexes, but it reveals the underlining structure of Dora's hysteria.

In his rereading of Freud's Dora case study, Lacan maintains that the real interest in Frau K. for Dora lies not in her as an individual, "but a mystery, the mystery of her femininity."[18] Dora's real investment in the triangular exchange in which she plays the part of a willing participant parallels the woman's interest from the cafe for the coupled woman. Even though Dora's father's impotence stems from his syphilitic condition, for Dora it symbolizes her growing independence from the familial paternal structure. Distrustful of, and without, a strong paternal function, Dora has virtually no idea what it means to be a woman. Since there is no essence to womanhood, how does a girl become a woman? There simply are no ready-made answers.[19] So, just like the woman in the cafe, Dora studies someone else's desire: Frau K.'s. This more accurately explains her investment in the triangular relationship. Dora studies desire through the relationship between her father and Frau K, but the particular reason why Frau K. is chosen by Dora as embodying the mystery to femininity centers around Dora's father's impotence. If her father is impotent and therefore cannot have coitus with Frau K., why would he still desire her? Since he cannot enjoy Frau K., she must have something else so attractive — so womanly — that catches her father's desire. Frau K., in a sense, is in "the position of someone who knows what it is to be a woman."[20] Dora attempts to maintain this structure for as long as it can persist, so she can study its dynamic of desire. Because their relation is wholly one of desire, and because Dora uses it as a model, she becomes repulsed at Herr K.'s sexual advances. She wants to keep Herr K. at a distance; she wants to keep him desiring in the way his wife has captured her father's desire. This is why the root cause of Dora's hysteria can be traced to a lack of knowledge concerning femininity.

While discussing Dora's second dream, Freud draws a connection between a scene in the dream where Dora wanders about alone in a strange town and a scene in Dora's actual life when she wandered about alone in a strange museum:

> The wandering about in a strange town was over-determined. It led back to one of the exciting causes from the day before. A young cousin of Dora's had come to stay with them for the holidays, and Dora had had to show

him around Vienna. This cause was, it is true, a matter of complete indifference to her. But her cousin's visit reminded her of her own first brief visit to Dresden. On that occasion she had been a stranger and had wandered about, not failing, of course, to visit the famous picture gallery. Another cousin of hers, who was with them and knew Dresden, had wanted to act as a guide and take her round the gallery. *But she declined, and went alone*, and stopped in front of the pictures that appealed to her. She remained *two hours* in front of the Sistine Madonna, rapt in silent admiration. When I asked her what had pleased her so much about the picture she could find no clear answer to make. At last she said: "The Madonna."[21]

Notions of the "wandering womb" aside, there is little doubt, during this scene within the Dresden picture gallery where Dora is enraptured by the Madonna, that Dora is fascinated with the mystery of femininity. Because he does not yet realize that the mystery of femininity is also a mystery for women, Freud overlooks this crucial observation. When Dora eventually answers that she was pleased with the Madonna, she merely tells Freud the name of the *objet d'art* that caught her admiration. But what really catches her undivided attention for two hours is femininity as something irreducible to any linguistic utterance except a tautology. She is attracted by something in the Madonna more than the Madonna — something connected to noble virginity. This view of the Madonna parallels Dora's earlier aesthetic description of Frau K.'s "adorable white body." Both have a profoundly sublime effect on Dora, and the "wandering womb" of hysteria refers to the subject's desire fated to an endless search for an impossible satisfaction.

In *A Sicilian Romance*, Julia, the main character in Radcliffe's first wholly Gothic family romance, finds herself in a situation very analogous to that of Dora. Not only is she eighteen at the start of the novel, but she is herself caught up in a similar game of exchange as Dora. Early in the novel, Julia finds herself, much like Dora, with an absent mother and a father whose heart has become "dead to paternal tenderness," showing a preference for his new love Maria de Vellorno (*SR* 3). Because Julia's father has left his two daughters' care to their governess Madame de Menon and left them behind in his virtually abandoned castle in Sicily while he, his new wife, and son reside on the mainland in Naples, the reader is left with the initial impression that Julia and her older sister Emilia maintain, and perhaps even enjoy, an ambivalent relation to paternal authority. As with the feminine side of the Oedipal structure, both sisters have lost their mother in early childhood without ever fully being "adopted" by their father, the figurehead of the symbolic order.

Early in the novel, however, the reader realizes that there is something different about Julia. Radcliffe develops some characteristic differences between

Julia and her older sister Emilia in order to portray the former as the type of modern woman who does not fully trust the paternal law to keep her connected to the symbolic order. For instance, later in the romance and throughout Radcliffe's other romances the constant lampooning of the Church echoes theology's waning support, indicating the breakdown of traditional power structures. This breakdown is dramatized throughout the entire narrative through Julia's endless physical and emotional wandering. Emilia is described as inheriting most of her mother's qualities. She has a "mild and sweet temper, united with a clear and comprehensive mind" (*SR* 4). Julia, however, is described as of a livelier cast: "Her temper was warm, but generous; she was quickly irritated, and quickly appeased; and to a reproof, however gently, she would often weep, but was never sullen. Her imagination was ardent, and her mind early exhibited symptoms of genius" (*SR* 4). Although many critics are easily tempted to view the typical Gothic heroine as a weak feminine figure wholly in conformity with patriarchal desires, Radcliffe draws this distinction between the two Mazzini sisters in order to indicate how women are actually double. On one level, women can assume a phallic position in society and even partake in phallic enjoyment. But, as Lacan points out, the signifier is non-all in relation to women. As the paternal order becomes more "phallic" during the breakdown of traditional power structures, as the signifier becomes increasingly the final authority, what the signifier is inadequate to becomes increasingly difficult to discern. This character trait distinction between Emilia and Julia used by Radcliffe effectively depicts the non-all of the symbolic in a woman's life.

Madame de Menon, the benevolent caretaker of Emilia and Julia, has the job of counteracting "those traits in the disposition of her young pupils, which appeared inimical to their future happiness" (*SR* 4). She, in other words, has the job of curbing enjoyment. Madame de Menon works to set up the reality principle as the guiding force of regulating enjoyment. The respective arts in which the two sisters develop an interest display the degree to which Emilia and Julia adapt to this regulation. Emilia, the more phallically defined of the two, picks up drawing as her main form of aesthetic expression. Julia, on the other hand, being naturally less bounded than her sister, develops into quite the connoisseur of music. It is, of course, not accidental, nor irrelevant, that Radcliffe chooses these two particular art forms for these sisters. Since drawing is two-dimensional in nature and conforms to an existing framework and a realistic aesthetic, it accurately reflects Emilia's personality and behavior throughout the novel. Music, on the other hand, being less bounded, less representational and more overtly relational, faithfully renders Julia's temperament and less constrained desires. Reductively speaking, drawing privileges objects, where music relies more on relations between sounds. Since Julia appears more attuned to relation, she is more observant of the relational aspect of the signifier, and, therefore, takes less stock in its authoritative function. Because of this early characterization of Julia, the reader suspects that she possesses a much more complex relation to her environs than her sister.[22]

The difference between these two sisters also plays itself out in their respective emotional contentedness within the confines of the Castle of Mazzini. One could argue that the supernatural occurrences that haunt the castle in the early part of the novel are a result of a certain discontent inhabiting the domestic space rather than a cause of discontent. What initially appears as a cause of distress — the late night moans, the mysterious lights, etc.— is actually the figurative effects of an already existing distress in the heroine. Furthermore, the unexplained light emanating from the locked southern wing of the castle, the weird underground moans, or any of the supernatural haunting, consistently occur after the customary hour of repose. The witnesses to these terrific happenings only perceive them because they have transgressed protocol. There appears to be some direct correlation between Radcliffe's use of the supernatural and the transgression of codified behavior. When a tremor suddenly seizes Julia late one night in response to an obscure sound emanating from the closed wing of the castle, the affect is in direct proportion to her violation. The somatic affect appears to be caused as much by the obscurity of the late hour as by anything supernatural inhabiting the castle. Keeping in mind that this primary supernatural disturbance occurs when Julia is alone in her little personal pleasure "closet," the reader allows him or herself to see that this little room as well as the late hour contributes to a space beyond the domestic sphere necessary for the desired disturbance. Furthermore, these supernatural disturbances, always occurring before Julia's father's return from Naples, signify the absence of the paternal anchor within the domestic sphere. Because the supernatural turns out in the end to be not so supernatural, one is inclined to read these early happenings as much as a figurative manifestation of Julia's discontent with her future domestic role as the literal sounds of her mother's real discontent. But, because she is unaware of her discontent, because she is literally unconscious at this point of her lack of satisfaction, it rears its head as a bodily symptom of the castle itself, making her domicile's uncanniness the effect of her inner torment. Later, when the marquis returns and arranges an unwanted marriage for Julia, her discontent no longer seeks a circuitous route through the castle's uncanny machinery. It is only with the father's return that Julia's discontent can be played out directly within the parameters of the narrative structure.[23]

Even though the narrative tries to convince the reader of a rivalrous relation between Julia and her stepmother, Maria de Vallorno, the details of the text display something different. When the marchioness first arrives at the Castle of Mazzini amongst all the pomp and circumstance of a festival celebration, Julia appears at first affected in a manner that is out of character:

> In a few days the marchioness arrived at the castle. She was followed by a numerous retinue, and accompanied by Ferdinand, and several of the Italian noblesse, whom pleasure attracted to her train. Her entrance was proclaimed by the sound of music, and those gates which had long rusted on their hinges, were thrown open to receive her. The courts and halls, whose aspect so lately expressed only gloom and desolation, now shone with sudden splendor, and echoed the sounds of gaiety and gladness. Julia surveyed the scene from an obscure window; and as the triumphal strains filled the air, her breast throbbed; her heart beat quick with joy, and she lost her apprehensions from the marchioness in a sort of wild delight hitherto unknown to her. *The arrival of the marchioness seemed indeed the signal of universal and unlimited pleasure* [*SR* 15; italics added].

The very arrival of Julia's supposed antagonist actually opens Julia's world to an unlimited form of enjoyment. Maria, the marchioness, is even given the name of the Madonna, the very figure which confronted Dora with the riddle of femininity. From this point on, Julia grows more and more coherent regarding her discontent over the domestic sphere. On the level of all straightforward accounts, the marchioness appears to play the role of Julia's nemesis. But in reality, the marchioness breaches the mystery of femininity in Julia's life much the way Frau K. did in Dora's. The marchioness, a woman with supposedly unbarred access to enjoyment, actually becomes the figure through whom Julia organizes her desire. The undeveloped veil of mystery that enveloped the castle as a sign of Julia's lack of satisfaction is transformed by the arrival of the marchioness into the mystery of femininity itself. Shortly after this arrival, Julia becomes "enchanted with the new world that was now exhibited to her" (*SR* 20). Even though this new world is predominated by pain, "it was so exquisitely interwoven with delight, that she could not wish it exchanged for her former ease" (*SR* 21). When she meets Hippolitus for the first time, love teaches her disguise. Her old innocent bliss becomes tiresome as she realizes that her new world has an added symbolic dimension.

This added dimension of Julia's experience correlates to the super-added dimension of the castle itself: the locked wing, the one Gothic convention of Radcliffe's novel not wholly borrowed from Walpole. Even though initiated by Clara Reeve, the locked-up wing of the castle plays a much more ambiguous role in *A Sicilian Romance*. Should the locked southern wing of the Castle of Mazzini, for instance, be viewed as a prohibited space or as an open space?

If the locked southern wing, where the supernatural appears to originate, is viewed as a locked-up space because it possesses some deep dark mystery within its bowels, the marquis's sovereignty is universal. In other words, by closing off a section of the castle, the marquis is able suture his hold over the domestic scene. The locked wing holds a sublime mystery which has to be kept as strictly unthinkable, as belonging to another realm: the supernatural. The rule of the domestic space is secured precisely by taking that which is beyond this rule and incorporating it into its domain as a sort of locked-up unruliness. This is how the locked southern wing of the castle appears at the beginning of the romance, and any reader would be hard-pressed at this point to argue differently. But, by the end of the narrative, thanks to Julia's unruly, wandering womb, the reader realizes how the locked-up wing, because it opens through a cavern to the outside, has really always existed as an open space. Since the locked wing remains opened at one end, it illustrates the fact that the marquis's rule possesses an inherent gap, an inherent inconsistency. And it is this inherent inconsistency that not only produces Julia's conflict over her desired role, but also keeps open the doubt that fuels Julia's hysterical reaction to the riddle of femininity.

With the arrival and permanent residence of the marchioness, Madame, Emilia, and Julia are forced to give up their apartments in turn for more desolate and less desirable accommodations within the castle. Not accidentally, the marquis moves Julia to a chamber that actually forms part of the buildings of the locked southern wing of the castle. If this locked and mysterious wing where all the uneasy supernatural occurrences originate marks that part of the domestic space that is incongruous with the castle's blueprint, so to speak, it appears Julia is somehow more in touch with this excessive aspect of her father's rule: "Julia observed that her chamber, which opened beyond Madame's, formed part of the southern building, with which, however, there appeared no means of communication. The late mysterious circumstances relating to this part of the fabric, now arose to her imagination, and conjured up terror which reason could not subdue" (*SR* 27). There only appears to be no communication between Julia's chamber and the enigmatic southern wing of the castle, but, as the narrative continues, the reader and characters alike discover Julia herself to be the key to this communication between the marquis's sovereign paternal space and its limit.[24]

Julia's father figuratively attempts to shut down this open-ended aspect of his sovereignty when he arranges the marriage between Julia and the duke de Luovo. It is almost as if the marquis surmises that all the recent drama and commotion surrounding the supernatural happenings issuing from the southern apartments, threatening his castle's stability, are a displacement of Julia's growing discontent; the arranged marriage is, in essence, a way of reducing Julia's emerging femininity to maternity. The unwanted arranged marriage is his attempt to curtail this apparently minor, but potentially devastating deviation. Once the marquis breaks the news of the arrangement to Julia, she sits "motionless — stupefied and deprived of the power of utterance" (*SR* 55). Julia here acquires Dora's aphonia while she falls into a "state of *horrid* stupefaction" (*SR* 55; italics in original). When the mystery of femininity produces a conflict in Julia's psyche, she is always seized with sudden tremors of terror. But now that her father has given her something externally to fear, she lapses into a state of horror. Countering Julia's protest, the marquis launches into a tirade against Julia's repulsion:

> "Yet hear me, my lord," said Julia, tears swelling in her eyes, "and pity the sufferings of a child, who never till this moment has dared to dispute your commands."
>
> "Nor shall she now," said the marquis. "What — when wealth, honor, and distinction, are laid at my feet, shall they be refused, because a foolish girl — a very baby, who knows not good from evil, cries, and says she cannot love! Let me not think of it — My just anger may, perhaps, outrun discretion, and tempt me to chastise your folly. — Attend to what I say — accept the duke, or quit this castle for ever, and *wander* where you will" [*SR* 55–6; italics added].

The option articulated in this "my way or the highway" ultimatum is clearly that between the full acceptance of the paternal signifier of "wife" or the "wandering womb" of hysteria. Julia's metaphoric wandering, which was underway since the beginning of the narrative, becomes literalized onto the body of the narrative as she takes up the position, throughout the rest of the romance, of the one who questions why she is what the Other says she is. Julia appears from all superficial accounts to be caught between a decision for the duke or for Hippolitus. But either decision will only put her into the position defined by the signifier "wife." Therefore, her discontent with the signifier will still haunt her. Her decision between the duke and Hippolitus is actually a decision between becoming the object of the Other's enjoyment in the case of the duke or becoming the object of the Other's desire in the case of Hippolitus. Hysterically inclined, Julia naturally desires the latter. But in this case, she cannot immediately elope with Hippolitus. Her desire is to keep him desiring. This is why, later in the narrative, when Julia is on the run and eventually reunites with Hippolitus, she rebukes his offer. Her desire, the desire that is humiliating the marquis's sovereignty, is a desire for an unsatisfied desire. Even when she initially disobeys her father's planned arranged marriage with the much older duke, "the union proposed would have been hateful to her, even if she had no prior attachment" (*SR* 56). The duke is hateful not because he is not Hippolitus, but because of the obnoxious enjoyment he represents. Her "prior attachment" should not be conceived as an attachment to Hippolitus but rather as a persistent regard for the Other *jouissance* that Julia was exposed to during the arrival of the marchioness.

Whenever any characters enter the labyrinthian corridors of the locked southern apartments, they invariably become perplexed by the obscurity and intricacies of the environment, wandering about in a vain endeavor to find their way. There is little doubt for the reader that this mysterious and baffling realm, so long locked up, designates a space not wholly congruent with the realm of the marquis's rule. It is one of those excessive spaces often used in Gothic romance where, to use Lacanian terminology, fantasy touches onto something of the real. Radcliffe eventually literalizes this figurative space through Julia's subsequent escape from her confines at the Castle of Mazzini. When the wandering through the perplexing corridors of the southern apartments metamorphoses into the metonym of Julia's wandering through the obscure wilds of Sicily, then the mystery surrounding the southern apartments retroactively appears to be associated with limitlessness. This is precisely the role of the sublime scenery of the chase sequences from the latter half of the romance. Julia, much like Little Red Riding Hood, deviates from her filial duty of proceeding directly from one man (father) to the other (husband). She, in a sense, stops to smell the roses or, at least, to explore a possibility opened to her beyond the so-called limits of the law.

Because Julia's desire, the subject matter of the romance, is the desire of the Other, because Julia is more attuned to relation than to objects, the narrative focuses more on setting than on character. Once the narrative itself privileges relation over object, its atmosphere becomes much more sublime and registers an obscurity at the farther reaches of the paternal law and the law of the signifier. The reader's journey through the limited information offered by the narrative parallels the confused search for Julia that numerous characters pursue.[25] Radcliffe's privileging of setting over character — her privileging of the characters' relation to each other over the characters themselves — creates a narrative that is itself less certain than the traditional omniscient narrative. Because her narrative relies heavily on suspense, Radcliffe utilizes a third-person narrator whose omniscient perspective seems limited to the reader more than any specific character. The mysteries that the characters encounter throughout the novel are also encountered by the reader as mysteries. When, for instance, Julia manages her escape with the help of another woman after Ferdinand and Hippolitus fail to find their bearings and end up under the control of the marquis, the narrative does not directly present

Julia's actual escape scene. For 25 pages, the reader remains ignorant of exactly how Julia accomplishes this seemingly impossible feat. Her escape, however, occurs somewhere between pages 70 and 71. But once Julia's wandering begins, the perplexity that previously attended the navigation of the southern apartments of the castle becomes displaced onto the natural obscurity of the wild landscape as the setting for the rest of the narrative. Julia's wandering is a wandering that has no objective course; it is a wandering into a realm that possesses no clearly definable coordinates. Not only is the duke's pursuit described as "uncertain," but Julia herself "was perplexed which way to chuse" (*SR* 82, 83). The entire final two-thirds of the novel is an attempt to force uncharted ground into an orderly narrative. Radcliffe strategically uses the obscure sublimity of nature as a way to narrate that which is in excess of the law. The scenes that take place beyond the castle or any monastery reflect the uncharted regions of the feminine sublime as that which outstrips comprehension. Not only is this sphere one that is inhabited by outlaw groups of banditti singing songs devoted to Bacchanalian enjoyment, but this sphere is constantly described as primitive. The banditti themselves are described as being in a state of pre-civilized barbarity "before knowledge had civilized" (*SR* 85).

Once the mad pursuit after Julia is initiated, the duke, as the head of the search party, is consistently displayed, much like the marquis earlier, as powerless and incompetent in his search for Julia. Radcliffe even rhetorically emphasizes the duke's impotence as he feebly attempts to navigate the mystery of femininity by dropping the capital letter of his title. When lost one night in the uncertainty of their surroundings, a monastery bell heard in the distance allows the duke and his party to situate themselves. Because it is inhabited by a group of men who have forsaken the Other sex, the monastery becomes the only anchor point which these lost men can utilize to find their bearings in an otherwise obscure environment. After spending several arduous days on a seemingly impossible quest in search of Julia, the duke finds himself, after "reaching the summit of some wild cliffs," gazing upon "the picturesque imagery of the scene below" (*SR* 93). Unable to situate himself within this obscure region outside the limits of the law, the duke finds himself suddenly viewing a seemingly imaginary "beautiful romantic country" (*SR* 93). Within his fantastic and picturesque landscape, the duke's "attention [is] quickly called from the beauties of inanimate nature, to *objects* more interesting; for he observed two persons, whom he instantly recollected to be the same that he had formerly pursued over the plains" (*SR* 93; italics added). Unable to surmise that Julia escaped with the help of another female, the duke quickly believes that the male/female couple he spots within the frame of his fantastic scene to be Julia and whatever man chivalrously aided her escape. Upon catching up with the two fugitives, the duke discovers his error when he notices that the lady he thought was Julia turns out to be only a stranger — apparently another hysteric running amok and exploring the Other *jouissance*, the mystery of femininity not completely controlled by the signifier. This comical case of mistaken identity is replayed later in the narrative when Julia is erroneously captured by the search party out looking for this woman whom the duke mistakenly captures some 20 pages earlier. It is as if this obscure realm beyond the law is teeming with hysterics who are discontent with the signifying paternal space. However, the search parties can only find a modicum of stability by concocting fantasy scenarios (the all-male community of the monastery or a picturesque tranquillity) that are out of place given the limitlessness of their surroundings.

In her editor's introduction, Alison Milbank illustrates how the scenes set around Julia's wandering are narrated in the language of pictorial description. There are essentially two asymmetrical ways, according to Radcliffe's depiction, in which a character can situate itself with regard to the confusing landscape of Julia's desire. Milbank maintains that the duke's consciousness constructs a Claude Lorrain–styled picturesque pastoral landscape as a means to concoct a semblance of control over an otherwise hostile or indifferent sublime environment. But, as noted above, the duke's picturesque fantasy frame dissolves once he attempts to actually enter this frame. Instead of finding Julia in the imagined "picturesque imagery of the scene below," he encounters his own misrecognition in the form of a different wandering hysteric. Milbank contrasts this projected picturesque undertaking of the duke with Madame de Menon's more fruitful search for Julia. After quitting her post at the Castle of Mazzini over a misunderstanding with the marchioness, Menon finds herself in a similar romantic topography as the duke. Milbank notes how, unlike the duke with his definite objective, Menon "seemed without interest and without motive for exertion" (*SR* 103). It appears Madame de Menon is less distressed by a lack of boundaries and more attuned to the limitlessness of her surroundings:

> The evening was remarkably fine, and the romantic beauty of the surrounding scenery invited her to walk. She followed the windings of a stream, which was lost at some distance amongst luxuriant groves of chestnut. The rich coloring of evening glowed through the dark foliage, which spreading a pensive gloom around, offered a scene congenial to the present temper of her mind, and she entered the shades. Her thoughts, affected by the surrounding objects, gradually sunk into a pleasing and complacent melancholy, and she was insensibly led on. She still followed

the course of the stream to where the deep shades retired, and the scene again opening to day, yielded to her a view so various and sublime, that she paused in a thrilling delight and wonder. A group of wild and grotesque rocks rose in a semicircular form, and their fantastic shapes exhibited Nature in her most sublime and striking attitudes. Here her vast magnificence elevated the mind of the beholder to enthusiasm. Fancy caught the thrilling sensation, and at her touch the towering steeps became shaded with unreal glooms; the caves more darkly frowned — the projecting cliffs assumed a more terrific aspect, and the wild overhanging shrubs waved to the gale in deeper murmurs. The scene inspired Madame with referential awe, and her thoughts involuntarily rose, "from Nature up to Nature's God." The last dying gleams of day tinted the rocks and shone upon the waters, which retired through a rugged channel and were lost afar among the receding cliffs. While she listened to their distant murmur, a voice of liquid and melodious sweetness arose from among the rocks; it sung an air, whose melancholy expression awakened all her attention, and captivated her heart [*SR* 104].

The melodious and melancholic voice, of course, will turn out to be Julia's as Madame is by chance reunited, however temporarily, with her own wandering desire. Radcliffe's description of Madame's little excursion qualitatively differs from her depiction of the duke's surroundings in a couple of ways. As Milbank notices, this scene does not reflect the pastoral tranquility of a Claude Lorrain landscape; rather, it does take on the aura of the "irregular sublime" associated with the works of the Italian landscape painter Salvator Rosa, a conventional comparison. Unlike the Claudian landscape, the terrain of Salvator's work is utterly indifferent to any meaningful arrangement. This picture of grotesque rocks, towering steeps, projecting and receding cliffs, and deep murmurs betrays any attempt at the stable orderliness that the duke projects onto the alienating environment that he encounters. Milbank asserts that Madame, because she gives herself over to the power of the sublime experience, does not become disappointed and frustrated like the duke. In fact, she even accomplishes what appears impossible for the duke: she finds Julia.

Although Milbank insists that Madame succeeds where the duke fails because she does not follow the duke in penetrating the frame of the picturesque landscape, I would contend that, in the case of Madame, there is no frame at all. Rather than view Madame as entering the frame of the Salvator landscape, one should view her as part of a sublime landscape without a frame.[26] The unlimited landscape in which Madame finds herself, and to which she gives herself over, designates in a pictorial metaphor the non-all character of woman's desire. Since Julia flees the castle because she somehow feels the non-all character of her desire, one would have to become a cartographer without a map in order to find her. Any framing of Julia's desire, any attempt to understand what she wants, will only result in missing her. Since Madame is not actively pursuing Julia, since Madame is proceeding through the wilderness aimlessly without direction, she coincidentally runs into Julia. It is as if she proceeded far enough along a mobius strip that she ended up on the other side.

The manner in which Radcliffe depicts Madame's surroundings also says something significant about this Other terrain. The duke, perhaps because he is in search of a specific object and is object-oriented in the first place, stands outside the very environment from atop a mountain, maintaining that very divinesque perspective essential for the masculine sublime. The "beautiful romantic country" spotted through the "picturesque imagery of the scene below" is a scene that appears to exist regardless of the duke. But, as Radcliffe portrays him descending to the depths of his observation, she makes the scene collapse like some traversed fantasy. The scenery surrounding Madame, however, makes a completely different point. The sinking melancholy of the surrounding objects, the retiring shades, the towering steeps, and the receding cliffs are just a few of the personifications Radcliffe utilizes to bring the setting to life. The scenery seems to come to life as Madame wanders through it. There is an utter lack of any objective viewpoint here. Rather, the scenery appears to be nothing other than a reflection and dramatization of the particular closeness between Julia and Madame at this moment. Here, only ten pages after the duke's debacle, Radcliffe appears to be illustrating how such a setting reflects the truth that there is no truth at the level of representation. The signifier always operates on the level of the performative. This, in turn, is the fundamental claim of the hysteric: "Why am I what you say I am?" In order to display Julia's wandering desire, Radcliffe has foregrounded her adventure in a hysterical setting. The wilds where Julia runs amok are actually the effect of the inadequacy of the signifier to wholly situate Julia, a signifier to which the duke seems to erroneously attribute complete authority.

The discontent Julia suffers is epitomized in the scenes where she seeks refuge in the Monastery of St. Augustine. Entering the abbey, Julia seeks asylum as much against the excessive enjoyment associated with feminine sexuality, personified in the natural scenery, as against those searching for her. Why else would she seek security in an abbey entitled with the signifier of one of Catholicism's most important paternal figures? Julia's discontent, however, quickly rears its ugly head again when she is confronted with the paternal ultimatum, this time by the abbot. In his selfish benevolence, he offers Julia what he thinks is an either/or choice. But, in reality, as reflected in Julia's eardrums, his either/or choice transforms into a neither/nor forced choice.

Her supposed option between being returned to her father or taking the habit amounts to no choice at all. "We grant you three days to decide upon this matter," pronounces the abbot, "at the expiration of which, the veil, or the Duke de Luovo, awaits you" (*SR* 141–2). Julia, faced with the non-choice of either becoming the "wife" of the duke or becoming the "wife" of God, once again seeks escape from an all-too-limiting conflict. Robert Miles describes this neither/nor scenario as a dramatization "of male power and female resistance."[27] But I would argue that this type of forced choice more dramatizes male impotence than male power. If males possessed actual power in this narrative space, they would not need to resort to force. Although the setting of this neither/nor scene is the monastery of St. Augustine — a space akin to the castle and also ruled by paternal authority — the entire, almost comical, dramatic scene is drawn out as a childish confrontation between the abbot and the marquis during the latter's siege of the convent. Hippolitus's hand is also no solution to the discontent Julia suffers over having to become the wife of the duke or of God. Marrying Hippolitus would still designate Julia a "wife," which itself is the root of the problem.[28] As mentioned briefly above, when Julia eventually reunites with Hippolitus in the ruins where a group of bandits commit their nightly crimes, the obvious and most efficient solution to Julia's problems is rejected by her. She tells Hippolitus she cannot instantly run off and marry him because of the too-recent fate of her brother Ferdinand. But within this unreasonable reaction, one should hear an echo of the depths of Julia's discontent.

What all these men chasing Julia through the wilds cannot accept is Julia's ability to libidinalize absence. They fail to notice the essence of femininity: "femininity is defined not as an essence but *as a relation*."[29] As Darian Leader reads Lacan, feminine *jouissance* is not infinite, rather it is infinite in relation to the phallic function, in relation to the signifier. In other words, this Other enjoyment, this one which Lacan insists women experience without knowing anything about it, is unfixed, much like the scenery and setting of most of the final two-thirds of *A Sicilian Romance*. It is irreducible to the signifier, but the signifier's existence is necessary for the presence of the Other *jouissance*: "If she is in the phallic function, she is not everywhere there, and if she has a relation to S(Ⱥ) [desire outside the limits of the law] it is nonetheless in castration."[30] Therefore, the indeterminate space Radcliffe sets up as the major setting — the chaotic and savage wilderness between the domiciles ruled by men — is a literary depiction of Julia's partner as solitude. Being alone for Julia has more to do with not being with the father than it has to do with being with Hippolitus. As Leader argues elsewhere, even though a woman is essential for a man's sexuality, the reverse is hardly the case.[31] In the case of a woman, the very absence of a man is sexualized. Man directly desires an object, where women's desire is always a desire of the Other's desire. Julia's real partner within the wilds beyond paternal authority is solitude itself. She gets more enjoyment out of the renunciation of Hippolitus than she could ever get, within this environ, from delivering herself over into Hippolitus's hands. She, in fact, will defer her ultimate matrimony with Hippolitus until they are on the more stable shores of mainland Italy. This is why even those who attempt to aid Julia, those who by all accounts are assisting Julia, inevitably fail. Madame, for instance, delivers Julia into the hands of the ego-maniacal abbot, and Ferdinand takes her on a disastrous voyage to Italy:

> The magnificence of the scenery inspired Julia with delight; and her heart dilating with high enthusiasm, she forgot the sorrows which had oppressed her. The breeze wafted the ship gently along for some hours, when it gradually sunk into a calm. The glassy surface of the waters was not curled by the lightest air, and the vessel floated heavily on the bosom of the deep. Sicily was yet in view, and the present delay agitated Julia with wild apprehension. Towards the close of day a light breeze sprang up, but it blew from Italy, and a train of dark *vapours* emerged from the verge of the horizon, which gradually accumulating, the heavens became entirely overcast. The evening shut in suddenly; the rising wind, the heavy clouds that loaded the atmosphere, and the thunder which murmured afar off terrified Julia, and threatened a violent storm.
>
> The tempest came on, and the captain vainly sounded for anchorage: it was deep sea, and the vessel drove furiously before the wind. The darkness was interrupted only at intervals, by the broad expanse of vivid lightnings, which quivered upon the waters, and disclosing the horrible gaspings of the waves, served to render the succeeding darkness more awful. The thunder, which burst in tremendous crashes above, the loud roar of the waves below, the noise of the sailors, and the sudden cracks and groanings of the vessel conspired to heighten the tremendous sublimity of the scene.
>
> > Far on the rocky shores the surges sound,
> > The lashing whirlwinds cleave the vast profound;
> > While high in air, amid the rising storm,
> > Driving the blast, sits Danger's black'ning form.
>
> Julia lay fainting with terror and sickness in the cabin, and Ferdinand, though almost hopeless himself, was endeavoring to support her, when a loud and dreadful crash was heard from above. It seemed as if the whole vessel had parted. The voices of the sailors now rose together, and all was confusion and uproar. Ferdinand ran up to the deck, and learned that part of the main mast, borne away by the wind, had fallen upon the deck, whence it had rolled overboard [*SR* 152–3; italics added].

Throughout this passage, in rather exaggerated fashion, Radcliffe exposes the reader to the truth of Julia's desire. This scene begins with Julia's and Ferdinand's embarkation to Italy and is portrayed in the ostensible tranquil atmosphere associated with Julia's escape from the supposed tyranny that is oppressing her. As the passage proceeds, however, the narrative again moves from the tranquility of a Claude Lorrain painting into all the chaotic indetermination and obscurity associated with Salvator Rosa's landscapes. Upon Julia's attempted escape, her high feeling of enthusiasm in leaving all the sorrows which have been oppressing her begin to conflict with her previous characterization as one who "loved to indulge the melancholy of her heart in the solitude of the woods" (*SR* 42). Significantly, the waters and wind surrounding the ship initially remain calm as long as Sicily is still in view. But once the calm becomes too manifest, once Sicily disappears over the horizon, Julia inexplicably becomes agitated. Coincidently, at the moment Julia suffers some agitation, so, too, does the atmosphere. The "dark vapours," which here function as the first sign that nature is enjoying, is a thinly masked metaphor for the vapors that were traditionally thought to emerge from the uterus as the cause of hysteria and that was still being used synonymously for hysteria in Radcliffe's day. Also, that nature is here symptomatically acting out Julia's natural drive is further reinforced by Radcliffe's choice of a storm-tossed sea for the central metaphor. A ship tossed by the sea was a common simile to describe the hysteric when losing mastery of her own affections.[32] Radcliffe is further figuratively arguing the then growing belief that marriage was not a proper cure or treatment for hysteria and the old fashioned idea that the vapors may in fact cause such disorders.[33]

Even though Julia appears content when embarking for Italy, she remains literally unconscious of her real desire to remain in touch with the solitary sorrow that is supposedly oppressing her. In fact, the entire shipwreck scene reflects the fundamental obscurity of feminine sexuality. The sudden and unexpected fury of the tempest, which tragically blows the escaping ship back to the island of Julia's father's authority, acts out Julia's true desire. Julia lies below deck in fainting terror as if all her energy has been psychically displaced onto the strength of the tempest's rage. Her real enjoyment lies within the wilderness of her father's rule and is here transferred to the sublime scenery of the tempest where nature is pictured as itself enjoying. Julia herself is probably unconscious of the particular enjoyment she wishes to return to in Sicily, but, nonetheless, the gratification of the tempest betrays her real desire. Her desire to return to Sicily, a desire she remains unconscious of as she lies unconscious below deck of the storm-tossed ship, illustrates that her desire may not be wholly accountable by the signifier, but neither does it exist outside of the symbolic realm.

Unlike the typical reading of the Gothic heroine, which purports that her suffering occurs at the hands of a tyrannical father, Julia testifies to the truth that her (and perhaps all Gothic heroines') suffering is not only one she paradoxically enjoys, but it is caused by her father not being symbolic enough. Because Maria, the very woman who indirectly opened Julia to a possibly limitless experience, pulls the strings in the marquis's relation to his daughters, Julia, following Dora, instinctively notices her father's impotence. She, in a sense, like all good hysterics, notices that the father is defective in plugging the hole in the symbolic order. If he cannot close it, Julia becomes susceptible to an indeterminate and unfathomable enjoyment. Radcliffe uses the sublimity of nature not only to illustrate nature enjoying, but to show that the hysteric's most intimate enjoyment takes place beyond the signifier on the letter of the text. In fact, not only does the tempest's rage coincide with Julia's change in emotional state and depletion of physical energy, but Radcliffe's narrative alters its voice in compliance. Her language becomes much more rhetorical with its heavy overuse of personification as the raging tempest climaxes. The overdetermined connection between Julia's discontent, the weather's fury and the narrative's play becomes only accountable on the level of the chronicle as Radcliffe's prose lapses into poetry. In the narrative's attempt to represent and account for Julia's desire as something outside the signifier, it resorts to verse, a form of language that is itself on the border of representation.[34]

Not limited to her use of the "explained supernatural" throughout her narratives, Radcliffe's writing, particularly her use of the sublime, often seems to reveal more than is contained by the actual signifiers on the page, poetically revealing the suspension of the law of the signifier. J.M.S. Tompkins maintains that the chaste propriety of Radcliffe's phrasing is always accomplished in "voluptuous coloring." Tompkins writes: "Her books are full of the half-revealed, of objects that are betrayed sufficiently to excite curiosity but not sufficiently to allay it, of hints and traces that lead the mind into a region of vague sublimity."[35] Tompkins even suggests that if there is suspense in Walpole, in Radcliffe, everything is suspended.[36] Radcliffe's theme, as Tompkins further indicates, is not some dreadful happening. Describing things directly limits the imagination, where suggestion stimulates. Many recent critics have noticed how these suspensions inherent in Radcliffe's narratives are patterned on feminine eroticism. Ann Ronald goes so far as to claim that the movement of Radcliffe's narratives "invite the reader to think about sex."[37] Radcliffe hints at the fact that the obscure wilds of Sicily outside the Castle of Mazzini have something in common with feminine sexuality when she describes the unlawful nature of the environ. While the duke, surrounded by shadowy uncertainty, chases the wandering Julia, he encounters a light which issues "from the mouth of a cavern, and cast a bright reflection upon the overhanging rocks and shrubs" (*SR* 84). It does not take much imagination to realize that not only is Radcliffe's narrative painting a picture of female genitalia, but, because this cavern is filled with banditti, her narrative suggests the unlawful nature of feminine sexuality. Cynthia Griffin Wolff indicates that Radcliffe expresses the dilemmas of feminine sexuality in a disguised form.[38] This is done by Radcliffe's narrative, however, not as much for censorship purposes as to point out the signifier's inadequacy in portraying much about feminine sexuality.[39]

These claims can be further articulated by specifying a marked distinction between male and female eroticism. Leader maintains that, as far as sex goes, men do their best to avoid disappearing. Men's masturbation fantasies always center on the man being in control of sexual enjoyment. To masturbate with an image in one's head means not having to confront the woman in a real sexual encounter: "It is the latter that will make him disappear and hence the relative security of a sexual relation not with a woman but with one's own body."[40] Only in this way can a man focus on pure *jouissance*. It is completely different for a woman. Leader maintains that the woman's masturbatory fantasy centers around asking her husband for intercourse, his refusing and leaving her for another woman. According to Leader, "there is no manifest representation of what we might call sexual pleasure."[41] The key, of course, is that the woman finds enjoyment in a lack of enjoyment. Leader calls this structure of feminine sexuality *the sexualization of her own disappearance*.[42] The disappearance staged in this masturbatory fantasy is not wholly different than Radcliffe's staging and restaging of Julia's disappearance throughout *A Sicilian Romance*. Julia inexplicably disappears first from the castle, then from her hideout where Madame de Menon finds her, then from Saint Augustine, and finally from the banditti dungeon. One could even be tempted to read the entire body of the novel as the repetitive disappearance of Julia, as an extended masturbatory fantasy Julia engages in one night "beyond the hour of customary repose" in her "small closet."[43]

Discussing femininity, Willy Apollon theorizes that there are four men in a woman's life. The first is customarily her father or some sort of father figure. He, as a man of the signifier, offers his daughter love in a word or gesture that divides her between maternity and femininity. This love itself functions as a "prop against the failings of the signifier."[44] Apollon even maintains that, in the little girl's fantasy of seduction by the father, one should recognize the very structure of the search for the signifier as a pure offering of love. Love, which Apollon claims the father bears witness to, guarantees the certainty the little girl requires from the signifier. That is, until the arrival of the second man. There comes a time, Apollon contends, where man, including the father, in some instances, represents something of a danger for the girl.[45] Apollon offers an example from one of his analysand's narratives. An 11-year-old girl who, one summer vacation, picked up her cousin's book and opened to a scene not for her naive eyes: "I must have opened it up to any page to read a bit. After several minutes, I quickly closed it. I had fallen on a love scene. I had never imagined anything like that could happen."[46] Apollon notes that this case illustrates "that surprising discovery for a girl of that peculiar strangeness rising up in her body and opening it to a space she was not previously aware of at that point in her life. At this point the girl departs the imaginary of her childhood and arrives at adolescence by means of access to a knowledge that has been kept apart from her life until then. But from then on, that knowledge will inhabit her questioning of the signifier and of any love discourse addressed to her."[47]

In a sense, Julia is bombarded with this discovery at the moment when Maria enters the narrative. This obscure discovery for Julia is also emphasized in the unwanted terrifying arranged marriage with the duke and in the inset tales within the novel's primary narrative. The first inset tale of the novel is Madame's history of Louisa, Julia's and Emilia's dead mother. Through this tale Julia both learns about the gloriousness and disappointment of love for the first time. Her mother lost her beloved and was systematically killed by the marquis's contemptuous love. From here on out, Julia will display a certain distrust of the signifier and any love discourse addressed to her. The inset tales themselves (Louisa's story, Madame's story, Cornelia's story, and the story concerning the daughter of Marquis Murani) all represent love's incapacity to adequately prop up the failings of the signifier. Functioning the same way as the romance novel did for Apollon's analysand, these inset stories expose Julia to the inconsistency of the signifier and the Other *jouissance*. Furthermore, the inset tales of Radcliffe's narrative are microcosms for her romance as a whole. One could argue that the "reading" of these tales by Julia coincides with the reading of *A Sicilian Romance* itself. Radcliffe's romance figuratively functions as one of those tales of chivalry that exposed someone like Saint Teresa to that Other *jouissance*, to which she spent her entire life being uncontrollably haunted. Regardless, these inset tales, because they uncover the inability of love to fully support the signifier, expose Julia not only to a knowledge that language fails to hail, but also to an enjoyment other than the one imaginable on the basis of sex.

This disarray of femininity in which Julia finds herself with the entrance of Maria is something her family attempts to curtail. The marquis knows that the most effective way to restrict the Other *jouissance* under the rules of the signifier is through the reproduction of Julia in the family romance. By arranging a marriage, the marquis hopes to give Julia a signifier ("wife," "mother") that will compensate for what she loses of femininity with the acquisition of a symbolic status. By reducing femininity to spousal duty, the marquis hopes Julia's femininity will be reduced to maternity. Realizing that she would have to give up the Other *jouissance* upon entering this marriage and realizing that it would be impossible for the duke or Hippolitus to offer her a satisfaction for this lost part, Julia flees the castle into the obscurity of the Other enjoyment. Following Apollon, the second man exposes the girl to the fact that the "delimitation of the sexual field by the signifier of the Law makes a remainder, it constitutes an exteriority which is the site of the other *jouissance*, the one sex does not rule."[48] As Apollon insists, this outsider, which Julia becomes, "has no center, has no border either"; it is fugitive.

In the middle of the narrative when Julia and Madame are bound up and brought to a deserted and decadent mansion, "the broken battlements, enwreathed with ivy" betray the sexual innuendo of Radcliffe's narrative. Even though Matthew Lewis is the Gothic novelist who supposedly gives the reader the sexual in all its presence, one can argue Radcliffe does exactly the same. Only, for Radcliffe, since she is presenting feminine sexuality — something the signifier is inadequate in displaying — she can only do so indirectly. Innuendo, as Radcliffe utilizes it throughout her novels, is the sublimated manner in which the Thing, to use the language of Freud, shows up on the level of the objective narrative. Radcliffe's expert sense and depiction of sublime scenery coincides with her poetic display of feminine desire. Julia's repetitive disappearing illustrates precisely how the realm of the signifier remains always non-all in relation to her. Her disappearances indirectly manifest the very inconsistency of the symbolic order by illustrating the impotence of the various male characters in their attempt to find Julia along the grid of the signifying chain.

Under the traditional rule of law, Julia would simply tend to seek the love of God as that one unconditional love which can never betray her as she foolishly attempts mid-way through the romance when she seeks asylum in the Convent St. Augustine.[49] As Alenka Zupančič has pointed out, the convent used to function as that one refuge for women who have lost their honor, who have lost their place in the configuration of symbolic roles.[50] The wandering woman is, within the confines of a symbolic order, dead. As Zupančič confirms, "a woman who has to enter the convent because she has lost her honour is already dead in the symbolic, but is still alive in reality."[51] Such an amok woman is unbearable. She must be removed from circulation and prevented from appearing as a "loose" woman — a creature who is symbolically dead (that is, with no symbolic attachments that would define her), but who continues to wander around. A woman who has "sinned, but does not go into the convent, is like the living dead, a spectre, a being with no place in the symbolic."[52] This is incidentally why these men searching for these "loose" women, or women on the loose, throughout the wilds of Sicily have such a terrible time properly locating them. The men can only navigate their way around by using an ordered grid which itself is inconsistent to the space being mapped. Julia, on the other hand, can elude detection precisely because she is somewhat attuned to the non-all character of this space. Only with her overly poetic prose filled with subliminal landscapes, innuendos, and half-revealed appearances is Radcliffe able to accurately depict this non-all landscape.[53]

Zupančič admits that this exposure of women as the "living dead" in this sense is abundantly present in much eighteenth-century literature. But, she is quick to add, we must be overly cautious in linking the fading of this type of woman since the eighteenth-century to some sort of liberation. Rather, Zupančič concludes that we should notice that a new signifier has been invented to cover what was left out by the previous signifiers "mother," "daughter," "sister," "wife" and "nun." According to Zupančič, "in romantic literature, it is love that reconnects loose women to the symbolic order. As long as she is really in love with a man, she can live outside the realm of the law without disturbing it."[54] Since Radcliffe portrays the fading of the Church's traditional authority throughout her Gothic narrative, Julia's only means of avoiding the signifier "wife" without being pejoratively reduced to the signifier "whore" is to finally accept "love" from Hippolitus. This explains the overly contrived happy ending suspiciously supplied by Radcliffe as a means to testify to the untrustworthiness of the symbolic order without Julia or Radcliffe herself posing a direct terrifying threat. This is also, of course, Radcliffe's manner of producing Lacan's second notion of sublimation as desublimation—finding the sublime in something inconsistent within the symbolic, like love, rather than in something otherworldly.[55]

6

⚜

Matthew Lewis and the Gothic Horror of Obsessional Neurosis

Tantalized by the possibilities she found in Horace Walpole's inaugural and immature Gothic romance, Ann Radcliffe focused her Gothic fiction primarily on what she found to be the more sophisticated literary devices of terrifying scenes and mysterious occurrences. Her writing cuts through the chaotic supernatural display of *The Castle of Otranto* in an attempt to salvage the "explained supernatural" as the only device necessary for the genre. By creating terrifying scenes whose full explanation was deferred until the end of the romance, she crafted hysterical narratives, as argued in the previous chapter, where sense was completely severed from affect. In this manner, Radcliffe's narratives thematically and subliminally point to their own inability to "say it all." Begrudgingly influenced by the works of Radcliffe, Matthew Lewis attempted to improve a genre that he felt was not explicit enough. As far as Lewis was concerned, Radcliffe's romances basically cheat the reader in the end.[1] Through her use of suspense, she is able to lure the reader into a captive state only to pull the rug out at the last minute by displaying the rational reason behind the supposed supernatural occurrences that have captivated the reader's imagination. Lewis's literary reaction to Radcliffe parallels a 19-year-old man's reaction to being rebuffed by a woman. Radcliffe, in a sense, teases, tantalizes, and leads on the young, teenaged author only to deny him his desire in the end. Lewis, therefore, decides to write his own Gothic romance in order to do without the Other sex. Like the true obsessional neurotic, he will search for what he wants without involving the Other's desire.

The Monk goes to the opposite extreme of Radcliffe's narratives. Where Radcliffe appears to hold everything back, Lewis's romance offers everything in its obscene presence. His technique turns the Radcliffean terror of suggestion into the horror of demonic rape, incest, and murder. According to Fred Botting, Lewis describes "in lurid detail the specters that Gothic fiction had previously left to the superstitious or explained away."[2] In so doing, Lewis disregards and often even parodies the sentimentality found in Radcliffe's work. Borrowing from the vulgarity of German writers like Lorenz Flammenberg and Karl Grosse, Lewis offers the reader a pornographic Gothic in which the previously ambiguous supernatural is now given in all its obnoxious presence. What was formerly left hidden, half-revealed, and suggested now takes center stage in the sensationalism of excess. Where Radcliffe's narratives did not give enough, Lewis's romance simply gives too much. Radcliffe refined and perfected the one aspect of Walpole's inaugural Gothic romance that she felt worth salvaging, and Lewis resurrected and cultivated another aspect of Walpole's narrative for which he felt a strong affinity. Together they split Walpole's work — castrated it, if you will — and developed it into its mature generic status by the end of the century.

Lewis's reaction to Radcliffe's Gothic and his development of Walpole's Gothic machinery can be explained by the Freudian structure of obsessional neurosis as a strategy of dealing with a foundational lack, keeping in mind that aesthetic productions, especially overtly sublime ones, are always a means of demarcating the contours of some lack in our symbolic economy. As mentioned earlier, in Bruce Fink's distinction between hysteria and obsessional neurosis as the two forms of neurosis, the breast in breast-feeding is the sight where the infant initially has all his immediate needs satisfied. At first the infant considers the breast as merely part of himself.[3] It is not, of course, until separation from the mother that the infant realizes that his main source of satisfaction comes from a source outside himself. Once this separation happens in the development of the infant's life, he realizes that the breast can never be possessed in the same unimpeded manner again. Therefore, the object that now is lacking becomes eroticized. How the infant deals with this initial loss, this separation, how the child finds a substitute for the mother and thereby completes the Oedipus complex, determines the difference between the obsessional neurotic and the hysteric — the difference between being aligned on the masculine or feminine side of sexual difference. For the hysteric, separation is overcome as the subject constructs herself as the erotic object that substitutes for the loss suffered by the mother, or the Other. In fantasy, she becomes that which can complete the Other. This is why the hysteric's desire is always the desire of the Other. Radcliffe's narratives illustrate this structure by creating worlds that are in themselves incomplete and inconsistent. The universe that the Radcliffean Gothic heroine inhabits is a world of the "non-all," an open-ended universe that creates an unsettling effect on both characters and readers.[4]

In the end, Radcliffe's strategic use of the "explained supernatural" illustrates how the incompleteness that allows for even the surmising of something supernatural is both inherent and endemic to our symbolic economy itself.

The obsessional, however, tries to compensate for his initial loss in another way. Separation is overcome by the obsessional by eroticizing the breast itself as the object that functions as the cause of his desire. This fantasy allows the belief that the object, which is now eroticized, can reproduce the original full satisfaction. But, as Fink notes, the obsessional refuses to acknowledge that the breast is part of, or comes from, the Other, or that it bears any relation to the actual woman who becomes his sexual partner. This is why on the masculine side of sexual difference in his formula of sexuation, Lacan writes masculine sexuality with his matheme for fantasy ($\mathcal{S}$<>a, the lacking subject in relation to the fantasmic object that causes him to desire). The man aims for the woman but only comes up with the object. This, I will argue, is the role of the sublime objects within the horrific narrative of Lewis. Because feminine sexuality is "non-all" in relation to the signifier, Radcliffe offers narratives that structurally cannot offer it all. Since masculine sexuality strives for it all and only comes up with the object, Lewis's narrative begs to be read as offering sublime objects in all their vulgar presence as materializations of the more definable enjoyment associated with the obsessional neurotic. The supernatural entities and horrific gore scattered throughout Lewis's Gothic romance aesthetically represent libido outside the body. In hysteria one is confronted with affect without sense, without any reason for the affect (the repressed returns on the body); therefore, Radcliffe's use of terror as a supposedly sublime fear where one is frightened without knowing what one is frightened of works perfectly in delimiting a feminine Gothic aesthetic. Since in obsessional neurosis one has meaning without affect (the repressed returns in thought), Lewis tidies up any confusion or indeterminateness in his story line by giving the reader an actual supernatural realm. His narrative lacks the refined suspenseful tone of Radcliffe's because, by offering the supernatural in all its unbelievable existence, Lewis's narrative remains virtually without affect. Once the narrative establishes a supernatural realm, wonder becomes obsolete and irrelevant. The characters and readers simply know immediately why such strange things happen.[5]

According to Fink, the obsessional neurotic, through his obsessively ritualistic performatives, "attempts to neutralize the Other."[6] The Other is precisely what the obsessional negates in his infantile endeavor to sever the breast from her whose breast it is. The obsessional's erotic object, his *petit a*, is the objective correlate to the Other's desire. It at once covers over and exposes the Other's desire. The obsessional's compulsive behavior is initially geared toward regulation of the Other's desire and inevitably geared toward regulation of the Other's enjoyment. For the neurotic, obsessional actions are an attempt to create an existence that is so regulated by routine that all room for accident is eliminated. Whenever an obsessional is exposed to the desire of the Other in a forceful manner, he invariably slips into the mode of compulsive behavior. This is precisely what happens to Freud's most famous obsessional, the Rat Man, when he encounters the "Cruel Captain." After hearing about the excessive enjoyment the Captain obtains from horrifying types of torture, the Rat Man turns any of the Captain's requests into tormenting internalized demands. According to Fink, "the obsessional is shaken up by such manifestations of the Other's desire, and can no longer successfully nullify or neutralize the Other and his dependence on the Other."[7] Rather than face the abyss of the Other's desire, the obsessional will tend to read the emptiness of the Other's desire as a demand. In this manner, the unfathomable desire can be materialized into something tangible. But this tangibility is almost always something horrifying.[8]

The mother as a desiring figure is situated at the center of the nodal complex of the obsessional. This desire is precisely what the obsessional attempts to regulate by choosing to see the breast as his object. The obsessional's fantasy schema ($\math$<>a) allows the obsessional to remain fundamentally ignorant of the Other as desiring. This structure can be seen at work in an incident in the personal life of Matthew Lewis. Laurie Langbauer tells of a comical and potentially terrifying incident within the Lewis household. This incident revolved around a romance that caused an even bigger scandal than *The Monk*. After Lewis published his Gothic romance, the Lewis family was thrown into more disgrace than *The Monk* could ever cause. It seems Matthew Lewis's mother penned a little book of her own. When this terrible fact reached Lewis, he implored his mother to suppress her romance. According to Langbauer, "Lewis warns his mother of the injuries publication of her romance would cause: his father would be shattered, his unmarried sister left an old maid, his married sister disgraced in her husband's family, and Lewis himself would have to flee to the Continent."[9] Langbauer suggests that Lewis objects to his mother's authorship out of a fear that it would overshadow his own. But, more importantly, Lewis fears his mother's writing will threaten her role as a mother. In other words, her writing makes her inconsistent with the signifier "mother"—the signifier that represents her for Lewis. Lewis's horror does not so much concern the simple fact that his mother has penned a romance, but, rather, over the fact that her writing opens up the space of her desire beyond her desire for him as son—the very space that horrifies the obsessional. Lewis even writes to his mother that he always considered female authors as half-male.[10] Because of her authorship, Lewis's mother begins to appear to him as some sort of unnatural, if not supernatural, being.

In "Notes Upon a Case of Obsessional Neurosis," the Rat Man tells Freud that his neurosis began as a young boy when he looked up his governess's skirt. Charles Melman notes that what the Rat Man saw up this skirt must be the cause of his neurosis. The Rat Man describes this incident himself:

> My sexual life began very early. I can remember a scene during my fourth or fifth year. (From my sixth year onward I can remember everything.) This scene came into my mind quite distinctly, years later. We had a very pretty young governess called Fraulein Peter. One evening she was lying on the sofa lightly dressed, and reading. I was lying beside her, and begged her to let me creep under her skirt. She told me I might, so long as I said nothing to any one about it. She had very little on, and I fingered her genitals and the lower part of her body, which struck me as very queer.[11]

The Rat Man in fact saw two things up F. Peter's skirt: the feminine sex and nothing. In other words, the Rat Man at an early age was confronted with the feminine sex as a question — a fundamentally unplumbable question. What he felt was so unfathomable that it could only be dealt with through conceptualization. Therefore, according to Melman, the lack that the Rat Man encountered becomes transformed, through his obsessional regulation, into an object that designates the lack as such, as a positivization of the very inability to demarcate it.[12] The devastating lack that perplexes the Rat Man gets transformed into a crime he committed. Therefore, when the Rat Man later encounters the excessive enjoyment of the "Cruel Captain," he stands accused, to himself, of a crime he must correct or those he loves — his father and beloved — will meet an untimely death. It appears that, for the obsessional, the only way to curb the Other's desire and to keep the Other's enjoyment at bay is to convince oneself of the omnipotence of thoughts. Once confronted with something out there beyond his control, the obsessional relies on the security that his thoughts affect reality and that he can control these thoughts up to a certain point. This self-torturing, this pleasure in suffering is the paradoxical manner in which the obsessional enjoys.

Because this fundamental lack that constitutes the Other's desire is so anxiety-producing, the obsessional will do anything to transform this unfathomable desire into a demand. As long as the obsessional is faced with a demand, he can directly face what confronts him. The unfathomable obscurity that readers and characters confront in Radcliffe's narratives is the specific aspect of her literary technique against which Lewis reacts. When Lewis implicitly complains that Radcliffe, through her use of terror, refuses to take her sensations far enough, he is complaining about his own confusion when confronted with what he thinks is the enigma of woman. To make up for the lack of pain, the lack of the graphic, and the lack of horror in Radcliffe's Gothic world, Lewis offers the reader a sublime apparatus with more substance. He, much like the obsessional, essentially transforms what Radcliffe's romances lack into sublime objects. By giving the reader the supernatural and gruesome details in all their presence, Lewis virtually eliminates any of the obscurity associated with the desire of the Other for both the readers and his characters.

As with *Otranto*, *A Sicilian Romance,* and the Gothic romance in general, the prefatory remarks of *The Monk* play a vital part in the romance's textual machinery. Even though Jacques Derrida has formulated the manner in which prefaces, or what he calls the *hors livre*, haunt texts in ways that go beyond merely offering outside assistance to the reader,[13] the authorial opening remarks in Gothic romances, which are themselves part and parcel of the Gothic textual convention, may play a more substantive role than in most literary genres because Gothic romances deal primarily with haunting. Walpole uses his two authorial prefaces to first pretend that his romance is a translation of an ancient Italian manuscript and then to write a mini dissertation on the literary benefits of combining ancient and modern romance. First he attempts to mask the absurdity associated with his romance's immaturity, and then he attempts to illustrate precisely how this absurdity is really a sophisticated philosophical and literary experiment. Radcliffe, in *A Sicilian Romance*, also uses her authorial preface to strategically situate her romance in an uncanny superstitious past. Since prefaces logically precede the text proper and are contained somewhat before the beginning of the text, outside of the text, they play the role in the Gothic tradition of that which has been left out — repressed, if you will. The material that makes up these Gothic prefaces is not so much neither within nor without the romance proper as much as it is extimate to the text (to use a Lacanian term, introduced earlier). These prefaces are both external to the text and also its most intimate aspect. This is also true for Lewis's introductory remarks to *The Monk*.

Lewis's preface consists of a poem in imitation of Horace. This poem, as the first thing the reader is greeted with, is a sort of ode to the very romance that the reader is about to read. The first stanza consists of the author's initial nervousness about publishing his now finished manuscript. Even though he is hesitant about letting go of his production, the author understands his personified book's desire to stand amongst the important literary works in the windows of London's prestigious bookseller's shops. The second stanza further pronounces the author's deepest fears and anxiety about letting his book out into the world. (The book's maturation obviously parallels that of the 19-year-old author).

Go then, and pass that dangerous bourn
Whence never Book can back return:
And when you find, condemned, despised,
Neglected, blamed, and criticised,
Abuse from all who read you fall,
(If haply you be read at all)
Sorely will you your folly sigh at,
And wish for me, and home and quiet.[14]

It seems Lewis, as author, is grudgingly willing to let his hideous progeny go forth, as Mary Shelley will allow many years later, especially not without the warning that it is potentially dangerous out there. Unlike Shelley, who in her preface to *Frankenstein* feels that to release her romance, her creature, into the public bodes dangerous for society, Lewis's hesitation stems from his fear that this public offering may prove catastrophic for his romance and himself. Lewis is apparently overly concerned with the potential retaliatory abuse the public may heap on his literary production. In his words of advice to his young romance, he seems to anticipate the uncertain nature of public response.

In the third stanza of the prefatory ode, Lewis attempts, by "assuming a conjuror's office," to forecast his romance's reception: "Soon as your novelty is o'er, / And you are young and new no more, / In some dark dirty corner thrown, / Mouldy with damps, with cobwebs strown, / Your leaves shall be the Book-worms prey" (*M* 3). According to Lewis's verse, the long-term future of his romance appears rather bleak. The reader will notice that the very position in which Lewis puts his manuscript following public reception — in some dark corner eaten alive by worms — is the very place and position the Monk Ambrosio ends up in at the end of the romance after Satan casts him down from Old Testament heights. This would lead the reader to suspect that Lewis's romance, *The Monk,* is figured through its own character of the Monk, making the romance about nothing other than its own public demise. If Ambrosio — a character who goes from public fame to public infamy in a matter of 442 pages — is a figure for *The Monk* itself, one could speculate that Lewis may have attempted to write a romance that is so solipsistic that it would never need public release. Lewis, in a sense, writes a romance about the cruelty of public recognition so as to force any public complaints onto themselves. Public complaint against *The Monk* could only be public complaint about public complaint. In this sense, Lewis writes a romance that boldly, if also obsessively, attempts to nullify the Other, to nullify any potentially hostile audience.

That Lewis, much like the obsessional, fears the Other's unfathomable desire (the public's unknowable reaction) is further revealed by the rest of his prefatory ode. Stanzas four and five articulate the author's own character which otherwise would not accompany the romance. This is done, it appears, primarily to let the public know a little something about the author in order to ward off any hasty criticism. He mentions how he is graceless and dwarfish in stature, extreme in loving and hating, neither rich nor poor, and poor in judging. The author finally notes how he is "in friendship firm, but still believing / Others are treacherous and deceiving" (*M* 4). After explaining various personal characteristics, the author professes his fundamental distrust of others, specifically those others who figure in the public reception of his romance. Since he cannot forecast the desire of the public — how they will react to his work — the author views the Other as potentially evil in nature. The unfathomable nature of the Other's desire is so frightening for the author that he transforms it, through his ode, into a supernatural personified demand by his own book to be published.

In the advertisement to the romance, Lewis continues his attempt to tame the Other's elusive reaction. The advertisement is entirely designated for the author's recognition of plagiarism within the romance. Admitting that the narration's basic idea came from the story of *Santon Barissa*, that the myth of the *Bleeding Nun* is not wholly original, that the *Water-King* story comes from Danish legend, and that the *Belerma and Durandarte* section derives from Spanish poetry, Lewis hopes to counteract any potential criticisms rooted in charges of plagiarism. But by pointing out the more or less obvious literary borrowings of *The Monk*, Lewis opens his text up to more scrutiny. His borrowings from Jacques Cazotte's *Devil in Love* and Schiller's *The Robbers* are not accounted for. It appears that Lewis feels if he claims some plagiarisms, he will be either excused for others or they will go unnoticed. He ends his advertisement by claiming innocence: "I now made full avowal of all the plagiarisms of which I am aware myself; but I doubt not, many more may be found, of which I am at present totally unconscious" (*M* 6). Interestingly enough, Lewis uses the term "unconscious" here in its proper Freudian fashion.[15] What is unconscious in Lewis's romance is to be determined by the Other, in its reception. The truth of what Lewis intends to write in *The Monk* can only be determined "out there" in the desire of the Other. Its truth, in other words, is determined in how it is received, following Lacan's rather cryptic claim that the letter always reaches its destination.[16] This is precisely the one thing that gives Lewis anxiety. The very fact that he cannot control the significance of his romance — the very fact that the Other determines its merit — gives him the creeps. Both his prefatory poem and his advertisement are articulated not only to expose this anxiety but also to curb the public's desire. He is surreptitiously attempting to turn the unfathomable obscurity of public reception into an object that will tend to read his romance the way he sees fit, especially if this prefatory material constitutes a joke on the young author's part.

There is also a rather out-of-place scene in the middle of Lewis's romance where, once again, the narrative reveals the horrible fear of public reaction to the romance. Shortly after arriving back in Madrid after his supernatural bout with the Bleeding Nun, Raymond comes home to find his page Theodore completing a poem. Raymond decides to indulge himself as a critic of the young boy's fresh literary creation. After reading the poem, Raymond assures young Theodore that his writing pleases him very much but warns him that, since he is already in his personal favor, his criticism is tainted. This warning is then followed by a lecture about why Theodore should not waste his valuable time composing verse:

> An Author, whether good or bad, or between both, is an Animal whom every body is privileged to attack; For though All are not able to write books, all conceive themselves able to judge them. A bad composition carries with it its own punishment, contempt and ridicule. A good one excited envy, and entails upon its Author a thousand mortifications. He finds himself assailed by partial and ill-humored Criticism: One Man finds fault with the plan, Another with the style, a Third with the precept, which it strives to inculcate; and they who cannot succeed in finding fault with the Book, employ themselves in stigmatizing its Author. They maliciously rake out from obscurity every little circumstance, which may throw ridicule upon his private character or conduct, and aim at wounding the Man, since They cannot hurt the Writer. In short to enter the lists of literature is willfully to expose yourself to the arrows of neglect, ridicule, envy, and disappointment. Whether you write well or ill, be assured that you will not escape from blame [*M* 198–9].

Immediately following this diatribe, Raymond proceeds to lay some harsh criticism on young Theodore's use of rhyme and confusion of metaphors. But the reader can sense that Raymond's criticism is Lewis's own auto-criticism when it turns to the topic of plagiarism. Echoing The Advertisement, Raymond lets Theodore know that "most of the best ideas in his poem are borrowed from other Poets, though possibly you are *unconscious* of the theft yourself" (*M* 200; italics added). Raymond continues by excusing such unconscious plagiarisms when they occur in "a work of length," but not when they occur in a shorter piece like young Theodore's 20-stanza ballad. Lewis is, of course, making excuses through his characters for the potential criticism that awaits him. He seems to believe that if he acknowledges certain faults in his own young writer's literary production, the public will relax its ridicule of the young Matthew Gregory Lewis's text, especially since his romance is much longer than poor Theodore's doggerel.

In the advertisement, Lewis acknowledges some of his more overt plagiarisms and thereby nullifies them as plagiarisms. But he also neglects to
mention others under the guise of unconsciousness. It seems what he neglects
to mention most of all are his borrowings from contemporary German writers.
There's no doubt that the general tone and topic of *The Monk* is heavily
influenced by the fashionable style of the *Sturm und Drang* writers in Germany. But when Lewis pilfers scenes directly from Goethe, Schiller, Weber,
and Flamenberg, he is at least careful enough to set some of these lifted scenes
in that small part of the romance that takes place in Germany. So even though
he does not directly acknowledge his debt to these German writers, whom he
hopes few know of, he does manage to pay them some homage by not completely smuggling them out of their homeland, as if it is not really theft if he
does not rip them from their native soil. But by situating some of these purloined scenes in Germany, Lewis also indirectly informs his reader of their
original source. Like the true obsessional neurotic, Lewis is almost begging
to get caught by figuratively writing his own guilt into his romance's topography.[17]

At the outset of his "criticism of criticism" dissertation, with which he
confuses young Theodore, Raymond cautions the budding poet that his criticism may be worthless because Raymond himself is not very experienced in
the writing of poetry: "'Your little poem pleases me very much,' said He;
'However, you must not count my opinion for any-thing. I am no judge of
verses, and for my own part, never composed more than six lines in my life:
Those six produced so unlucky an effect, that I am fully resolved never to
compose another'" (*M* 198). The attentive reader will recall those six lines of
poetry composed to unlucky effect from Raymond's encounter with the Bleeding Nun recorded 43 pages earlier in the romance:

> *Agnes! Agnes! Thou art mine!*
> *Agnes! Agnes! I am thine!*
> *In my veins while blood shall roll,*
> *Thou art mine!*
> *I am thine!*
> *Thine my body! Thine my soul!* [*M* 155–6].

In this scene in which he thinks he is pronouncing marital vows to Agnes,
who is disguised as the legendary character of the Bleeding Nun in order to
escape the confines of her jealous Aunt's castle, Raymond is actually pledging
his love to the genuine specter of the Bleeding Nun. After the immediate carriage wreck and his subsequent rehabilitation — during which he is haunted
every night by the spectral nun — it is no wonder Raymond resists poetic com-

position. For this six-line poem — composed at the moment when he was taking Agnes unlawfully beyond the realm of parental or religious law, and perhaps soiling her reputation — appears to be what caused the chaotic events that followed. In other words, bringing Agnes outside the rule of law unleashes something beyond words. Raymond is literally faced with the Other's desire without any proper restrictions. Agnes, situated in limbo between being a "daughter," a "nun," or a "wife," poses a threat that within Raymond's imagination can only take a supernatural form. Just as his poem, when delivered, unleashed the chaos of the Other's desire, poetic composition, according to Raymond's argument with Theodore, can only unleash the unfathomable fury of the public's potential ill will, unless it is kept to oneself.

The romance proper opens with a semi-comical scene set during a Catholic mass in Madrid. As Leonella and her niece Antonia search the overcrowded church for seating, the two young cavaliers Don Lorenzo and Don Christoval are taken aback by Leonella's female voice. However, when they see that the voice they are enchanted by belongs to the old, squinting, redheaded Leonella, they simply ignore it and resume their conversation. But immediately their attention is once again seized by another feminine voice, this time that of Leonella's niece. Her voice, as described by the narrator, resounds with "unexampled sweetness" (*M* 9). But it also belongs to a woman worthy of Lorenzo's and Christoval's chivalric attention. Before we know her name, the narrative carefully describes how Antonia appears to the two young cavaliers: as a collection of partial objects. A beautiful and symmetrical neck, long fair hair, a below middle size figure, a carefully veiled bosom, a delicately proportioned foot, and a thickly veiled face all together give us something short of Antonia. But, as far as the narrative is interested in the desire of the cavaliers, especially Don Lorenzo, we are given an ample description of what they see. The face itself remains covered almost as if the narrative is letting the reader know that while Lorenzo may desire the woman, he only approaches the partial objects of his fantasy screen.

But a page or so later, after he has made repeated attempts to engage Antonia in conversation, only to be given short one-word replies to his questions, Lorenzo is confronted with something beyond his fantasy object: "By this time He had discovered that his Neighbour was not very conversable; But whether her silence proceeded from pride, discretion, timidity, or idiotism, He was still unable to decide" (*M* 10–11). Within a page or so of the narrative, Antonia, through the imagination of Lorenzo, has transformed from partial object of desire to an enigma. As the rest of the chapter will testify, Lorenzo, who at first is attracted to this object of his desire, is confronted with the horrific feeling of being exposed to the Other as desiring — the very unfathomable desire that the obsessional attempts to ward off with his compulsive practices.

As the scene proceeds, the two women learn from the cavaliers the reason the church is so overcrowded on this Thursday, of all days. It appears Ambrosio, abbot of the monastery and the most famous orator to speak in Madrid in years, is going to take the pulpit. His fame is behind the crowd's enthusiasm. He has even been dubbed "The Man of Holiness." He has spent his entire 30-year life in complete seclusion, only recently facing the public during his awe-inspiring sermons. When "The Man of Holiness" approaches the pulpit and the crowd gets a first glance at such embodied righteousness, Antonia feels "a pleasure fluttering in her bosom which till then had been unknown to her, and for which She in vain endeavoured to account" (*M* 18). Lewis uses the language and imagery of Radcliffe to illustrate the opening of feminine desire. But Lewis's narrative will react to it in a wholly different manner. Once this unfathomable feeling is exposed, coupled with the fact that Antonia exists as an enigma for Lorenzo, the reader is told that during Ambrosio's pious and damning sermon "his voice at once distinct and deep was fraught with all the *terrors of the Tempest*, while he inveighed against the vices of humanity, and described the punishments reserved for them in a future state" (*M* 19; italics added).[18] As soon as Lorenzo is exposed to the potentially unfathomable desire of Antonia, he is insensibly confronted with a pious sermon that warns one of the potential dangers of such desires. The Monk's voice carries all the terrors of the Tempest that Radcliffe displays in various heroines' disastrous flights of terror. But, most of all, Ambrosio warns about the possibility of eternal destruction — the very destruction embodied in the Other's enjoyment. One must pray and repent, keep an unsullied conscience, in order to keep this potentially catastrophic enjoyment at bay.

Freud, of course, makes the connection between obsessive actions and religious practices in his essay bearing that title. Obsessive practices like compulsive hand-washing possess the identical ceremonial quality as religious rituals. According to Freud, obsessional ceremonials have to be carried out by the obsessional in the same manner and in a regular routine: "These activities give the impression of being mere formalities, and they seem quite meaningless to us. Nor do they appear otherwise to the patient himself; yet he is incapable of giving them up, for any deviation from the ceremonial is visited by intolerable anxiety, which obliges him at once to make his omission good."[19] The intolerable anxiety that the obsessional is exposed to approximates the horror of the Other's enjoyment. If the obsessional deviates from his ritualistic compulsive actions, the order these regulative actions give to his life collapses. And if this order collapses, the obsessional fears he will be exposed to numerous accidents that paradoxically approach the Other's purpose: "The Other is out there to harm me, but as long as I appease him with my regulatory obsessional actions, it will leave me be. Any time I lapse in my actions, I am somehow and mysteriously once again drawn to the attention of the Other and its unfathomable desire." The divine justice of the Other's desire, as far as the obsessional is concerned, appears very close to the Freudian superego. This is perhaps why Lacan insists, "Christianity naturally ended up inventing a God such that he is the one who gets off (*jouit*)!"[20]

As soon as Lorenzo is marginally exposed to the incompleteness of the universe in the form of the enigma of Antonia, he is bombarded with super-egoic warnings emanating through the Monk's pious sermon. That Lorenzo is deeply affected by this exposure together with the sermon is corroborated by his dream immediately following the evacuation of the Church. While waiting to visit his sister, who is a nun at the adjoining convent, Lorenzo fuels his melancholy within the solitude of the now empty church and abandons himself to the delusions of his fancy: "He thought of his union with Antonia; He thought of the obstacles which might oppose his wishes; and a thousand changing visions floated before his fancy, sad 'tis true, but not unpleasing" (*M* 27). While in this state of contemplating his conflicting desire, Lorenzo falls asleep and dreams about a fantastic nightmare wedding with Antonia, where during the ceremony she is abducted by what is described as a "gigantic Unknown," only to flee to heaven without ever consummating the marriage (*M* 27–28). With the exception of the Monk's summoning of the superego in his sermon, this dream sequence is the first evocation of the supernatural in the romance. The unknown entity that rushes between Lorenzo and the utterly delightful Antonia is an oddity indeed. This initial supernatural manifestation of *The Monk* appears situated somewhere between Radcliffean terror and Lewis's use of horror. There is definitely an objective existence to this supernatural entity, but this object remains not wholly differentiated. Prior to the dream, the Monk conjures up the terror of the unfathomable, and within the dream this terror begins to assume shape. But since a dream is less an objective reality than it is a subjective reality, the enigma's ontological certainty remains in doubt. But what is not in doubt is the influence of the Monk's sermon on Lorenzo's obsessional conscience. The question Lorenzo is faced with when confronting Antonia mixes with the excessive piety of Ambrosio's speech to produce an unknown sublime figure hovering between terror and horror.

Because the Monk's sermon opens Lorenzo up to the possibility of the unfathomable desire of the Other, Antonia as enigma retroactively begins to turn into something horrific in the dream — the locus of Lorenzo's desire. In other words, the unknown gigantic creature figures as the devouring desire of Antonia. It acts as a hyperbole of the "blush of pleasure" that glows upon her cheek when she sees her bridegroom in the church during the dream. Her potentially unfathomable desire is so overwhelming for Lorenzo that he finds himself "involuntarily" advancing to the altar, unable to disobey her command. Being the obsessional he is, Lorenzo appears to be already transforming Antonia's terrifying, incomprehensible desire into a horrific demand that he must either comply with or resist. This is the reason for the enigmatic aspect of this unknown figure in the dream. It is itself situated in a liminal state somewhere between the two aspects of the frightening: terror and horror. By the end of the dream, when Antonia is split between the hellish whore, who is in the clutches of utter enjoyment figured as the Unknown, and the holy virgin arising to heaven, Lorenzo has already made the choice typical of the obsessional neurotic. A true obsessional can only have carnal relations with a whore and can only be in love with a virtuous virgin. And this imaginative split of Antonia into a whore and a virgin actually gets played out by Lewis's narrative through the split in Lorenzo himself activated in the separate but loosely connected story lines of the lecherous monk Ambrosio and the chivalrous Raymond de las Cisternas.

In "A Special Type of Choice of Object Made by Men," Freud maintains that, up until the time of psychoanalysis, the depiction of the necessary conditions for loving which govern people's choice of an object has been left to creative writers, who make the demands of the imagination conform to reality.[21] Writers possess the ability to be sensitive to hidden impulses and to draw on their own unconscious wishes in depicting their portraits of these "necessary conditions for loving," but they are also, according to Freud, under the additional necessity to produce intellectual and aesthetic pleasure — a necessity which prevents the creative writer from reproducing the stuff of reality unchanged. Accordingly, they must isolate portions of reality, remove disturbing associations, and tone down the whole. Moreover, according to Freud, "they can show only slight interest in the origin and development of the mental states which they portray in their completed form."[22] The Gothic romance, however, works at the margin of Freud's claim. By utilizing the supernatural in all its infantile associations, the Gothic romance attempts, however indirectly, to express in the form of literary enjoyment what is beyond the pleasure principle. In this vein, *The Monk* sublimates the disposition and object choice formulated by the obsessional neurotic.

In his *Three Essays on the Theory of Sexuality*, Freud maintains that the neuroses are the negative of perversion. When, during the course of development, a child reaches the mature genital stage of its sexual development, the polymorphous perversions that dominated its sexuality up until that point undergo repression. The neurotic's perverse tendencies do not, however, fully disappear. Rather, they are, in a sense, repressed, making the neurotic unconscious of them. A neurotic, therefore, is a neurotic to the precise extent that he dreams he is a pervert; his perversions are wholly relegated to fantasy. When any repressed perverse tendency resurfaces as out of conformity with one's fantasy screen, a neurosis is brought about. According to Freud, "a great shock in real life will perhaps bring about a neurosis even in an average constitution."[23] Darian Leader illustrates this basic Freudian idea through a comical story:

> A young man goes on a date with a woman he has met only briefly before. While they are dining in an elegant and expensive restaurant, his urbane conversation is interrupted when the lady reaches over and puts his fingers in her mouth. Yet the result is not a night with Eros but rather a two day stay in the hospital: the man is simply not built for encounters which don't fit with the frame of his phantasy. His libido was redirected to generate unbearable stomach pains. The woman here is not included in the sexual knowledge of the man: she stepped outside his conscious and, probably, unconscious, set of rules for how a partner behaves. He simply couldn't know what she was going to do.[24]

When confronted with the desire of the Other in this unexpected manner, the obsessional reacts with revulsion. Because he is primarily concerned with his own fantastic object, he simply cannot deal with that desire which breaks the frame protecting his object.

Following Freud's argument in *Three Essays*, a normal sexual life is only assured when there is an exact convergence of the two currents directed toward the sexual object.[25] These two currents are the affectionate current and the sensual current. The affectionate current, the one originally aimed at the mother, comprises what remains of the infantile efflorescence of sexuality. When the obsessional divorces the object that originally satisfied him — his mother's breast — from the mother in order to compensate for his loss, he forever severs his affectionate feelings for his mother from his erotic and sensual feelings for the object. In other words, the obsessional neurotic has a difficult time loving the same object that he has eroticized. Love and sex become irreconcilable within the same object. This is the precise deviation that makes the obsessional not feel normal. The affectionate currents, or ego drives, aim at a person, but the sensual currents, or sexual drives, do not have a person as their object; rather, they are structured around the various erotogenic zones of the body that have privileged erotic value.[26] Normality would be the result if these two currents could be aimed at the same object. But, because the obsessional is a neurotic subject, and therefore castrated,[27] directing his sexual drives at the object of his affection, his mother, is prohibited to him because of the incest barrier.

Leader maintains that at this point two things can happen. First, a mother substitute can be found in order to preserve the apparent assimilation of the two drives: "The result of this first alternative is that a relation is maintained involving both love and desire directed towards the same partner."[28] In other words, a normal sexual life can be established. But this normality rests on shaky ground. For, as Freud maintains, a shock can induce the second alternative, the alternative that determines obsessional neurosis. If the subject cannot assimilate the love and the sexual drives toward the same object, the object itself becomes double: "One woman is loved in an idealized way and another is desired sexually. The loved woman cannot be a sexual object while the sexual object incarnated in the second woman cannot be loved."[29] The object of the obsessional's desire is split between the wholesome virgin and the demanding whore.

This, in a sense, is the situation Lorenzo finds himself in during the first chapter of Lewis's romance. He initially finds Antonia to be a woman who can finally assimilate these two currents of his desire. His uncle has been after him for a while now to finally find someone to marry, and initially Antonia appears to be the perfect one. But shortly thereafter, when Antonia displays a confusing and erotic desire of her own for the monk Ambrosio, Lorenzo experiences his dream of the Unknown. It is easy to reconcile this Unknown that wells up to terrify Lorenzo with guilt as the maternal superego. The guilt displayed in the signifiers scripted on the Unknown's forehead — "Pride, Lust, Inhumanity" — betray Lorenzo's doubt about giving his affectionate current over to someone other than his mother. As Leader claims, incestuous dreams are usually a response to the presence of a new love object:

> One of Freud's patients dreamt that he was having intercourse with both his mother and his sister: Freud remarked to him that he must have been very much in love with a girl at the time of the dream. The key here is that all the unconscious knows about women is a collection of traits drawn from the mother, for example, "to belong to another man," "to have a certain color hair," and so on. When a woman is found who satisfies these criteria, there is nevertheless something more — she exists as a reality beyond the collection of preconditions, a reality for which nothing can possibly prepare the man. In the unconscious, beyond the image of the mother, the woman exists only as a gap, as a lack of representation.[30]

The Unknown is, then, a thinly disguised figure for the Other's desire, something unfathomable into which the obsessional would rather not lose himself. The dream, therefore, displays Lorenzo's inability to properly align his affectionate and sensual currents. The Unknown, which returns in this dream as the confluence of the affectionate and sensual feelings he once supposedly had for his mother, marks the return of the repressed. What returns in this neurotic dream is the supposedly outgrown perverse desire for the mother; perversion returns in the neurotic's dream. Lewis characterizes this Unknown, this return of the repressed, as "gigantic" as if it is the return of the gigantic spectre that haunted the perverse narrative of *The Castle of Otranto*. What so artlessly haunted Walpole's immature romance on the same level as the narrative reality returns in Lewis's romance on the level of the dream. Lorenzo's dream, in a sense, harkens back to some sort of pre-genital stage because repression forces enjoyment to return in roundabout ways.

In Radcliffe's narratives, the supernatural shows up only as the affect produced by the narrative. In Walpole, it shows up on the same level as the everyday reality. But in Lewis's narrative, the supernatural, at least in this first occurrence, shows up in a dream as the location where what is in excess of reality finds its place. In conformity with a masculine sublimation, Lewis constructs a narrative that symbolizes the real object, that object which is excised from the normal narrative field. Or, to put it in Kantian terms, *The Monk*, with all its horrifying actualities, attempts to articulate that which is an exception from the phenomenal field itself. Where Radcliffe's narrative is haunted by its own otherness, Lewis's narrative constructs something other than it that then haunts its interior.

This first supernatural occurrence in Lewis's romance — the terrifying Unknown erupting in Lorenzo's dream shortly after perceiving Antonia as a desiring subject — causes, I would argue, Lorenzo to wake up from his dream precisely so he can keep on dreaming, as Lacan said *apropos* of the father in Freud's dream of the burning child.[31] In other words, Lorenzo, and the romance itself, wakes up in order to avoid confronting the real of his desire in his dream. If dream-life is where the real is housed as the return of the repressed, then waking-life offers one an escapist adventure into fantasy. From this first supernatural happening, one centered more around terror than horror, the narrative spins off into two almost mutually exclusive narratives which interrogate the obsessional defensive doubling of the object that accompanies his confrontation with the desire of the Other. These two narratives of Ambrosio/Matilda/Antonia and Raymond/Agnes, between which Lewis depicts Lorenzo biding his time, are fantastic accounts indirectly depicting Lorenzo's mutually exclusive currents of desire: the affectionate and the sensual.

The Monk's two narratives, which have always confused commentators, revolve around Ambrosio's interest in the virgin and Raymond's interest in the whore. These two characters, which enter the narrative just prior to Lorenzo's dream, carry out the two conflicting paths of Lorenzo's desire in the dreamlike sequence of the romance. In a sort of wild psychoanalysis, one could say Ambrosio has a mother complex and Raymond has a prostitute complex. Ambrosio's role in Lorenzo's dream narrative is to force his sensual current into the path of his affectionate current. In other words, Ambrosio's excessive actions are the result of his impossible endeavor to find an erotic object that will conform to the ideal. Raymond, on the other hand, attempts, through the parallel narrative, to find love in his erotic object. The catastrophic results of both narratives illustrate in a hyperbolic manner the utter despair the obsessional neurotic faces when confronted with the conflict between love and libido.

Ambrosio's attempt to elevate the erotic object to the level of the ideal begins shortly after Lorenzo's dream. While meditating in his monastic cell immediately after his much-publicized sermon, Ambrosio reflects on his moral superiority. He views himself as the unique possessor of an untainted soul. But while in this megalomaniacal mood, Ambrosio begins to feel the same doubt concerning his moral constitution that Lorenzo expressed about him in the previous chapter. Confronted with Antonia's confused praise of Ambrosia immediately following the monk's sermon, Lorenzo had reacted with a bitter invective about how this holy man has not proven anything until he leaves his seclusion and enters the world of temptation. Until he undergoes a trial of temptation, Lorenzo adds, his holiness cannot be taken for granted. Ambrosio's self-doubt, which is really a rearticulating of Lorenzo's doubt, makes the pious monk wonder if he could survive an ordeal of temptation. When he eventually decides to use his fame to seduce women, Ambrosio turns to his painting of the Madonna and realizes the futility in such an endeavor: "As He said this, He fixed his eyes upon a picture of the Virgin, which was suspended opposite to him: This for two years had been the Object of his increasing wonder and adoration. He paused, and gazed upon it with delight" (M 40). The possible objects of temptation that Ambrosio might encounter by venturing beyond the confines of his monastic cell could never, it appears, live up to his ideal woman. By his own logic, Ambrosio is impervious to the temptations of his sensual currents, his sexual drives, because no erotic object can fit into the literal frame of the ideal. The Madonna as ideal not only reveals Ambrosio's model woman as mother, but it shows his ideal as something that he once possessed long ago. When he mentions to himself his desire to "press with his lips the treasures of that snowy bosom" (M 41), he is articulating a desire to regain that original satisfaction lost through maturation. Only now his original satisfaction has become, as evidenced by the framed portrait, an imaginary satisfaction. Much like the man in the restaurant with severe stomach pains, Ambrosio can only become interested in a woman who fits his previously established fantasy frame. And since this frame contains an ideal, something that cannot be found on earth, the Monk cannot reconcile his two mutually exclusive currents.

Shortly after learning the truth that little Rosario — the novice and constant companion of the monk — is really a woman named Matilda who disguised herself as a novice in order to penetrate the monastery solely to be close to her love, Ambrosio has a revealing dream where he brings his portrait of the Madonna to life with a kiss. Once again, the reader is exposed to a return of a similar scene from *Otranto*. Although quite a common conventional trope within the Gothic tradition, the portrait coming to life takes on a substantial dimension within this scene of Ambrosio's dream. What existed on the plane of reality in Walpole's narrative is located here in the dream realm where desire plays itself out. This return of a Walpolean scene from the original Gothic romance also marks the return of an original satisfaction, the satisfaction once provided by an over-proximate relation to the mother.

This dream sequence further blends the image of Matilda as erotic object with the Madonna as love object. Prior to Ambrosio's exposure to the shocking news that Matilda herself commissioned his portrait of the Madonna as a portrait of herself, thereby turning herself into his love object without him ever even meeting her, he already makes this maneuver himself. Later when Ambrosio does learn the truth about the origin of the portrait, it only conforms to and confirms his prejudicial favor for Matilda. When the truth of the portrait's commission is revealed, concrete reality and the ideal begin to overlap:

> [Matilda] started at the sound, and turned towards him hastily. The suddenness of her movement made her Cowl fall back from her head; Her features became visible to the Monk's enquiring eye. What was his amazement at beholding the exact resemblance of his admired Madona? The same exquisite proportion of features, the same profusion of golden hair, the same rosy lips, heavenly eyes, and majesty of countenance adorned Matilda! Uttering an exclamation of surprise, Ambrosio sank back upon his pillow, and doubted whether the Object before him was mortal or divine [*M* 81].

Immediately following Ambrosio's first actual sighting of Matilda's face, she reveals the secret behind her connivance. She, of course, arranged a painter to paint a portrait of her as the Madonna. And she further arranged it to be sold to Ambrosio.

When Ambrosio is confronted with the doubt concerning whether this object is divine or mortal, he is confronted with the Platonic repulsion brought on by the realization that his ideal is itself only a fantasy. Ambrosio also resists the truth he is confronted with and, therefore, believes that he has found his ideal in reality. His dream confirms as much:

> But the dreams of the former night were repeated, and his sensations of voluptuousness were yet more keen and exquisite. The same lust-exciting visions floated before his eyes: Matilda, in all the pomp of beauty, warm, tender, and luxurious, clasped him to her bosom, and lavished on him the most ardent caresses. He returned them as eagerly, and was on the point of satisfying his desires, when the faithless form disappeared, and left him to all the horrors of shame and disappointment [*M* 84].

This deferred satisfaction will, of course, turn out to be the perennial feature of Ambrosio's desire. Because of the incongruity of his two currents, any object will be inadequate. At this point, Matilda appears to have completely blended with the ideal image of the Madonna. Earlier, Ambrosio's dream consisted of an intimate encounter with Matilda alongside another with the Madonna; this dream, however, which only consists of an encounter with Matilda, displays the fusion of Ambrosio's two currents. He, it seems, has found a perfect mother substitute. But, as Lewis reveals, this fusion can only be a dream.

Later, when Ambrosio meets Antonia — who is to become his second incarnation of the ideal woman — for the first time, he compares her to Rosario, Matilda's masculine character. From here Matilda falls from grace, and Ambrosio searches for another virgin to approximate the ideal. He even convinces himself that his feelings for Antonia are completely different than those he harbored for Matilda. No provocations of lust or voluptuous desires rioting in his bosom taint his feelings for this new love object. To thwart the guilt associated with the violation of his priestly vows, Ambrosio persuades himself that this new love is more pure, filled with the sentiments of tenderness, admiration, and respect. His recent transgressions were merely the fault of a temptress: "Matilda gluts me with enjoyment even to loathing, forces me to her arms, apes the Harlot, and glories in her prostitution. Disgusting! Did She know the inexpressible charm of Modesty, how irresistibly it enthralls the heart of Man, how firmly it chains him to the Throne of Beauty, She would never throw it off" (*M* 243–3). It appears that the more Matilda shows a desire of her own, the more Ambrosio repulses in horror. As Matilda becomes more active in her relationship with the Monk, she mysteriously becomes more and more demonic, more and more some evil force enjoying at Ambrosio's expense. He eventually looks upon his portrait of the Madonna and tears it to shreds while screaming, "The Prostitute!" (*M* 244).[32]

The Monk's subsequent excesses of passion conducted under the rubric of pious respectability are well documented. With the assistance of Matilda's magic looking glass, Ambrosio is able to see Antonia dressing in her own private chamber. An obvious parody of the framed portrait of the ideal Madonna, this magical and impossible view soon inspires Ambrosio with all the lustful desires he once possessed for Matilda. Thanks to Matilda's sorcery and some minor assistance from a demonic force conjured up in the catacombs beneath the monastery, the pious Monk kills Elvira, Antonia's mother, and eventually entombs Antonia within the sepulcher which joins the monastery to St. Clare's convent. Having Antonia where he wants, Ambrosio rapes and kills her to prevent getting caught for his criminal activity, only to find out in the end the incestuous nature of his crimes. It turns out all along that Elvira was the Monk's long-lost mother and Antonia his own sister. It also turns out that Ambrosio found the ultimate erotic object in the image of his mother after all.

Unlike Ambrosio, whose love is inspired by the image of the Virgin, Raymond's desire for his love object, in the parallel narrative, is inspired by the image of a harlot. According to Raymond's own first-person narrative, while lounging around Lindenberg Castle in Germany with Agnes, Lorenzo's sister, Raymond thumbs through her sketches and becomes fascinated with one that "represented a Female of more than human stature, clothed in the habit of some religious order. Her face was veiled; On her arm hung a chaplet of beads; Her dress was in several places stained with the blood which trickled from a wound upon her bosom. In one hand She held a Lamp, in the other a large Knife, and she seemed advancing towards the iron gates of the Hall" (*M* 138). Upon Raymond's query, it turns out that Agnes's little sketch represents the Bleeding Nun, a legendary specter who supposedly haunts the interior of the castle. While the monk was originally seduced by a framed ideal, Raymond's framed image is far from the virtuous virgin. This terrifying female of more than human stature represents the Other as desiring, the very object Matilda becomes later in the romance when she becomes loathsome in Ambrosio's imagination. The image of the Bleeding Nun with a rosary in one hand and a bloody knife in the other represents the paradoxical portrait of a woman who is both virtuous and ruthless, a representation that can only appear to the obsessional as otherworldly. The Bleeding Nun, according to legend, appears every May 5 for one hour to haunt the domestic space. During the interim, her soul rests uncomfortably in a locked chamber of the castle.

When Raymond and Agnes decide to elope, they use the legend of this Bleeding Nun as a cover. Since the Nun, according to legend — a legend Agnes puts little credit in — appears every May 5 at midnight, walks through the castle, and exits through the front gates, Agnes will simply disguise herself as the Nun, and, when everyone in the castle is trying to avoid the specter, she will simply exit through the gates and meet Raymond on the other side. In this manner, Agnes can escape the jealousy of her aunt and the inevitable residence in a convent that is her terrible destiny. But, of course, something devastating happens on the fateful night. It turns out that this disguised specter is no disguise after all. Raymond has eloped with, and made his vows to, none other than the actual specter of the Bleeding Nun. Once the specter enters the carriage Raymond has provided for their escape, the carriage bolts like a bat out of hell until it inexplicably crashes a few minutes later some 400 miles away. When Raymond regains consciousness the following morning and sees the carnage around him, he is at a loss as to the whereabouts of his beloved Agnes.

It appears Raymond did not quite know what he was in for. By eloping with Agnes, he was bringing her out into a realm where, by all Gothic standards, she would be considered a whore. No longer under the confines of the signifier "daughter" and not yet under the convent roof, Agnes, and Raymond along with her, would have to exist, much like the Radcliffean runaway heroine, in a domain of lawlessness. Raymond must have had an inkling of this when Agnes previously warned him that if they eloped she would be under his protection and he therefore had to do right by her. It is safe for Raymond to desire Agnes when she is under the control of her aunt. Since a union is impossible while she is under her aunt's roof, Agnes exists almost as an ideal. But once freed from the tyranny of both her aunt and the nunnery, Agnes could only appear as the unlawful desiring harlot that the Bleeding Nun once was. Once exposed to the Other's desire in the form of Agnes out-of-bounds — not tied to a signifier — Raymond reacts much the same way as Leader's stomach-ailed obsessional. Raymond, while convalescing from his injuries caused by the carriage crash, is visited every night by the specter of the Bleeding Nun. This continues until the Wandering Jew figure opens (or closes) Raymond's eyes to the supernatural aspect of Agnes's desire. He explains to Raymond how Beatrice, the historic Bleeding Nun, once scandalized all Bavaria "by her impudent and abandoned conduct" as a prostitute and atheist (*M* 173). Until the Other's desire is seen as supernatural in nature, it will remain an object of terror. But once it is sublimated to a realm beyond by the Wandering Jew's narrative, it can be viewed as a disgusting object of horror.

The reader can begin to sympathize with Raymond's obsessional guilt when Agnes is later interred pregnant in the sepulcher of the convent of St. Clare by the prioress. Because Agnes was impregnated by Raymond while she was a nun at St. Clare's, the prioress determines to hide the scandal caused by this "whore" in order to save her convent's reputation. In captivity, Agnes sadly clings to her maggot-covered stillborn infant, which is being devoured by insects. Agnes, who started as a disguised Bleeding Nun, only to be mysteriously replaced by the actual Bleeding Nun, herself becomes, in the end, a bleeding nun chained up in the confines of the underground catacombs. The obsessional lesson for Raymond: you mess with the forces of the supernatural, and they shall enjoy at your expense. It seems, by all obsessional belief in the omnipotence of thought, that since Agnes masqueraded as the Bleeding Nun, since she ridiculed this legend, the legend itself became literalized to her detriment.

These two mutually exclusive narratives are only loosely held together by Lorenzo, the "hero" who merely plays a tangential role in the romance. However, in the end, their merging in the sepulcher of the monastery inventively allows for the merging of Lorenzo's two conflicting obsessional currents. Because Antonia is killed, and because Agnes is in need of care, the reader is introduced to the character of Virginia. Lewis artfully casts Virginia in a role uncannily similar to Isabella's in *The Castle of Otranto*. Here, however, Lewis throws in a twist. Virginia, who becomes Lorenzo's substitute love object following the gruesome death of Antonia, only appears at the time of Antonia's demise. It appears that since Lorenzo can no longer have his virgin in reality — she exists, as Ambrosio's narrative demonstrates, only as an ideal — he can at least have her in name. Virginia may not be an ideal virgin like the Madonna or Antonia, but she will be one at least at the level of the signifier. Lewis portrays Virginia at the end of the romance as an opportunistic figure; she cares for Agnes only because she thinks her benevolence will win some points with Lorenzo. She is far from virtuous. It cannot be accidental that Lewis gives this character the name he does. She is a perfect amalgamation of the framed images of the Madonna and the Bleeding Nun. In the happy ending of the Gothic romance, Virginia symbolizes the obsessional's compromise formation of the conflicting desire between the affectionate current and the sensual current.

Even though Lewis's romance may affect the reader with scenes of grotesque horror, this horror must be seen as already emerging out of a deeper anxiety, as an escape from something much more terrifying — the fact that there is nothing instead of something, as pointed out by the narratives of the Radcliffean school of terror writing. Lewis may assume he made an advance with his particularly masculine use of Gothic horror; however, his narrative, like the obsessional, creates an external sublime object of horror to cover a terror that has no external cause. Oddly enough, the lacking supernatural machinery of Radcliffe's Gothic universe becomes for Lewis its most monstrous and frightening dimension.

Conclusion: James Hogg, the Psychotic Doppelgänger, and the Foreclosure of the Gothic

Since psychosis is the only one of the psychopathologies yet to be discussed, I want to finish by briefly outlining a possible connection between psychosis and the Gothic. In order to illustrate the Gothic novel's relation to psychosis, my analysis will have to move to the margins of the genre. Since the period of the genre customarily spans from 1764 to 1820, Robert Maturin's *Melmoth the Wanderer* is customarily considered the final romance of the Gothic tradition. After *Melmoth*, the Gothic shifts from a genre proper to a mode. *Melmoth*, in a sense, is already a *wandering* Gothic novel. Maturin's ultimate obsessional novel — filled with tales within tales framed by other tales, all in order to painstakingly keep the genre afloat, to keep inevitable collapse at bay — illustrates perfectly how much the Gothic as genre can expand without losing its identity. After *Melmoth*, the Gothic becomes gothic — a mode in fiction, something existing only tangentially in the novels and stories in which it appears. From the Brontës to Stevenson and Wilde up to Faulkner and O'Connor, gothic becomes merely an ingredient.[1] Unable or unwilling to maintain an entire Gothic atmosphere, the so-called Gothic writers after Maturin tend to use Gothic devices and situations in the service of other new genres ranging from history-romance, romantic realism, and the sensational novel to the neo-gothic.[2]

There is one novel, however, that appears to be situated in a liminal sphere discernible by the disintegration of the Gothic's generic identity. This generic disintegration, in fact, appears to be allegorically what James Hogg's *The Private Memoirs and Confessions of a Justified Sinner* is all about. Published four years after *Melmoth*, Hogg's romance signals the disintegration of the Gothic within the disintegration of the mind of its main character. This marginal Gothic romance — empty of any heroes or heroines — chronicles, like a case study, the sins of an overly devout Calvinist.[3] The doppleganger theme of this novel points to a certain dissolution of the Gothic romance itself. The recent tragic demise of the genre, which should exist as a story outside the novels themselves, appears to have magically emerged at the heart of this final Gothic, making it a Gothic romance existing in a sort of limbo outside the symbolic space of the genre itself. If one follows Frederick Frank's suggestion that this is a novel about schizophrenia, it is evident that Hogg's novel does not fully fit within the standard relegating practices of the Gothic romance. Much like Robert Wringhim within the narrative, *Justified Sinner* finds itself as an outcast in the tradition.[4] If the supernatural is explained in Radcliffe and appears only in a sort of dream world in Lewis, it returns in the form of the real in Hogg's narrative.

In perversion, the paternal function is disavowed, while it is repressed in neurosis. But in psychosis, the paternal function is foreclosed (*Verwerfung*). According to Bruce Fink, "the absence of the paternal function is the single most important criterion to consider in diagnosing an individual as psychotic."[5] In the psychotic structure, the father's "no" (the *nom-du-père*), as both the prohibition against the child's desire for the mother and as the name of the father, is never instilled in the way it is for the neurotic. Therefore, the castration complex is never initiated, and the psychotic subject never passes through primary and secondary repression (alienation and separation in Lacan's reconfiguration). In this manner, as Lacan points out, the name-of-the-father never attains the place of the Other, never establishes the symbolic realm for the psychotic, and, instead, appears in the real in opposition to the subject.[6] Robert Wringhim, the main character of Hogg's novel, has not only been downright rejected by his father, but he has been brought up by his severely pious mother.[7] In fact, shortly after her marriage to Laird Dalcastle, Robert's mother "turn[s] her head away disgusted" at the hearing of her new name Colwan, setting in motion the foreclosure of the name-of-the-father that will ultimately affect young Robert and lead to his delusional behavior (*JS* 3). Robert, like the psychotic in general, is left prey to the mother's unregulated desire.[8] Early in the novel, even Robert determinedly rejects the name of his father when first meeting his brother George in Edinburgh: "'No, not Colwan, Sir,' said Robert, putting his hands in his pockets, and setting himself still farther forward than before, — 'not a Colwan, Sir; henceforth I disclaim the name'" (*JS* 23).[9] This precarious status and the burgeoning psychotic structure of Robert may explain his oddly described youthful behavior, his rivalry with classmate M'Gill, his delusions of grandeur, and his conventionally Gothic malignant eye (*JS* 19, 109, 114, 21).[10]

Since castration never separates Robert from the Other's desire, he is constantly bombarded by the Other's enjoyment in the form of the antinomian discourse of Calvinist predestination. As Kevin Cameron has pointed out, since Calvinism is largely based on a collapse of mediation between the subject and the divine and a loss of the comfortable detachment that comes with cleric arbitration, it "forces the individual into the precarious trust of his/her own devices in order to justify his/her relation to God."[11] Because of this, "God incarnates the failed symbolization of the mother's desire, that is, the failure of the paternal law."[12] Since the father function is literally foreclosed in Robert's universe, it returns as the reified word of God, much as it did for Schreber.[13] In other words, Robert's double, as he emerges in the narrative, should be viewed less as some sort of demonic entity haunting him than as the word of God stripped of any symbolic significance.[14] Gil-Martin, the name the double takes, is the form the word of God takes when it is foreclosed. To paraphrase Russell Grigg, Robert's hallucinated double Gil-Martin should be understood as the reification of the discourse of predestination.[15] Or as Lacan claims about the psychotic, "something has taken the form of speech and speaks to him."[16]

Robert's psychotic break takes place immediately after he finds out from his pastor Robert Sr. (probably his mother's secret lover and Robert's biological father) that he is one of the saved and, therefore, predestined to go to heaven. It is so upsetting, it appears, for Robert to be accepted into such a symbolic community, to be included into the Book of Names, that he is immediately haunted by a hallucination that will hound him throughout the romance. Indeed, Robert's break emerges over the question of what paternal name, Colwan or Wringhim, is to be written in his spot in the Book of Names. Rather than emerging into the symbolic order in a more or less normal manner, Robert has the symbolic order, the master signifier, thrown at him by Robert Sr. What was previously foreclosed in Robert's psychic makeup simply returns from outside, to use Freud's phrasing.[17] Bruce Fink describes the psychotic trigger that leads to the psychotic break: "It is the encounter with the One-father, with the Father as pure symbolic function (and this often takes the form of an encounter with a particular person, male or female, who plays or tries to play a symbolic role), that leads to the triggering of psychosis — that is, to a psychotic break."[18] Therefore, from early in Robert's own confessional narrative, there is no relegation of enjoyment. Gil-Martin, as the hallucinatory real, constantly bombards young Robert with the need to murder in the name of God the Father. In Robert's universe, the signifier simply follows him and terrorizes him.[19] Robert is basically coaxed into his criminal activity because the law does not apply to one of the sinless, to one of the predestined, to one with a foreclosed paternal law.

Robert's trigger almost immediately gets transformed into the delusion that he uses to cover the hole that has now appeared in the external world.[20] Since psychotics do not have a symbolic register like the neurotic, they only have their imaginary to ward off the onslaught of real *jouissance*. Imaginary delusion, therefore, becomes for the psychotic, oddly enough, his only form of defense. "Reality itself initially contains a hole," as Lacan puts it, "that the world of fantasy will subsequently fill."[21] Lacan calls this filling the delusional metaphor, and its purpose is to imaginarily substitute for the foreclosed paternal metaphor: "It is the lack of the Name-of-the-Father in that place which, by the hole that it opens up in the signified, sets off a cascade of reworkings of the signifier from which the growing disaster of the imaginary proceeds, until the level is reached at which signifier and signified stabilize in a delusional metaphor."[22] The psychotic essentially sets up an artificial imaginary reality, albeit a reality the psychotic is certain of, in order to prevent reality from collapsing from the intrusion of the real, as happens during the psychotic break. This is what leads to the conclusion that the psychotic is imprisoned in the imaginary.[23] Since language remains real for the psychotic, since it never becomes symbolic, and since there is no paternal metaphor organizing the psychotic's reality, psychotics are unable to generate or comprehend metaphor, or any symbolic use of language.[24] This is seen in Robert, shortly after his break, at the moment he meets his doppelgänger for the first time and attempts to insert his delusional metaphor, which leads to his delusions of grandeur. After meeting Gil-Martin for the first time, Robert's parents recognize that he is ill and comment about his "crazed head," indicating a change in Robert tantamount to a break (*JS* 120). The following day, when meeting up with Gil-Martin for the second time, Robert begins to forge his delusional metaphor through his literalizing of Gil-Martin's metaphor about becoming God's "two-edged weapon" (*JS* 122). Rather than devoting his life to conversionary preaching, as it appears Gil-Martin is requesting, Robert devotes his life to literally slaying those deemed sinners:

> From that moment, I conceived it decreed, not that I should be a minster of the gospel, but a champion of it, to cut off the enemies of the Lord from the face of the earth; and I rejoiced in the commission finding it more congenial to my nature to be cutting sinners off with the sword, than to be haranguing them from the pulpit, striving to produce an effect, which God, by his act of absolute predestination, had for ever rendered impracticable [*JS* 122–23].

At this point the Calvinist discourse of predestination is taken by Robert to even further extremes than it is with his "severe and gloomy" mother, as it becomes the very imaginary delusion that will organize Robert's reality throughout his *Confessions*.

Because Robert's separation from his mother remains incomplete, his doppelgänger Gil-Martin functions both as a hallucinatory sign of this lack of separation and as an uncastrated version of himself.[25] Mladen Dolar points out not only that the double realizes the subject's hidden desires but also how this marks itself out in Freud's topology: the double "constitutes the essential part of the ego; he carries out the repressed desires of the Id; and he also, with a malevolence typical of the superego, prevents the subject from carrying out his desires — all at the same time."[26] Essentially, the internal psyche of the subject is projected outward as a quasi-independent being. The paternal signifier, which is lacking in Robert's case, guarantees the objective world of reality by keeping the *objet a* — the subject's kernel of being — out of it. Otherwise, if the *objet a* appears in reality, reality loses its consistency, as happens during a psychotic break. However, the doppelganger initially emerges for Robert as his mirror image that includes *objet a*. When the lost part of reality, *objet a*, is included in reality it paradoxically destroys reality instead of completing it.[27] Robert's own summary of his initial encounter with Gil-Martin reeks of this doppelgänger convention:

> That stranger youth and I approached each other in silence, and slowly, with our eyes fixed on each other's eyes. We approached till not more than a yard intervened between us, and then stood still and gazed, measuring each other from head to foot. What was my astonishment, on perceiving that he was the same being as myself! The clothes were the same to the smallest item. The form was the same; the apparent age; the colour of the hair; the eyes; and, as far as recollection could serve me from viewing my own features in a glass, the features too were the very same. I conceived at first that I saw a vision, and that my guardian angel had appeared to me at this important era of my life; but this singular being read my thoughts in my looks, anticipating the very words that I was going to utter [*JS* 117].

Initially, Robert's doppelgänger appears to him as the shadow appears to the primitive, according to Otto Rank. His double exists as a guardian angel, as a protective, benevolent spirit. But, as Rank also points out in his famous study of the double, in the modern era, the double transforms into a terrorizing malevolent enemy, eventually turning into an image of the subject's own evil propensities.[28] In fact, the aggression Robert displays toward M'Gill and even toward his brother George duplicates the aggressivity that Lacan claims possesses the subject upon the insertion into the imaginary order during the mirror stage of development when the alter ego becomes the measure of the ego's boundaries.[29] Normally the imaginary recognition of the child is accompanied by the symbolic recognition of a parent as the representative of the field of the Other, the symbolic order. But, since Robert never reveals to his parents the existence of Gil-Martin, his imaginary reality is never sublated to the symbolic realm.[30] This lack of a symbolic sublation prevents young Robert from triangulation, leaving him stuck in an imaginary dyadic structure with his doppelgänger.

The early nineteenth century was the era of the doppelgänger. Not only did Jean Paul adopt the term for his 1796 novel *Siebenkäs*, but this was the era of Hoffman, Chamisso, Tieck and Kleist. In his editor's introduction to Rank's doppelgänger study, Harry Tucker contends that the quest into the mind, the investigation into the integrity of the self began during this period, and the doppelgänger was used by various literary writers in an attempt to dramatize and expose the "obscurely understood drives and impulses" of the human mind.[31] The dyadic relation in which the hero of the doppelgänger narrative finds himself forces the hero to confront a part of himself heretofore ignored or foreclosed. As Rank asserts about the doppelgänger, "the pathological disposition toward psychological disturbances is conditioned to a large degree by the splitting of the personality, with special emphasis upon the ego complex, to which corresponds an abnormally strong interest in one's own person, his psychic states, and his destinies."[32] Clinical studies have verified the narcissistic nature of the doppelgänger phenomenon.[33] They testify to the fact that the stalling of development in an imaginary primary narcissism prevents the subject from attaching his or her libido to an external object, making the externalized alter-ego the object of libidinal attachment.[34] The double, therefore, provides a means for the subject who is trapped in the imaginary to attach to an external object, and Robert's initial meetings with Gil-Martin reproduce this type of narcissism. When he speaks of his "spiritual pride being greatly elevated" (*JS* 17) during his first meeting with his awe-inspiring Gil-Martin and how his own alter ego "seemed to have more knowledge and information than all the persons I had ever known put together" (*JS* 118), the reader, who readily realizes that Robert is merely thinking out loud, cannot help but notice the self-congratulatory nature of such boasting. But later, when Robert realizes that Gil-Martin has prevented him from praying, he reveals, at least to the reader, his own lack of concern for religious formalities once he has been proclaimed one of the saved (*JS* 128). The doppelgänger, therefore, becomes the closest thing to an external object for the subject and the hallucinatory means of purging and confronting his own hidden self as something foreign.[35] In his double, the hero confronts precisely what has been overlooked in his own self-conception.[36] The double, therefore, not only personifies the uncanny possessor of hidden secrets within the doppelgänger narrative, but it also functions to fictively dramatize the nature of "conflicting feelings and impulses."[37]

Narcissism is also a primary characteristic of psychosis. According to Freud, in psychosis the ego detaches itself from the external world because it never surmounts the stage of primary narcissism.[38] Essentially, the battle of the split ego that takes place in psychosis between the ego and the id is dramatized by the doppelgänger narrative as the conflict between the hero and his double. Where the hero ends and the double begins is about as easy to discern as where the ego ends and the id begins in psychosis. In Bruce Fink's examination of Rachel Corday, "a psychotic who has made an extremely instructive videotape entitled *Losing the Thread*," he notices the breakdown of the ego's boundaries that constitutes the psychotic's symptom. According to Fink,

> [Corday] "loses herself" during psychotic breaks.... She tells us that she can then no longer relate to other things, as there is no *I* to do the relating, no longer any recognizable center of intentionality. "Everything in reality disintegrates, including my own body," she says, detailing how difficult it becomes to move from one point to another without the "CEO in her office," that homunculus known as the ego which gives us the sense that our bodies are organized wholes that move harmoniously, as a unit. The nerves, muscles, and tendons in her body still have all the same connections that allowed her to execute complicated movements before, but the sense of self that allowed her body to function as a whole dissipates.[39]

Fink is basically describing an individual who has remained stranded in the Lacanian imaginary mirror stage, where the child's own feeling of fragmentation seems contradicted by the seemingly whole, complete, and unified body of the mirror image. When Belle Calvert is questioned by Mrs. Logan if she could identify Robert as the possible murderer of his brother George, she describes his hasty departure from the murder scene in strikingly similar terms: "I think I could [identify him], if I saw him walk or run: his gait was very peculiar: He walked as if he had been flat-soled, his legs made of steel, without any joints in his feet or ankles" (*JS* 80). This description alludes to the possibility that Robert is not in complete control of his body and that some part of his own ego has been projected out, making it difficult for him to maintain that sense of self necessary for complete and harmonious motor control. Fink further elaborates on the disintegration of the sense of the self inherent in psychosis:

> The disintegration of the ego is not always so complete in psychosis, and we perhaps more often witness a confusion between self and other, a difficulty in determining who is speaking.... The "boundaries" of the ego

are not simply flexible, as they are sometimes described in neurosis, but virtually nonexistent, leading to a dangerous sense that another person or force is trying to usurp one's place ... imaginary relations predominate.[40]

Immediately following Robert's first encounter with the stranger Gil-Martin, his pastor Robert Sr. notices how he has changed since the morning when he told young Robert the supposed good news concerning his predestination. The reverend father comments, "I could not have known you for the same person. Have you met with any accident?" (*JS* 120). By all outward appearances, Robert is simply not the same after his bizarre encounter with Gil-Martin. It is as if he does not fit in with the chain of signifiers, which are quilted by the paternal signifier. A few pages later, Gil-Martin reveals to Robert his secret ability to take on another's features merely by looking at a person attentively. Throughout his narrative, Robert constantly feels he is being displaced by some outside force. The "unnatural joy" Robert first sees in Gil-Martin's face soon becomes an enjoyment at Robert's expense. Shortly after coaxing Robert to murder his brother in Edinburgh, Gil-Martin literally takes over Robert's being in order to rape a young woman and kill his own overbearing mother. Robert seems at a loss concerning the accusations made against him, and goes on the run as an outlaw until the conclusion of his narrative: "My state both of body and mind was now truly deplorable. I was hungry, wounded, lame; an outcast and a vagabond in society" (*JS* 218). Robert, it appears, has no symbolic role. And without a symbolic, without a language to delimit, Robert eventually falls prey to the uninhibited enjoyment of the real.

Understanding of the structure of psychosis through the breakdown of the ego's boundaries reveals the doppelgänger Gil-Martin as the hallucinatory symptom of Robert's psychotic state. Fink also mentions that the hallucinatory voice that the psychotic hears often speaks in interrupted phrases that break off just before the utterance of a vital term or phrase, requiring the subject to supply the missing part.[41] This may explain the "riddling ambiguity" of Gil-Martin's speech.[42] But, it also explains why young Robert rarely, if ever, supplies the reader with Gil-Martin's supposedly sublime, awe-inspiring, and utterly convincing arguments, the very arguments that also supposedly justify Robert's criminal acts.[43]

Bodily disintegration and loss of the sense of self, however, are only two of the effects of the split ego psychosis shares with heautoscopy. Rank has also indicated that the double both represents the subject's past and indicates a connection between this past and the superstitious beliefs of primitives, further forging a connection between the double and the uncanny.[44] N. Lukianowicz likewise argues that the double reanimates the make-believe nature of children's imaginary companions.[45] In young Robert's case, his doppelgänger's very presence reaffirms the fact that Robert has never surmounted the dyadic structure that constitutes the imaginary order prior to alienation and separation from the mother. This would explain why Keppler concludes that Gil-Martin is bound to young Robert "as the mother to her child."[46] Gil-Martin, as previously mentioned, stands in for the original lost object (the mother); only, due to Robert's psychotic state, this object is not lacking from his reality. It is actually too present, providing a certain sense of unreality for Hogg's antihero. But, following Rank's understanding, the doppelgänger also represents, for Robert, his attempt to find a delusional father substitute for that name-of-the-father he never had substantiated.[47] In fact, near the end of Robert's *Confessions*, he indirectly confirms that his delusional doppelgänger emerged as his attempt to imaginarily enact the separation from his constricting and suffocating mother's desire:

> In this state of irritation and misery, was I dragging on an existence, disgusted with all around me, and in particular with my mother, who, with all her love and anxiety, had such an insufferable mode of manifesting them, that she had by this time rendered herself exceedingly obnoxious to me. The very sound of her voice at a distance, went to my heart like an arrow, and made all my nerves to shrink [*JS* 184].[48]

Shortly after this acknowledgment, Robert attempts to literally enact separation. Through his doppelgänger, of course, he murders his mother, resulting in the complete unraveling of his life for the rest of his narrative.

One of the truly fantastic aspects of Hogg's narrative is the ambiguity surrounding Gil-Martin's existence. If he is only the product of Robert's abnormal psychology, as I have been pursuing thus far, how can the reader account for the other characters in the romance that appear to see this chameleon-like character?[49] Since the name-of-the-father has never been substantiated in the symbolic, Robert has no defense from the onslaught of the real of enjoyment, and the romance cannot regulate the enjoyment of its narrative. It is virtually impossible to tell how much of Gil-Martin is hallucination (what is foreclosed in the symbolic returning in the real) and how much is actual. Although Robert is the only one who sees Gil-Martin as Peter the Great, other characters testify to seeing Robert constantly in the company of some stranger. But this confusion may only add to the idea that the Gothic genre itself has had a psychotic break — that it has lost its legitimacy. Even if others testify to seeing Robert in the presence of some stranger, three things must be kept in mind. One, these witness accounts all take place within the first part of Hogg's split narrative. This first part of the romance, "The Editor's

Narrative," itself purports to be almost exclusively based on tradition or legend. Therefore, the editor may be as unreliable of a narrator as the psychotic and delusional antihero who narrates the second part of the romance. Two, the characters who do recall seeing Gil-Martin and claim he is the devil in disguise, might themselves be subject to the folkloric superstitious beliefs that once ruled in Scotland's past.[50] Madness was, afterall, traditionally understood as demonic possession.[51] Third, even if one were to grant that Gil-Martin is the devil in disguise,[52] one must keep in mind that Freud argued that the devil himself is simply the projection of "instinctual impulses" into the external world.[53] But what is most interesting is that Hogg's romance not only structurally reproduces the doppelgänger motif by doubling its narrator into two seemingly distinct personas, but also the split narrative exhibits signs of the splitting of identity that is the hallmark of psychosis.

Is the "Editor's Narrative" so easily to be understood as the truth of Robert's *Confessions*? The Ettrick Shepherd's own cameo appearance in the second "Editor's Narrative" near the completion of the romance and the satirical ridicule of the narrator that is implied in the author's cameo seem to undercut this configuration.[54] Furthermore, the justified sinner himself claims that his narrative is not autobiographical but a "religious parable such as Pilgrim's Progress" (*JS* 221). This might be his own subterfuge, his attempt to get the permission to print his manuscript from his boss Mr. Watson at the printing house where he works, knowing full well that no reasonable publisher will print such an obviously fantastic tale as nonfiction. Watson even tells Robert that allegories are "the very rage of the day" (*JS* 222).[55] On the surface, then, it may appear that Robert fabricates the allegorical nature of his manuscript for marketing purposes, but its shear outlandishness puts the editor, in his concluding remarks, into the very same position as today's contemporary Gothic critic:

> That the young Laird of Dalcastle came by a violent death, there remains no doubt; but that this wretch [Gil-Martin as Satan] slew him, there is to me a good deal. However, allowing this to have been the case, I account all the rest either dreaming or madness; or, as he says to Mr. Watson, a religious parable, on purpose to illustrate something scarcely tangible [*JS* 254].

Either the text is to be understood as a religious parable, understood allegorically to illustrate something that could be told more directly, or it is to be understood as a romance, as revealing something about the nature of psychopathology that can only be revealed indirectly. Andrew Webber has argued that doppegänger literature gauges this very shifting relation between realism and fantasy, calling the doppelgänger figure itself a triumph simultaneously

of mimesis and monstrosity.[56] Mimesis, or realism, relies on the repression of
the fantastic enjoyment of the uncanny in order to maintain its coherence and
verisimilitude. The doppelgänger, however, embodies the familiar and the
strange together, indicating, as in psychosis, that its narrative space remains
stranded in an imaginary realm divorced from the very reality to which allegory refers.

The difference between enjoyment as it is relegated by neurosis and
enjoyment as it is not relegated in psychosis is clearly articulated by Fink:

> Lacan asserts that the body, in neurosis, is essentially dead. It is written
> with signifiers; in other words, it has been overwritten or codified by the
> symbolic. The body as a biological organism is what Lacan calls the "real,"
> and it is progressively socialized or "domesticated" to such an extent that
> libido retreats from all but a very few zones: the erogenous zones. Only
> in these zones is the body still alive, in some sense, or real. Here libido
> (or jouissance) is channeled and contained. This is not the case in psy-
> chosis: the hierarchy of drives achieved imaginarily can collapse when
> the imaginary order that supports it falters. The body, which has been
> for the most part rid of jouissance, is suddenly inundated with it, invaded
> by it. It comes back with a vengeance, we might say, for the psychotic
> may well experience it as an attack, an invasion, or forcible entry.[57]

The body here is Robert's corpse as a figure for the corpus of Gothic literature
up to the period of Hogg's romance. At first, with Walpole, enjoyment had
some meaning, but it was rampant. There was clearly some concerned use of
the supernatural in Walpole's Gothic universe, but it was not really regulated
in any serious, non-confused manner. With the maturing Gothic cosmologies
of Radcliffe and Lewis, along with all their respective imitators, the supernatural sublime, as the materialization of excessive enjoyment, was regulated
into a meaningful role. The supernatural existed for more than just its own
sake. Its very regulation was the practice upon which the narrative realities
maintained any sense of realism. But with Hogg's romance, which both
announces the end of the Gothic and comes after the Gothic proper, enjoyment takes over. Not so much in the way it does in *Otranto*, but in a way in
which one can never be sure of whether anything supernatural occurs. "The
Editor's Narrative" is a feeble attempt to anchor "The Sinner's Narrative" in
some external reality, but even it is too filled with contradictions to be reliable
and is based largely on legend, making it no more reliable than the direct discourse of a psychotic obviously suffering from graphamania (*JS* 254). "The
Editor's Narrative" should perhaps be read as just another hallucinatory tale.
With Hogg's romance, the Gothic no longer wears the supernatural on its
sleeve. It has begun its journey into the realm of the psychological that will

culminate in the Gothic of the 1890s. Behaving much like Robert, Hogg kills off a genre that has flourished too long by making the symbolic importance of the Gothic collapse just like the psychotic's. And much like Robert's corpse, the Gothic lay buried until it was dug up by the late twentieth-century's revived critical interest in the genre.

Chapter Notes

Introduction

1. Michelle Massé, "Psychoanalysis and the Gothic," 230.

2. Diane Long Hoeveler, *Gothic Feminism: The Professionalization of Gender from Charlottte Smith to the Brontës*, 58.

3. Jacques-Alain Miller, "The Experience of the Real in Psychoanalysis," 9.

4. In the astute words of Marshall Brown, "Freud had developed a logic, a locale, and a method for analyzing what the Enlightenment barely found a primitive means to suggest in representation." Marshall Brown, *The Gothic Text*, 55. For an examination of the scientific origins of the unconscious in eighteenth-century science, especially mesmerism, see Henri F. Ellenberger, *The Discovery of the Unconscious*, 3–109. For an account of the literary discovery of the unconscious in late eighteenth and early nineteenth-century literature, see Lancelot Law Whyte, *The Unconscious Before Freud*. For a study of the roots of the unconscious in late eighteenth and nineteenth-century philosophy, see Angus Nicholls and Martin Liebscher, eds., *Thinking the Unconscious: Nineteenth-Century German Thought*.

5. Kalu Singh, *Sublimation*, 18. Singh adds, "The stories of Oedipus, Elecktra, Hamlet and Faust induce a sense of inexhaustible wonder which seems to fit the puzzling taste for the dark side of family life."

6. Robert Rogers, *A Psychoanalytic Study of the Double in Literature*, 29.

7. Ibid.

8. Lionel Trilling, *The Liberal Imagination*, 50.

9. In fact, Townshend's fear of anachronism and his crippled desire to keep his Lacanian analysis within the historicist hegemony of current criticism lead him to the following paradoxical claim: "If formalized, theoretically enshrined psychoanalytic notions of the unconscious post-date eighteenth-century Gothic by a considerable period of time, Foucault's category of the modern unthought provides a less anachronistic critical alternative." Dale Townshend, 32. Leaving aside the extent to which Foucault's notion of the "modern unthought" itself derives from Freudian psychoanalysis, it seems more logical to claim that since Freud's discoveries predate Foucault's by nearly three-quarters of a century that the use of Foucault's categories for an analysis of eighteenth-century Gothic fiction would likely be more historically suspect than the use of Freud's categories. The phallic nature of such a claim intimates the parallel claim that all ideas are historically determined, except those that posit the historically determined nature of thought. For some reason, in Townshend's analysis, Foucault's claims seem to escape and even transcend the parameters of his own historical situation, whereas Freud's are allowed only a historically-limited range.

10. For instance, while claiming that psychoanalysis helped define the modern subject, Townshend argues that "subjectivity ... is nothing other than the sum-total of its cultural representations" (ibid., 22–23). While his definition of subjectivity might well be accurate, the subject, as psychoanalytically defined, is actually what remains of the human after being stripped of all his or her cultural representations. Likewise, Townshend sees the gaze as not how I see myself but as how others see me: "As Lacan explains, if the subject can be gazed upon from so many different positions upon the social horizon, his ego construction is profoundly relativized" (ibid., 305). For Lacan, however, the gaze is not how others see me; rather, it is how I see others seeing me, a giving to be seen, as Lacan would have it. The gaze in Lacan is virtual because it originates in the Other, which is itself virtual, not disciplinary. As Townshend himself quotes Lacan, "The gaze I encounter ... is not a seen gaze, but a gaze imagined by me in the field of the Other" (ibid., 305).

11. For Lacan, the *jouissance* (enjoyment) of the Other is imaginary; it is what the neurotic believes others are exclusively enjoying, usually at his expense. The Other *jouissance*, however, is linked, by Lacan, to feminine sexuality; it is a form of enjoyment that is not tied to the signifier and is real. Also, by translating Lacan's *plus-de-jouir* as "excessive *jouissance*" instead of as "surplus *jouissance*," Townshend leads the reader to believe that Lacan's concept embodies a prohibited enjoyment that requires some sort of transgressive act to achieve. However, Lacan's notion of surplus enjoyment marks that everyday partial *jouissance* that supplements for the original lost *jouissance*. For more on the different modalities of *jouissance* in Lacan's teachings, see Jacques-Alain Miller, "Paradigms of *Jouissance*."

12. Fred Botting, *Gothic Romanced: Consumption, Gender and the Technology in Contemporary Fictions*, 7–8.

13. Ibid., 8.

14. For instance, while discussing Francis Ford Coppola's romantic post-modern adaptation of *Dracula*, Botting argues, as it frames gothic, seems to clean up its darker counterpart, sanitizing its depravations; it tries to transform, even ennoble, violent gothic excesses in the name of the heterosexual couple" (ibid., 1).

15. Connecting the pathological to the passions, Punter claims: "We need to recall that the word 'passion' comes from the same common Greek root as 'pathology,' and so in approaching the passions one is simultaneously approaching a pathology.... The crucial difference is one of emphasis: where pathology emphasizes precisely the *logos*, seeks truth through mechanism and reason, the word and the law, passion stands for an approach through the organic" (Punter, *Gothic Pathologies*, 60).

16. In his analysis of literary writers, American psychoanalyst Edmund Bergler has noted that the literary writer "differs both from the neurotic and the healthy by his ability to express personal conflicts in a form which makes them enjoyable to others without making it too noticeable that they originate from repressed human wishes. Hence he creates by giving artistic form to his unconscious phantasies, which, through the process of repression, have become unpleasurable, but which, in art, find and retain a more sublime method of gratification and pleasure" (Edmund Bergler, 10).

17. Jacques Lacan, "Homage to Marguerite Duras, on *Le ravissement de Lol V. Stein*," 124. For more about this claim, see Malcolm Bowie, *Freud, Proust, and Lacan: Theory as Fiction*; Colette Solar, "Literature as Symptom," 213–18; Jean-Michel Rabaté, *Jacques Lacan: Psychoanalysis and the Subject of Literature*; and Ehsan Azari, *Lacan and the Destiny of Literature*.

Chapter 1

1. Sigmund Freud, "The 'Uncanny,'" in *The Standard Edition of the Complete Psychological Works of Sigmund Freud* [hereafter cited as *SE*], vol. 17, 217–55

2. Harold Bloom, "Freud and the Poetic Sublime: A Catastrophe Theory of Creativity," in *Freud: A Collection of Critical Essays*, 218.

3. David B. Morris, "Gothic Sublimity," 300.

4. Vijay Mishra, *The Gothic Sublime*, 71.

5. Andrew Smith, *Gothic Radicalism: Literature, Philosophy and Psychoanalysis in the Nineteenth Century*, 161.

6. Dale Townshend, *The Orders of the Gothic*, 324.

7. Kathy Justice Gentile, "Sublime Drag: Supernatural Masculinity in Gothic Fiction," 22. At the beginning of *Civilization and Its Discontents*, Freud himself draws an implicit connection between the sublime and the uncanny. While examining a peculiar feeling many people have experienced ("a sensation of 'eternity,' a feeling as of something limitless, unbounded — as it were, 'oceanic'" as Freud describes it), Freud concludes that this feeling is a "shrunken residue" of an earlier feeling that was prevalent before the formation of the ego. Therefore, this peculiar feeling of sublimity is itself based on a return of something that should have remained hidden; it is, in a word, uncanny. Sigmund Freud, *Civilization and Its Discontents*, in *SE*, vol. 21, ed. and trans. James Strachey (London: Hogarth, 1964), 64, 68. I want to acknowledge Gentile's article for bringing to light this implicit connection between the sublime and the uncanny in Freud's *Civilization and Its Discontents*.

8. Terry Castle, *The Female Thermometer: Eighteenth-century Culture and the Invention of the Uncanny*, 8. Although, according to the *OED*, the specifically supernatural use of the term "uncanny" did not become common until the mid-nineteenth century, this particular usage originates in a poem by Scottish poet Robert Ferguson, written less than a decade after the publication of *The Castle of Otranto*, the first Gothic romance (*The Oxford English Dictionary*, 2nd ed., vol. 18, Oxford: Clarendon, 1989).

9. Ibid., 13.

10. Ibid., 15. In *Seminar VII*, Lacan articulates the three human discourses' relation to the unknown — the emptiness of our knowledge. Science forecloses this emptiness by articulating the unknown as not only immanent but as accessible. With more time, effort and technology, science believes it can uncover the unknown and make it known, transforming the Thing into mere things unknown. Religion avoids this emptiness by articulating the unknown as transcendental and therefore inaccessible. For religion, the unknown

can only be encountered in the eternal realm, making the Thing divine. Art, however, organizes itself around this emptiness by articulating the unknown as paradoxically immanent yet inaccessible. In this manner art is able to expose the unknown negatively as the limit of its own vision. Only in art, therefore, does the unknown become the Thing in the strictly psychoanalytic sense. Art, of course, is a means of sublimating the uncanny, exposing it while simultaneously providing the needed symbolic distance (Jacques Lacan, *The Seminar of Jacques Lacan, Book VII: The Ethics* of Psychoanalysis, 129–30). For a wonderful discussion of this Lacanian argument, see Alenka Zupančič, "The Splendor of Creation: Kant, Nietzsche, Lacan," 35–41. See also François Regnault, "Art After Lacan," 48–69.

11. Ibid., 5. One could argue that the return of the repressed as an essential ingredient of the Freudian uncanny is already intimated in the Longinian sublime. Longinus claims that when reading a sublime poet our soul comes to believe "it had itself produced what it has heard" and that we believe we already know what the sublime poet expresses for us. He is, in a sense, already articulating that strange form of intimacy of the uncanny. For Longinus, however, this feeling has not yet changed into the vision of terror that it does when the sublime becomes truly uncanny in the hands of the Gothic novelists. Longinus, "On the Sublime," 84.

12. Morris, "Gothic Sublimity," 306.

13. Even though Tzvetan Todorov claims that his notion of the uncanny bears a resemblance to Freud's, he insists there is not an entire coincidence between his and Freud's use of the term. In fact, there is really nothing psychoanalytic about Todorov's use of the term. According to Todorov's structuralist analysis, there are two basic ways in which the fantastic can slip into a neighboring genre. One occurs at the level of the nature of events depicted, and one occurs at the level of the very text that describes these events. If at the end of a reading, the reader makes a decision to opt for one solution or the other, whether or not the events portrayed stem from the common reality of the work or from outside it, he or she thereby emerges from the fantastic. Now, if the decision to end the hesitation cannot be fully supported from within the narrative itself, the reader cannot wholly emerge from the fantastic. If the reader decides that the seemingly supernatural events of the narrative can be explained away as natural, the work slips into the genre Todorov calls the uncanny. If, on the other hand, the reader decides that these certain events belong to a realm beyond the everyday reality supplied by the work, the work slides into the marvelous. Accordingly, the fantastic never seems to exist in a pure state. It is only, apparently,

housed in either a latent uncanny or a latent marvelous narrative. This then is the first level danger of the fantastic: "Either the reader admits that these apparently supernatural events are susceptible to rational explanation, and we shift from the fantastic to the uncanny; or else he admits their existence as such, and we find ourselves within the marvelous" (Tzvetan Todorov, 58). Todorov would naturally claim that Ann Radcliffe's use of the "explained supernatural" situates her novels within the genre of the uncanny. But just because Todorov's analysis of genre lacks a psychoanalytic edge, this does not preclude Radcliffe's narratives from being understood through Freud's notion of the uncanny. For an account that attempts to link Todorov's uncanny with Freud's, see Maria Tatar, "The Houses of Fiction: Toward a Definition of the Uncanny," 167–82.

14. Mishra, *The Gothic Sublime*, 64.

15. Borrowing Milton's phrase, Northrop Frye argues that because of its structure and conventions, romance suggests alternative meanings. This "symbolic spreading" of meaning "expresses the haunting sense of what is often called allegory in romance, but it seems to me that the word allegory here is misleading: I should prefer some such phrase as 'symbolic spread,' the sense that a work of literature is expanding into insights and experiences beyond itself." Spreading a symbolic meaning onto a literary work, according to Frye, "begins by detaching the literary work being studied from its context in literature. After that, the work may be discussed in relation to its historical, social, biographical, and other nonliterary affinities. Such a method, inadequate as it is, is often rationalized as a proper emphasis on the 'uniqueness' of the work" (Northrop Frye, *The Secular Scripture: A Study of the Structure of Romance*, 59). Anne Williams also prefers Milton's "symbolic spread" over "allegory" in her analysis of the Gothic (Anne Williams, *Art of Darkness: A Poetics of Gothic*, 81–86). Milton's term nicely captures the movement of symbolic meaning from the literary text to critical understanding that characterizes the process of interpretation.

16. "Political Vampyres," 24–26.

17. Ibid., 25.

18. Ibid.

19. Ibid.

20. Ibid.

21. It could, however, be argued that just as the classical allegorical interpreters — the Stoics, Philo and Origen — found indicators of allegory in Homer and the Hebrew Bible that justified their interpretive method, current Gothic criticism also makes the interpretive decision to recognize that the obvious outlandishness of the Gothic must, because of its outlandishness, symbolize something beyond the literal, thereby, making allegoresis an inevitable mode of Gothic

criticism. For more on the Classical reasoning behind allegoresis, see Jean Grondin, *Introduction to Philosophical Hermeneutics*, 25–27.

22. Northrop Frye, *Anatomy of Criticism: Four Essays*, 89.

23. Peter Berek, "Interpretation, Allegory, and Allegoresis" *College English* 40.2, 125.

24. Morton W. Bloomfield, "Allegory as Interpretation," *New Literary History* 3.2, 301–02.

25. Franco Moretti, *Signs Taken for Wonders: Essays in the Sociology of Literary Forms*.

26. Judith Halberstam, *Skin Shows: Gothic Horror and the Technology of Monsters*.

27. Stephen Arata, *Fictions of Loss in the Victorian Fin de Siècle*; Burton Hatlen, "The Return of the Repressed/Oppressed in Bram Stoker's *Dracula*," in *Dracula: The Vampire and the Critics*, 117–35; and Christopher Craft, "'Kiss Me with Those Red Lips': Gender and Inversion in Bram Stoker's *Dracula*," *Representations* 41, 19–46.

28. Kim Ian Michasiw, "Charlotte Dacre's Postcolonial Moor" in *Empire and the Gothic: The Politics of Genre*, 35–55; Stephanie Burley, "The Death of Zofloya; or, The Moor as Epistemological Limit," in *the Gothic Other: Racial and Social Constructionin the Literary Imaginaiton*, 197–211; Massimiliano Demata, "Discovering Easter Horrors: Beckford, Maturin, and hte Discourse of Travel Literature' in *Empire and the Gothic*, 13–34; and Renée Bergland, *The National Uncanny: Indian Ghosts and American Subjects*.

29. See, for instance, H. L. Malchow, *Gothic Images of Race in Nineteenth-Century Britain*; Cannon Schmitt, *Alien Nation: Nineteenth-Century Gothic Fictions and English Nationality*; J. Gerald Kennedy and Lilian Weissberg, *Romancing the Shadow: Poe and Race*; Allan Lloyd Smith, "'This Thing of Darkness': Racial Discourse in Mary Shelley's *Frankenstein*," 208–222; Laurie Langbauer, *Women and Romance: The Consolations of Gender in the English Novel*; Donna Heiland, *Gothic and Gender: An Introduction*; Joseph Adriano, *Our Ladies of Darkness*; Eugenia C. DeLamotte, *Perils of the Night*; Kate Ellis, *The Contested Castle*; George Haggerty, *Queer Gothic*; and Eve Kosofsky Sedgwick, *Between Men: English Literature and Male Homosocial Desire*.

30. Moretti, *Signs Taken for Wonders*, 101 (emphasis in original).

31. Ibid.

32. Ibid., 101–02.

33. Ibid., 102. This return of what should have remained dead and buried is Freud's definition of the uncanny as a particular form of the frightening. Freud, "The 'Uncanny,'" in *SE*, 17:224.

34. Freud asserts that the uncanny pertains to an affect much more specialized than what excites fear in general. Freud, "The 'Uncanny,'" in *SE*, 17:219.

35. For an account of the inherent connection between the uncanny and anxiety in Freud, Heidegger and the Gothic, see Kathy Justice Gentile, "Anxious Supernaturalism: An Analytic of the Uncanny," 23–38.

36. David Punter even claims that the literary uncanny offers a means of rendering in narrative that which is naturally resistant to linguistic or rational appropriation, thereby implying that the uncanny figure of Gothic romance itself figures that which cannot so easily be identified with a terrestrial object of fear. David Punter, "The Uncanny," 134.

37. Jacques Lacan, *Seminar X: Anxiety*.

38. Moretti, *Signs Taken for Wonders*, 105.

39. Ibid.

40. Ibid., 89. However, as Northrop Frye has pointed out, "the happy ending exists only for readers who finish the book, and, within the book, only for characters who survive to the end of the story." Frye, *The Secular Scripture*, 135.

41. This method of interpretation echoes the Stoics' systematic rationalizing of the outlandishness of myth through allegorical interpretation. See Grondin, *Introduction to Philosophical Hermeneutics*, 24.

42. See, for instance, Slavoj Žižek, *The Sublime Object of Ideology*; and Slavoj Žižek, "The Spectre of Ideology," 1–33.

43. Quoted in Halberstam, *Skin Shows*, 19.

44. Maureen Quilligan even claims that allegory forces us to realize what kind of readers we are (Maureen Quilligan, *The Language of Allegory*, 24). Peter Szondi argues that "allegorical interpretation ... is kindled by the sign which has become alien, to which it gives a new meaning born not of the conceptual world of the text, but rather belonging to that of its interpreter" (Peter Szondi, "Introduction to Literary Hermeneutics," 24). This close attention to the *sensus spiritualis* at the expense of the *sensus litteralis* that characterizes much current Gothic allegorical criticism has prompted Chris Baldick and Robert Mighall to claim that much Gothic interpretation congratulates itself on its own enlightenment more than it illuminates anything objective about the Gothic mode of literature (Chris Baldick and Robert Mighall, "Gothic Criticism," 210). In their uncanny return to a sort of Hirschian objective criticism, Baldick and Mighall argue that much current Gothic criticism suffers from severe de-historicizing because of its collapsing "of history into universal psychology" (ibid., 218). Although there are many redeemable criticisms made in this highly touted essay, its general critique of psychoanalytic approaches to the Gothic is never worked out from a knowledgeable position; indeed, many of the critics the essay tends to lump together as working under "the dominant Freudian agenda" are themselves Foucauldian critics, sometimes explicitly hostile to psycho-

analysis. Moreover, the critics' enthusiastic call for a "return to careful historical specification" in future Gothic studies proves underwhelming since they also complain about how current critics tend to give more weight to the metaphorical, the hidden, and the symbolic than they do to the literal and the ostensible, as if the object of study itself isn't literature. What is literature, after all, if not a medium that specifically privileges the metaphorical over the literal? Isn't this why interpretation is endemic to literary studies in the first place? Of course, if it is pointed out that the literal is, in fact, the supreme figure, a whole other can of worms is introduced. But, this can is never even implicitly opened by Baldick and Mighall in their critique. For an explicit Hirschian critique of allegoresis, see Berek, "Interpretation, Allegory, and Allegoresis."

45. Again, in Freudian psychoanalysis, anxiety, as a fear of nothing, is much more free-floating and disturbing than a fear of something identifiable. Anxiety tends to paralyze one where fear makes one react. This distinction is also articulated as the difference between traumatic anxiety and castration anxiety — the latter being of a secondary order. See, for instance, Sigmund Freud, *Inhibitions, Symptoms and Anxiety*, in *SE*, vol. 20.

46. Slavoj Žižek, "Grimaces of the Real, or When the Phallus Appears," 57. See also, Slavoj Žižek, *Enjoy Your Symptom*, 113–46.

47. Ibid., 64.

48. Ibid.

49. Žižek adds, "The analysis that focuses on the 'ideological meaning' of monsters overlooks the fact that, before signifying something, before serving as a vessel of meaning, monsters embody enjoyment qua the limit of interpretation, that is to say, *nonmeaning as such*" (ibid., 64, emphasis in original).

50. Lacan, *Seminar VII*, 99. In a recent article, Gary Farnell argues in favor of "a powerful new theory of the Gothic," one incorporating the psychoanalytic notion of *das Ding* (the Thing). The Thing, "as absolute otherness," is, according to Farnell's analysis, not "of the order of signifiers within the symbolic order; hence its un-nameability" (Gary Farnell, "The Gothic and the Thing," 113). Farnell further argues that the Gothic Thing "both resists and provokes symbolization" in a manner similar to what I have been arguing above. Farnell's plea at the conclusion of his essay for a "reconceptualisation of the Gothic that is possible within the framework of Thing theory" seems to imply that Gothic studies is currently "traversed by a split between the symbol and the Thing" (ibid., 122, 117). Since I am basically arguing that allegorical interpretations of Gothic sublimity tend to symbolize that which resists symbolization, my study might fall within the "new theory of the Gothic" that Farnell is

championing. Farnell's strict focus on the Thing, while important, forces his analysis into a primarily masculine notion of the sublime and sublimation. Since he focuses only on the first and most famous of Lacan's notions of sublimation (the elevation of the object to the dignity of the Thing) from *Seminar VII*, he does not acknowledge the difference between masculine and feminine sublimation. This distinction is the subject of Chapter 4 below. See also my essay "The Moral Value of Gothic Sublimity," 119–37.

51. Mladen Dolar, "'I Shall Be with You on Your Wedding Night': Lacan and the Uncanny," 6.

52. Gothic narratives invariably revolve around a crisis in the realities of their characters' lives. This crisis functions as the narrative's libidinal force (what Lacan renamed *jouissance*) that seduces character and reader alike. The prophesy that opens *The Castle of Otranto*, for instance, not only inaugurates Gothic uncanny sublimity, but also throws the existing reality (the symbolic space) of Manfred and his family out of joint. Because the real can never be recognized symbolically (except negatively), it always appears monstrous or utterly foreign. The negative insistence of the real within symbolization further explains the Gothic investment in the sublime and its capacity for negative revealing.

53. Dolar, "'I Shall be with You on Your Wedding Night,'" 7.

54. Ibid., 19.

55. In accord, Dale Townshend claims that Gothic enjoyment is much darker than its contemporary mainstream theories of aesthetic pleasure promulgated by Jeremy Bentham, David Hume, Joseph Priestly, Tamworth Revesby, Robert Lowth, et al. Townshend, *The Orders of the Gothic*, 254.

56. Alenka Zupančič, *The Shortest Shadow*, 76–7.

57. Slavoj Žižek, "'In His Bold Gaze My Ruin Is Writ Large,'" in *Everything You Always Wanted to Know About Lacan*, 239.

58. See Jacques Lacan, *The Four Fundamental Concepts of Psycho-analysis*, 56–64, 216–29.

59. Žižek, "'In His Bold Gaze My Ruin Is Writ Large,'" 239.

60. Dolar, "'I Shall be with You on Your Wedding Night,'" 19. David Punter even claims that the Gothic renders the uncanny incapable of interpretation or explanation. David Punter, "Shape and Shadow," 194. Likewise, Marshall Brown argues that the significance of a Gothic literary work always lies ahead of it, that it always means more than what is realized at the time (Marshall Brown, *The Gothic Text*, xix).

61. Lacan, *Seminar VII*, 130.

62. Horace Walpole, *The Castle of Otranto*, ed. W.S. Lewis (Oxford: Oxford University Press,

1996), 9. Hereafter cited parenthetically in text as *O*.

63. Angus Fletcher, *Allegory: The Theory of a Symbolic Mode*, 5.

64. Ibid., 3.

65. Quilligan, *The Language of Allegory*, 15.

66. For a late eighteenth-century distinction between the new novel and the lingering romance, see Clara Reeve, *The Progress of Romance*; James Beattie, *Dissertations Moral & Critical*, 505–74; Samuel Johnson, *The Rambler*, no. 4, in *Samuel Johnson: The Major Works*, 175–79; and Ioan Williams, ed., *Novel and Romance*.

67. David Punter has argued that the Gothic text terrifies, in part, because "the madness exemplified in the text may end up by removing some of our own usual life coordinates and leaving us adrift, the victims of a transgression which can no longer be healed" (David Punter, "Narrative and Psychology in Gothic Fiction," 7).

68. E.J. Clery, "The Genesis of 'Gothic' Fiction," 22. For more on this issue, see Clara McIntyre, "Were the 'Gothic Novels' Gothic?" 644–66; Alfred E. Longueil, "The Word 'Gothic' in Eighteenth-Century Criticism," 453–56; Frederick R. Karl, "Gothic, Gothicism, and Gothicists," 235–74; and Townshend, *The Orders of the Gothic*, 80–91.

69. Ibid., 23.

70. Nicholas Royle, *The Uncanny*, 13. This confusing of the imagination and reality parallels the confusion of the figurative and the literal in much Gothic language.

71. Barbara Fuchs, *Romance*, 38.

72. Frye, *The Secular Scripture*, 163.

73. Frederic Jameson, "Magical Narratives: Romance as Genre," 153.

74. Ibid., 154. While Jameson is mostly concerned with interrogating the ideological nature of romance as a literary form and how the archaic character of romance "suggests a nostalgia for a social order in the process of being undermined and destroyed by nascent capital," his essay displays an interest in moving away from the Marxist allegorical reading of texts and into an affinity with psychoanalysis (ibid., 158–59).

75. Frye, *The Secular Scripture*, 29.

76. Ibid., 53.

77. Ibid., 57. Frye also contends that romance conjures a world that is "older than history" yet "younger than the present moment" (ibid., 126). This seemingly paradoxical claim appropriately captures the persistence of not only the archaic in the Gothic but also the persistence of the primitive in the unconscious that is resurrected in the uncanny.

78. Anne Williams, *Art of Darkness*, 81.

79. Ibid., 81–82.

80. Ibid., 82.

81. Ibid.

82. The equation of romance and the primitive or childlike is echoed by numerous critics: Fuchs, *Romance*, 79; Frye, *Secular Scripture*, 51; Jameson, "Magical Narrative," 154; Erich Auerbach, *Mimesis: The Representation of Reality in Western Literature*, 133; Gillian Beer, *The Romance*, 8; Jean Radford, "Introduction," in *The Progress of Romance: The Politics of Popular Fiction*, ed. Jean Radford, 17; Ian Duncan, *Modern Romances and the Transformations of the Novel*, 16; David Fairer, "The Faerie Queen and Eighteenth-Century Spenserianism," 199; and David Punter, *Gothic Pathologies*, 13.

83. Williams, *Art of Darkness*, 82.

84. Slavoj Žižek, "Psychoanalysis This Side of the Hermeneutic Delirium," 140.

85. Anne Williams, 86.

86. Sigmund Freud, "Creative Writers and Day-Dreaming," in *SE*, vol. 9, 149.

87. Sigmund Freud, "Instincts and Their Vicissitudes," in *SE*, vol. 14, 117–40.

88. Mary Ann Doane, *Femme Fatales: Feminism, Film Theory*, 249.

89. Lacan, *Seminar VII*, 301.

90. One should point out that the German language does not normally extend the alchemical meaning of sublime into figurative uses as in English. Modern German uses of any of the derivatives of *sublim* are specifically chemical terms. (One will note that the chemical process of sublimation has to do with purifying a solid substance by directly transporting it into a gaseous substance, bypassing the intermediary liquid stage.) All aesthetic and figurative German terminology has historically been translated into native words: variations of *erhaben*. See Jan Cohn and Thomas H. Miles, "The Sublime: In Alchemy, Aesthetics and Psychoanalysis," 293. Oddly enough, only Goethe, Schopenhauer, and Nietzsche use the Latin *sublim* in an aesthetic context. *Erhaben* is the term Kant uses in his aesthetic investigation throughout the Third Critique and the term Freud uses in his one reference to the sublime in his aesthetic essay "The 'Uncanny.'" However, when Freud develops his idea of sublimation from "'Civilized' Sexual Morality" to *Civilization and Its Discontents*, he consistently uses the term *sublimierung*, borrowed from the "chemical-scientific vocabulary" (ibid., 301). So, at least in Freud, it appears that the sublime and sublimation, although sharing the same root meaning of "above the limit," deviate at some point — a point that might be initially characterized as the intersection of aesthetics and ethics. But Freud also considered his particular use of the term *sublimation* as unique, indicated by his italicizing of the term. In fact, in his 1908 paper "'Civilized' Sexual Morality and Modern Nervous Illness," when he claims that sublimation has to do with elevating desire to a purer aim, he be-

gins to sound like a number of eighteenth-century aesthetic theorists who claimed that that which is sublime is likewise lofty and elevated. Therefore, even though Freud consistently uses two different root words for the sublime and sublimation, this difference may be more a matter of linguistic custom than one of conceptual difference.

91. Lacan, *The Four Fundamental Concepts of Psychoanalysis*, 165.

92. Joan Copjec, "The Tomb of Perserverance: On *Antigone*," 251–2.

93. Ibid., 253. Edmund Bergler clams that "sublimation denotes an unconscious process of shifting psychic energy from something infantile and 'forbidden' to something culturally approved." Edmund Bergler, *The Writer and Psychoanalysis*, 19. In this manner, the Gothic literalizes the sublimation process by making an archaic and infantile form of literature culturally acceptable in an era that should have outgrown such childish nonsense.

94. Ibid.

Chapter 2

1. Michel Foucault, *Power/Knowledge: Selected Interviews & Other Writings*, 153.

2. Ibid., 154.

3. Michel Foucault, "What Is Enlightenment?" in *The Foucault Reader*, 39.

4. Ibid., 34.

5. Immanuel Kant, "What Is Enlightenment?" in *Immanuel Kant: Philosophical Writings*, 263.

6. Ibid.

7. Foucault perceptively realizes that these three criticisms pertain to the three challenges "what can be known," "what must be done," and "what may be hoped for" at the heart of Kant's three *Critiques*.

8. Kant, "What Is Enlightenment?" 264.

9. Ibid., 265.

10. Mladen Dolar, "The Legacy of the Enlightenment: Foucault and Lacan," 49.

11. The university's structural split automatically inhabits students the moment they attend college. Unlike secondary school, college students are not required by external authority to attend. If a student is not happy with the educational program, he or she can easily leave; there is no compulsion to attend. It is only when students are not compelled by external authority to attend school that they become utterly responsible for their own education. One no longer needs to give an excuse for missing class or not doing one's assignments. In a sense, there has to be some sort of arbitrariness of rule in order for academic freedom to exist.

12. Dolar, "The Legacy of the Enlightenment," 51.

13. Ibid., 46.

14. The Enlightenment, much like democracy and technology, is the cure for its own ills. In other words, the only cure for the problems caused by the Enlightenment is more enlightenment. Criticism of the Enlightenment project on any grounds itself paradoxically participates in the Enlightenment project. There appears to be no "outside" to the Enlightenment. But at the same time, it is far from a totalizing system. Its inherent contradiction, the rift of universality, is precisely what prevents the Enlightenment from slipping into a totalitarian endeavor. And it is because of this aspect of the Enlightenment that we have Freud as one of its greatest disciples.

15. The actual name "Oedipus complex" does not appear until 1910 in "Contributions to the Psychology of Love." The analysis and use of Sophocles's character shows up in letters to Fleiss dating from roughly three years before the publication of *The Interpretation of Dreams*, but by this time virtually the entire text was already complete.

16. Sigmund Freud, *The Interpretation of Dreams*, in *SE*, vol. 4, 262.

17. Ibid. It has been said that Oedipus is the only figure in history who never suffered from the Oedipus complex, making him truly anti–Oedipus. He neither wanted to kill his father nor marry his mother. These were retroactive projections that he never actually felt at the time of his actions. But, I would counter, this is precisely how the unconscious works. As Lacan argues, "The fact that Oedipus absolutely does not know that he has killed his father, nor that he causes his mother to enjoy, nor that he enjoys her, changes nothing about the question, since, precisely, it is a fine example of the unconscious" (Jacques Lacan, *The Seminar of Jacques Lacan, Book XVII: The Other Side of Psychoanalysis*, 114). Just like Oedipus, none of us, according to Freud, actually know we want to marry our mother and kill our father; one never realizes the structures of one's life. But unlike Oedipus, most of us do not actually fulfill this non-recognized desire. We merely set up some sort of enjoyable return, some form of surplus *jouissance*, for not fulfilling this desire. The unconscious only rears its head when it is too late. It is only when we do something we did not necessarily intend, like Oedipus, that we realize we did intend doing it. See also Cynthia Chase, "Oedipal Textuality: Reading Freud's Reading of Oedipus," in *Decomposing Figures: Rhetorical Readings in the Romantic Tradition*, 175–95.

18. This "no" is referred to by Lacan as the famous *nom-du-père*. Lacan's pun captures both the "no" of the father, the prohibition that sets up

alienation or primary repression, and the "name" of the father, the paternal signifier that introduces the symbolic order by instilling separation, or secondary repression. Of course with psychotics the "no" appears lacking. Likewise, with perverts and phobics, in different ways, the "no" is present without the paternal signifier making itself sufficiently felt. See Jacques Lacan, "The Function and Field of Speech and Language in Psychoanalysis," in *Écrits*, 230; Jacques Lacan, "On a Question Prior to Any Possible Treatment of Psychosis," in *Écrits*, 464–65; and Jacques Lacan, *The Seminar of Jacques Lacan, Book III: The Psychoses, 1955–1956*, 96, 193, 306.

19. At this point, I leave the complex process where one becomes a sexed subject in the Oedipal scenario, along with the Lacanian reading of the complex that goes with it, for the following chapters.

20. Freud, *The Interpretation of Dreams*, in *SE*, 4:263. It will be remembered that Oedipus himself gouges out his eyes at the end of the tragedy.

21. Sigmund Freud, *Totem and Taboo*, in *SE*, 13:126–7.

22. Joseph Addison, "*Spectator*, No. 419," in *Essays in Criticism and Literary Theory*, 170. "Nature" in the sense used here by Addison functions as a synonym for the probability and plausibility of realism, not to be confused with a Freudian use of "nature" as demarcating a pre–Oedipal or pre-symbolic realm.

23. Addison borrows this phrase from John Dryden.

24. Addison, "*Spectator*, No. 419," 171. Here, Addison is using the modifier "naturally" in a more Freudian fashion as referring to a time before the child was fully socialized, Oedipalized.

25. Ibid.

26. Ibid., 172.

27. Ibid.

28. Ibid.

29. Ibid., 173.

30. See Montague Summers, *The Gothic Quest: A History of the Gothic Novel*; Devendra Varma, *The Gothic Flame*; Linda Bayer-Bernbaum, *The Gothic Imagination*; Maggie Kilgour, *The Rise of the Gothic Novel*; and David H. Richter, *The Progress of Romance: Literary Historiography and the Gothic Novel*. Baldick and Mighall are very critical of this attempt to assimilate "Gothic fiction into romantic and pre-romantic nostalgia for the Middle Ages," calling it "one of the cardinal errors of Gothic Criticism" (Baldick and Mighall, "Gothic Criticism," 213). While they seem correct in criticizing critics like Summers and Varma for seeing the eighteenth-century Gothic as a revival of medieval spirituality, they fail to see the unconscious ambivalence inherent in Gothic writers' tendency "to display a thoroughly modern distrust of past centuries as ages of supersti-

tion and tyranny" (ibid., 213). For an analysis of the eighteenth-century Gothic's paradoxical and ambivalent marriage of contemporary Protestant ethics and medieval Catholic aesthetics, see Emma McEvoy, "Introduction," in Matthew Lewis, *The Monk*, vii–xxx.

31. For an analysis of the political uses of the term "Gothic" in late eighteenth-century Britain, see Robert Miles, "The 1790s: The Effulgence of the Gothic,"41–62.

32. Arthur Johnston, *Enchanted Ground: The Study of Medieval Romance in the Eighteenth Century*, 2.

33. Ibid.

34. Ibid., 4. The five literary historians of Johnston's study are Thomas Percy, Thomas Warton, Joseph Ritson, George Ellis and Walter Scott. Of the five, only Ritson was neither a literary writer nor an antiquarian.

35. For a further analysis of the shifting connotative meaning of the term "Gothic," the shifting cultural value allotted to the term "Gothic," and the shifting debate between the classical and the Gothic in the middle of the eighteenth century, see David Punter and Glennis Bryon, *The Gothic*, 7–12.

36. Johnston, *Enchanted Ground*, 21.

37. Incidentally, the more medieval romance was studied in the eighteenth century, the more it became clear that it owed its own origins to Eastern fables. It became believed by many that the drive for romance exhibited in the Middle Ages was something that was imported during the Crusades. Ibid., 55–6.

38. See also E. J. Clery, *The Rise of Supernatural Fiction*, 68–69; Richard Davenport-Hines, *Gothic: Four Hundred years of Excess, Horror, Evil and Ruin*, 133–34; Markman Ellis, *The History of Gothic Fiction*, 23–4; and David Punter and Glennis Bryon, *The Gothic*, 8–9.

39. Richard Hurd, *Letters on Chivalry and Romance*, 4.

40. Fred Botting, *Gothic*, 37.

41. Hurd, *Letters*, 2.

42. Ibid., 3.

43. Ibid., 88.

44. See Lacan's analysis of the story of Choang-tsu, the man who could not be sure if he was really a butterfly dreaming he was a man (Lacan, *The Four Fundamental Concepts of Psycho-analysis*, 73–77).

45. Hurd, *Letters*, 89.

46. Ibid., 95.

47. Freud's conception of repression was developed early in his career and was illustrated in his 1895 *Project for a Scientific Psychology*. In his Emma case, Freud discusses the latency inherent in repression. Emma, who was sexually molested in a shop as a child, later, after puberty, develops a fear of shopping. Since the symptomatic fear

appears temporally severed from the supposed event that is its cause — the sexual assault — Freud concludes that the sexual aspect of the original event only exists for Emma after she became sexually mature enough to recognize it. When the original event happened, she was still too young to understand the event's sexual content, its true traumatic aspect. Her normal everyday existence existed precisely because it was based on this event not being properly recognized as sexual. The event was not so much repressed as much as the everyday is based on repression. This is repression in the strictly Freudian sense. There is no repression until its return. Return, plain and simple, constitutes repression. And the Gothic novel, I would argue, brings the return back onto the same synchronic plane as the reality that is based on this exclusion (Sigmund Freud, "Project for a Scientific Psychology," in *SE*, 1:347–59.

48. Incidentally, by writing a critique of the nobility by way of an entertaining ghost story, Walpole is also able to get his message to the masses who might otherwise not be concerned with politics proper.

49. Hurd, *Letters*, 118.

50. Along with Hurd, the scholarly work of the Warton brothers on Pope and Spenser, Macpherson's Ossian poems and, perhaps, even Chatterton's faux antiquarian poetry indirectly led the way for the Gothic's fusing of romance's imagination with Richardson's realism.

51. Northrop Frye, *Anatomy of Criticism*, 186.

52. Margaret L. Carter, *Specter or Delusion?*, 7.

53. David Punter, *The Literature of Terror*, 53.

54. Freud, "The 'Uncanny,'" in *SE* 17:219.

55. Ibid., 220.

56. Only the English "uncanny" fully approximates the German *das Unheimlich*.

57. "'*The Zecks* [a family name] *are all 'heimlich.'" "'Heimlich'? ... What do you understand by 'heimlich'?*" "*Well ... they are like a buried spring or a dried-up pond. One cannot walk over it without always having the feeling that the water might come up there again.*" "*Oh we call it 'unheimlich'; you call it 'heimlich'*" (ibid., 223; italics in original).

58. Ibid., 224; italics in original. Later on in the paper when Freud again quotes Schelling's definition, he apparently erroneously credits the quotation to Schleiermacher. The editor perceptively catches Freud's mistake and corrects it, leaving the reader only a note explaining the error. Of course, it is easy, if not inevitable, for anyone, even Freud, to confuse one's eighteenth-century Friedrichs. But on closer examination, one can begin to speculate that Freud's original error may have been unconsciously deliberate. For in German "Schleiermacher" literally means "veil maker," itself a nice definition of the uncanny. As in the famous scene from *The Mysteries* *of Udolpho*, is not a veil perfect for highlighting what should remain hidden and secret? It might be perceived as unfortunate that this seldom-found slip in Freud's own writing went undetected as a specifically Freudian slip by his editors.

59. Ibid., 227.

60. E.T.A. Hoffman, *Tales of Hoffman*, 87. That the servants possess a stronger belief in the supernatural than the masters originates with *Otranto* and is itself a long-term convention of the Gothic by the time Hoffman wrote his tale.

61. Freud, "The 'Uncanny,'" in *SE* 17:228.

62. The metaleptic structure of Hoffman's narrative is patterned the same way as the *Nachtraglickeit* nature of an analysand's uncanny free association.

63. Terry Castle, *The Female Thermometer*, 215.

64. For a succinct analysis of how modernity begins with the "killing" off of patriarchy, a theory itself borrowed from Max Horkeimer, see Juliet Flower MacCannell, *The Regime of the Brother: After the Patriarchy*.

65. See Sigmund Freud, "A Seventeenth-Century Demonological Neurosis," in *SE*, vol. 19, ed. and trans. James Strachey (London: Hogarth, 1961), 69–105.

66. Freud, "The 'Uncanny,'" in *SE* 17:233.

67. Ibid., 236.

68. Freud relates an example from analytic experience that he feels provides a paradigmatic confirmation of his theory of the uncanny: "It often happens that neurotic men declare that they feel there is something uncanny about the female genital organs. This *unheimlich* place, however, is the entrance to the former *Heim* [home] of all human beings, to the place where each one of us lived once upon a time and in the beginning. There is a joke saying that 'Love is home-sickness'; and whenever a man dreams of a place or a country and says to himself, while he is still dreaming: 'this place is familiar to me, I've been here before,' we may interpret the place as being his mother's genitals or her body. In this case too, then, the *unheimlich* is what was once *heimisch*, familiar; the prefix '*un*' ['un-'] is the token of repression." Freud, "The 'Uncanny,'" in *SE* 17:245. This, of course, is how and why a house itself becomes inhabited by the uncanny. According to Darian Leader, because the homey is always imbued with a latent uncanny, we should recognize the inevitability of the haunted house: "If houses don't always come with ghosts, ghosts always come with houses" (Darian Leader, *Promises Lovers Make When It Gets Late*, 116).

69. Freud, "The 'Uncanny,'" in *SE* 17:242.

70. Julia Kristeva, in an attempt to ward off the subreption of evil, asserts: "To worry or to smile, such is the choice when we are assailed by

the strange; our decision depends on how familiar we are with our own ghosts" (Julia Kristeva, *Strangers to Ourselves*, 191).

71. Dolar, "I Shall Be with You on Your Wedding-Night," 6.

72. Lacan, *Seminar VII*, 139.

73. Ibid., 71. Jacques-Alain Miller is most responsible for the further elaboration of Lacan's concept of *extimité*. In his essay so titled, Miller explains that *extimité* (extimacy) designates, for Lacan, the problematic manner of the real in the symbolic. Further, this term allows Lacan, and psychoanalysis in general, to avoid the "common ravings about a psychism supposedly located in a bipartition between interior and exterior" (Jacques-Alain Miller, "*Extimité*," 75). With this term Lacan proposed to show how the exterior is present in the interior. For instance, within the analytic experience, the most interior (the intimate) takes on a more than normally obvious exteriority. By projecting the fantasy screen onto the site of the Other — in this case the analyst — transference dramatically displays how what is most intimate to the subject takes on an exterior significance. In *Seminar XIII: Le Transfert*, Lacan illustrates this aspect of the analytic experience through Plato's *Symposium*. Alcibiades compares Socrates to a plain box that encloses a precious object (agalma). Of course, for Lacan the precious object that Alcibiades attributes to Socrates is really the object most dear to Alcibiades himself. Through a sort of transferential relationship to Socrates, that which is most intimate to Alcibiades comes to be located in the essence of Socrates — what is in him more than him. But of course this object is, for Lacan, that which is in Alcibiades more than Alcibiades — his *objet a*, his object cause of desire. Following this logic, Miller claims that extimacy should not be seen as the contrary of intimacy. Extimacy is obviously something more; it is an actual combination of the intimate and the exterior. According to Miller, "Extimacy says that the intimate is Other — like a foreign body, a parasite" (ibid., 76). In this sense, Miller maintains that the extimacy of the subject is the Other. He quotes a relevant passage from Lacan's essay "The Agency of the Letter" about "this other to whom I am more attached than to myself, since, at the heart of my assent to my identity to myself, it is he who stirs me" (ibid., 77). This quote is used by Miller to justify his further claim that the extimacy of the Other is tethered to the vacillation of the subject's identity to itself. Whenever the Other is flattened out in order to be understood as something tangible — as in Christianity with the concept of "neighbor"— there is an attempt to nullify extimacy. One chooses the signifier over what is its own inconsistency. Following Lacan, there is no Other of the Other, so the signifier is

inadequate to the Other of extimacy. Rather, "jouissance is precisely what grounds the alterity of the Other when there is no Other of the Other" (ibid., 79). Since the law of the signifier implies that one can always be substituted for the other (and this is what symbolism does), it is hopeless in representing enjoyment as the zero-sum of signification. It is a denial of the realm of the real at the heart of the symbolic.

74. Although used in a different context, Todd McGowan's words seem to resonate here: "Fantasy fills in the gap that haunts the social reality, but in doing so reveals that there is something not encompassed by this reality — a traumatic real. The very fact that we must have recourse to fantasy — that the social reality doesn't satisfy us — testifies to the existence of a real that haunts our reality. If the social reality were without fissure, if it could account for everything, it would not have a fantastic underside. And the turn to fantasy, the transition, makes the real evident because it reveals, however briefly, the point of fissure within the social reality" (Todd McGowan, *The Impossible David Lynch*, 165). Even though McGowan is directly referring to the films of David Lynch, a most Gothic filmmaker, by substituting the term "romance" for "fantasy" and "realism" for "reality" above, McGowan's insight could directly pertain to the Gothic.

Chapter 3

1. Horace Walpole, *The Yale Edition of Horace Walpole's Correspondence*, 1:88.

2. Montague Summers, *The Gothic Quest*, 408.

3. Devendra Varma, *The Gothic Flame*, 9–10.

4. Ibid., 67.

5. Ibid.

6. Martin Kallich, *Horace Walpole*, 102.

7. Sigmund Freud, *The Interpretation of Dreams*, in *SE*, 5:552–3; italics in original. The deleted section of this citation may have more to say concerning *The Castle of Otranto* than meets the eye. It reads: "These wishes in our unconscious, ever on alert, and, so to say, immortal, remind one of the legendary Titans, weighed down since primaeval ages by the massive bulk of the mountains which were once hurled upon them by the victorious gods and which are still shaken from time to time by the convulsion of their limbs."

8. Kallich, *Horace Walpole*, 102.

9. Ibid.

10. Ibid.

11. At least on the level of homonyms, it would seem that Conrad more appropriately represents Conway. He also seems to be the one to whom tyranny has served a blow. Interestingly enough,

Conway was seen by Walpole, as far as his actions towards him testify, as a creature incapable of doing things for himself. Whether this was really the dominant feature of Conway's personality or whether it was how Walpole needed his cousin to be in order for him to be the object of Walpole's own desire is difficult to say. The fact that Conway used to make his wife break potentially upsetting news to Walpole indicates the former. But Walpole's wish to financially support his cousin indicates that Conway's feebleness was more a matter of Walpole's own fantasizing. For more on the possible homosexual relation between Walpole and Conway and *Otranto* as stemming from Walpole's public outing, see Timothy Mowl, *Horace Walpole: The Great Outsider*, 178–89.

12. Kallich, *Horace Walpole*, 103.

13. Ibid.

14. It is debatable whether Horace was even Sir Robert's son. Stephen Gwynn speculates that he was really the son of someone whom Lady Walpole had more tender feelings for than Sir Robert. This speculation furthers the rumor that Horace was the son of Lord Hervey, who died in 1723, making Horace's father more absent than suspected. See Stephen Gwynn, *The Life of Horace Walpole*, 16; and Mowl, *Horace Walpole: The Great Outsider*, 88–89.

15. John Samson, "Politics Gothicized: The Conway Incident and *The Castle of Otranto*," 157.

16. Ibid., 145; italics in original.

17. Ibid.

18. Even though Samson fails to point it out, one can see the bloody arrow-shaped birthmark on Theodore, through which Jerome recognizes him, as a figure for the wound Walpole inadvertently inflicted on Conway—a sort of stab in the back. "As he [Theodore] stooped, his shirt flipped down below his shoulder, and discovered the mark of a bloody arrow. Gracious heaven! Cried the holy man [Jerome] starting, what do I see? It is my child! my Theodore" (*O* 57). Much will be said later concerning the relationship between Walpole and Conway. Suffice it to say now that Walpole, in a sense, attempts, after the death of his mother, to treat his cousin as a dependent.

19. Samson, "Politics Gothicized," 149.

20. Ibid.

21. Ibid., 150.

22. Ibid., 152.

23. "A clap of thunder at that instant shook the castle to its foundations; the earth rocked, and the clank of more than mortal amour was heard behind" (*O* 112).

24. For a Lacanian account of this distinction between ontogenesis and phylogenesis, see Paul Verhaeghe, "Causation and Destitution of a Preontological Non-entity: On the Lacanian Subject," 164–89.

25. Betsy Perteit Harfst, *Horace Walpole and the Unconscious*, 107.

26. In all fairness, it should be noted that Harfst's text was originally written three years before Kallich's book was published.

27. "By splitting his own ego into two different people, Walpole's unconscious self could project his own contradictory emotions.... Conrad represents the sympathetic emotions of admiration and love while Matilda portrays the antagonistic impulses. In this way, Walpole has projected his own warring impulses onto separate characters" (Harfst, *Horace Walpole and the Unconscious*, 74).

28. Jacques Lacan, *Écrits: A Selection*, 197–98.

29. Sigmund Freud, "Three Essays on the Theory of Sexuality," in *SE*, 7:150.

30. Jacques Lacan, "On Freud's '*Trieb*' and the Psychoanalyst's Desire," 418.

31. Lacan, of course, refers to this little object as the imaginary phallus as opposed to the symbolic phallus instilled by the Name-of-the-Father. In perversion, since the child recognizes that the mother lacks the phallus, he, in turn, literally becomes this object for the mother and, therefore, never completes castration. I will use the masculine pronoun throughout this analysis of perversion.

32. Jacques-Alain Miller, "On Perversion," 319.

33. For a careful analysis of this phenomenon in perversion, see Octave Mannoni, "'I Know Well, but All the Same...,'" 68–92.

34. If one reads the Genesis story of Adam and Eve's dilemma in the Garden of Eden as a myth of the origin of language, God's "no" in relation to the tree of knowledge is this same "no." God simply lays down the "no" necessary for alienation without naming why they cannot eat from the tree. Paradoxically enough, separation only came for the couple once they consumed fruit from the prohibited tree. This violation, in turn, gave Adam and Eve the knowledge necessary to name God's "no" as a prohibition. It also separated humankind from nature and God for good. Had Adam and Eve not succumbed to temptation, they would have remained stuck between alienation and separation. Stuck in this perverse space, they would have known full well what they were for God—that which fills in his lack. They would, perhaps, have remained what God created them to be: complete devotionals.

35. Bruce Fink, *A Clinical Introduction to Lacanian Psychoanalysis: Theory and Technique*, 165.

36. Ibid., 172.

37. Ibid., 173–4.

38. Ibid., 177.

39. Ibid.; italics in original.

40. This is why many neurotics think perverts enjoy (sex) more than they do. Neurotics have a difficult, if not impossible, time locating the ob-

ject that gets them off; it is by definition lost. The pervert, on the other hand, knows exactly what and where this object is. But the idea that the pervert somehow enjoys more than the rest of us, whether one is fascinated or disgusted with the pervert's enjoyment, is the neurotic fantasy *par excellence.*

41. Fink, *A Clinical Introduction,* 174.

42. Harfst, *Horace Walpole and the Unconscious,* 30.

43. Horace Walpole, "Walpole-Conway Letters," in *The Works of Horatio Walpole, Earl of Orford.* Cited in Harfst, *Horace Walpole and the Unconscious,* 28–9, 34.

44. Quoted in Harfst, *Horace Walpole and the Unconscious,* 37. Whether or not Lady Walpole herself suffered from what is today called Munchausen's by proxy, a nominal euphemism for the only form of female perversion, is up for speculation. Lacan, in fact, maintains that "the male sex [is] the weak sex in the case of perversion," precisely because, with women, there does not exist a "privileged place of jouissance" as there does with the male sex. As we shall see in the following chapters, the *objet a* plays a much more significant function on the male side of sexual difference than on the Other side (Jacques Lacan, "The Subversion of the Subject and the Dialectic of Desire in the Freudian Unconscious," *Écrits: A Selection,* 320).

45. This rivalry with his father, Sir Robert, is signified in Walpole's "willful perversity" in his "tactful evasion of his indifference" to the Palladian architecture of Houghton, Sir Robert's estate. According to Mowl, this "willful perversity" is responsible for Walpole's construction of his pseudo–Gothic Strawberry Hill, in direct rivalry with his father's more neo-classical architectural tastes (Mowl, *Horace Walpole: The Great Outsider,* 36–37).

46. Harfst, *Horace Walpole and the Unconscious,* 52.

47. Fink, *A Clinical Introduction,* 174. This conclusion drawn by Fink is concerning Freud's little Hans.

48. Freud, "The 'Uncanny,'" in *SE* 17:236.

49. One could argue that Walpole waited three more years until his first drama, *The Mysterious Mother,* before he attempted to approach perversion on a more thematic level.

50. For evidence of the former, see the unsigned review in *Critical Review,* January 1765. For an example of the latter, see John Langhorne's two unsigned reviews in *Monthly Review,* February 1765 and May 1765. All three are reprinted in *Horace Walpole: The Critical Heritage,* ed. Peter Sabor.

51. Sigmund Freud, "An Outline of Psychoanalysis," in *SE,* 23:204.

52. Walpole's claim that there is such a thing as modern romance intimates a critique of the authority of contemporary realist aesthetics. If the eighteenth-century novel is merely a modern type of romance, where is its realism in relation to the fantasy of the Middle Ages? Is eighteenth-century realism just the particular fantasy of the Age of Enlightenment?

53. For an analysis of how *Otranto*'s famous prefaces subvert the eighteenth century's attempt to gothicize English law generally and Blackstone's *Commentaries* specifically, see Sue Chapin, "'Written in Black Letter,'" 47–68.

54. It should be noted that only with the publication of the second edition of *Otranto* (the one where Walpole reveals himself as both author and fabricated translator) is "A Gothic Story" appended as a new subtitle. Even though it was originally published as a supposed long lost relic from the Middle Ages, it does not become properly Gothic until it is revealed as a modern dabbling in the aestheticization of medieval style. As E. J. Clery notes in her introduction to *Otranto,* "There is a dislocation: 'Gothic' is no longer a historical description; it marks the initiation of a new genre" (*O* xv). To take Clery's observation one step further, one would have to admit that "Gothic" never belongs to the past proper; rather, it only ever marks a "dislocation," to use Clery's term, of the modern. "Gothic" may take the form of some sort of a nostalgic reaction to the modern, but it really only marks, perhaps just more indisputably than any other form, the seamy side of the modern from within the modern.

55. Freud, "The 'Uncanny,'" in *SE* 17:244.

56. These supernatural events from the romance are respectively recorded in the following manner: "But what a sight for a father's eyes!— He beheld his child dashed to pieces, and almost buried under an enormous helmet, a hundred times more large than any casque ever made for human being" (*O* 19); "No, no, said Diego, and his hair stood on end — it is a giant, I believe; he is all clad in armour, for I saw his foot and part of his leg, and they are as large as the helmet below in the court" (*O* 35); "As they made the circuit of the court to return toward the gate, the gigantic sword burst from the supporters, and falling to the ground opposite to the helmet, remained immoveable" (*O* 66); "But I heard the rattling of amour; for all the world such a clatter, as Diego says he heard when the giant turned him about in the gallery-chamber ... cried Bianca" (*O* 103).

57. Paul de Man, it will be remembered, called this kind of confusing the materiality of the signifier with the materiality of what it signifies "ideology at its purest" (Paul de Man, "The Resistance to Theory," 11).

58. George Haggerty refers to the normativity of Manfred's paternal power as itself a perversion (George E. Haggerty, *Queer Gothic,* 25).

59. Lacan, "On Freud's '*Trieb*' and the Psycho-analyst's Desire," 419.

60. Jacques-Alain Miller, "Commentary on Lacan's Text," 426.

61. In the preface to the second edition of the *Old English Baron*, Reeve specifically validates her novel as the literary offspring of *The Castle of Otranto*. She further claims that her novel is an attempt, on her part, to correct what she calls the violent machinery of Walpole's most improbable romance. Reeve, in a sense, feels a need to relinquish the redundancy of the marvelous in order to relegate the enjoyment associated with the sublime within the limits of credibility (Clara Reeve, *The Old English Baron: A Gothic Story*, 3).

62. Ronald Paulson, "Gothic Fiction and the French Revolution," 532–54. This conclusion of Paulson's seems to make the *ancien regime*, the period of Walpole's writing, a sort of Gothic past of the true Gothic of the 1790s.

63. Anne Williams, *Art of Darkness*, 9–10.

64. Ibid., 11.

65. See Sigmund Freud, *Three Essays on the Theory of Sexuality*, in *SE* vol. 7.

66. Plato, *Symposium*, in *Lysis, Phaedrus, and Symposium*, 121.

67. Jacques Lacan, "On a Question Preliminary to any possible treatment of Psychosis," *Écrits: A Selection*, 197.

Chapter 4

1. In the preface to the second edition of *The Old English Baron*, Reeve, while claiming her novel as the "literary offspring of the Castle of Otranto, written on the same plan," emphasizes her calculated avoidance of what she calls the violent machinery of her novel's progenitor (Reeve, *The Old English Baron*, 3–6). Walpole, in a letter to William Mason, written the year the second edition of Reeve's novel was published, asks: "Have you seen *The Old English Baron*, a Gothic story, professedly written in imitation of *Otranto*, but reduced to reason and probability! It is so probable, that any trial for murder at the Old Bailey would make a more interesting story" (Walpole, *The Letters of Horace Walpole* 10:216–17). And nine months later, apparently still steamed by Reeve's overzealous genealogy, in a letter to Robert Jephson, Walpole complains, "I cannot compliment the author of *The Old English Baron*, professedly written in imitation, but as a corrective of *The Castle of Otranto*. It was totally void of imagination and interest; had scarce any incidents; and, though it condemned the marvelous, admitted a ghost. I suppose the author thought a tame ghost might come within the laws of probability" (Walpole, *Letters of Horace Walpole* 11:113).

2. Miss Aikin is, of course, the maiden name of Anna Laetitia Barbauld, who, in 1773, a year before her marriage, published *Sir Bertrand, a Fragment*, appended with the introductory essay "On the Pleasure derived from Objects of Terror." These two pieces were contained in the larger collaborative collection J. and A. L. Aikin, *Miscellaneous Pieces in Prose*.

3. Aikin, *Miscellaneous Pieces in Prose*, 123.

4. Ibid.

5. Ibid.

6. Ibid.

7. Ibid.

8. Ibid.

9. Ibid., 126.

10. Ibid., 127.

11. Ibid., 132.

12. In the same letters where Walpole complains about Reeve's imitation of *Otranto*, he has only praise for the acute observation of Aikin. "Miss Aikin flattered me even by stooping to tread in my eccentric steps. Her *Fragment*, though but a specimen, showed her talent for imprinting terror" (Walpole, *Letters of Horace Walpole*, XI: 113). Robert Miles argues that the Gothic of the 1790s deviates and makes new what Walpole had begun in 1764 (Miles, "The 1790s: The Effulgence of the Gothic," 58).

13. Ann Radcliffe, *The Mysteries of Udolpho*, 243.

14. Ibid., 512.

15. Ann Radcliffe, "On the Supernatural in Poetry," 149. Since many of the Gothic novelists were women, Radcliffe's use of "men" in this passage cannot be wholly accounted for by custom. As one will see, the distinction between "terror" and "horror" narratives becomes drawn around the lines of sexual difference.

16. Ibid.

17. Anne Williams draws a parallel between the narrative devices used by Radcliffe and Alfred Hitchcock: "As Alfred Hitchcock knew very well, what is implied but not shown is often far more disturbing than what the audience may actually see, no matter how expert the special effects" (Williams, *Art of Darkness*, 73).

18. Marquis De Sade, "Reflections on the Novel," in *The 120 Days of Sodom and Other Writings*, 108–9.

19. Ibid., 109.

20. Ibid.

21. Ibid.

22. Ibid.

23. Fred Botting, *Gothic*, 10.

24. Ibid.

25. Ibid., 64.

26. Ibid., 65.

27. Ibid., 76.

28. In his treatise-length study of the uncanny, Nicholas Royle makes a critique of the "explained

supernatural" similar to Botting's: "The uncanny is quite different from the gothic scenario in which (to quote Clery) 'apparently supernatural occurrences are spine-chillingly evoked only to be explained away in the end as the product of natural causes.' As I have been trying to suggest, the uncanny entails a sort of trembling of what is 'natural': it is an involuntary query, the experience of a hesitation and suspension concerning the very nature of the explicable" (Royle, *The Uncanny*, 30). As I am trying to argue, the explained supernatural, as perfected by Radcliffe and imitated by many other Gothic writers, produces the very "trembling," "hesitation" and "suspension" in the face of the inexplicable that Royle sees as the hallmark of an encounter with the uncanny. The "qualities of feeling," to use the words of Freud, evoked by the uncanny are those unleashed on both the character and the reader of the feminine Gothic. These feelings may dissolve at the end of the narrative when the supernatural is explained away, but they leave behind the uncanny curiosity (the "involuntary query" of which Royle speaks) for the reader as to why he or she felt these terrifying or titillating feelings over nothing. The explained supernatural may make the inexplicable in the text (castle groans, mysterious lights) explicable, but it provokes the reader and character to examine what it is in themselves that made them overreact and thereby produce a secondary, truly uncanny, inexplicable phenomenon. Unlike the masculine Gothic's externalization of the supernatural, the feminine explained supernatural forces reader and character alike to encounter something strange about themselves.

29. Frederick S. Frank, *The First Gothics: A Critical Guide to the English Gothic Novel*, xxvi.

30. Ibid., xvi.

31. This reading tends to show that Jane Austen's *Northanger Abbey* is less a parody than a copy of Radcliffe's work.

32. Frank, *The First Gothics*, xvi.

33. Edmund Burke, *A Philosophical Enquiry into the Origin of Our Ideas of the Sublime and Beautiful*, 103.

34. Ibid., 117–18.

35. David B. Morris, "Gothic Sublimity," 300.

36. Ibid.

37. Ibid.

38. Vijay Mishra, *The Gothic Sublime*, 80.

39. Samuel H. Monk, *The Sublime: A Study of Critical Theories in Eighteenth-Century England*, 6. Even though Kant's *Critique of Judgment* was first published in 1790, I use the term "anticipate" because no English translation existed until after the 1790s heyday of English Gothic fiction. I also use the term "anticipate" because the Gothic novelists of the 1790s, being fiction writers, are only interested in the limits of the imagination and

are not really concerned as much as Kant is with the ideas of reason.

40. Immanuel Kant, *The Critique of Judgment*, 130–31.

41. Ibid.,131–2.

42. Frances Ferguson claims that Burke's attempt to construct a version of scientific empiricism in order to set up a universal faculty of taste violates empiricism's most basic tenets. On one level, this maneuver offers Burke a defense against the charge that his ideas of the sublime and beautiful are merely his ideas, but, on the other hand, it all but invalidates the need for empirical evidence (Ferguson, *Solitude and the Sublime*, 41).

43. Kant, *The Critique of Judgment*, 90–1.

44. Ibid., 92.

45. Ibid., 93.

46. Ibid., 98.

47. Slavoj Žižek, *Tarrying with the Negative*, 47. Later in his text, Žižek further states: "In the Kantian Sublime, the boundless chaos of sensible experience (raging storm, breathtaking abysses) renders forth the presentiment of the pure Idea of Reason whose Measure is so large that no object of experience, not even nature in the wildest and mightiest display of its forces, can come close to it" (ibid., 248).

48. Kant, *The Critique of Judgment*, 119.

49. Jacques Lacan, *The Seminar of Jacques Lacan, Book XX*, 3.

50. Žižek, *Tarrying with the Negative*, 49; italics in original.

51. Alenka Zupančič, "The Logic of the Sublime," 59–60.

52. Ibid., 55.

53. As Gary Farnell points out, the Lacanian "Thing" is "a reworking of Kant's unknowable *Ding an sich*" (Farnell, "The Gothic and the Thing," 113).

54. Exposing the unfathomable is precisely the function of sublimation, psychoanalytically conceived. See Slavoj Žižek, "Surplus-Enjoyment Between the Sublime and Trash," 99–107.

55. See Jacques Lacan, "Kant with Sade," in *Écrits*, 645–68.

56. This defining purpose of the sublime is borrowed from Zupančič, "The Logic of the Sublime."

57. For a critique of the functionalist capacity of aesthetic works, see Terry Eagleton, *The Ideology of the Aesthetic*, 64–5.

58. Kant, *The Critique of Judgment*, 98; italics in original.

59. Ibid., 99.

60. Ibid., 101.

61. Ibid., 103; italics in original.

62. Lacan writes: "You know how much fun analysts have had with Don Juan, whom they have described in every possible way, including as a homosexual, which really takes the cake. But

center him on what I just illustrated for you, this space of sexual jouissance covered by open sets that constitute a finitude and that can, in the end, be counted. Don't you see that what is essential in the feminine myth of Don Juan is that he has them one by one" (Jacques Lacan, *Seminar XX,* 10). The relation between the mathematical and the feminine will be worked out below.

63. For an infinitely valuable reading of Don Juan, see Alenka Zupančič, "Kant with Don Juan and Sade," 105–25.

64. Don Juan is killed in the end because, as a feminine fantasy, he finds himself traversed onto the realm of the symbolic, the domain of the Law, which must regulate enjoyment.

65. Kant, *The Critique of Judgment,* 106.

66. Ibid., 108.

67. Ibid., 111.

68. Ibid.

69. The emergence of the dynamical sublime summons in us the feeling of our own insignificance in view of the whole of the universe, making the center of our existence insignificant. The sacrificing something of oneself, if not one's self, should be read as the diminishing of our ego in the face of the super-ego. The domination the subject feels over himself and the benefit that comes along with the sacrifice is tantamount to the surplus enjoyment associated with the super-ego. According to Zupančič, the super-ego forces "the subject, in spite of all the demands of reality, to act contrary to his well-being, to renounce his interests, needs, pleasure, and all that binds him to the sensitive world" (Alenka Zupančič, "The Logic of the Sublime," 11). Since this type of sentiment appears masculine, it might explain why Freud claimed that women suffered from a weaker sense of the super-ego.

70. Joan Copjec, *Read My Desire: Lacan against the Historicists,* 206.

71. Ibid., 213.

72. Ibid., 213.

73. Lacan, *Seminar XX,* 56–7.

74. Immanuel Kant, *Critique of Pure Reason,* 302.

75. Copjec, *Read My Desire,* 228.

76. Lacan, *Seminar XX,* 79.

77. Ibid., 79.

78. Ibid., 80.

79. Ibid.

80. I have decided to stick with Lacan's French symbols rather than designating *Autre* as "O."

81. Lacan, *Seminar XX,* 80.

82. Copjec, *Read My Desire,* 221.

83. Ibid., 225.

84. Ibid., 227.

85. Kant, *Critique of Judgment,* 108; italics added.

86. Ibid., 109.

87. Ibid., 115; italics added.

88. Copjec, *Read My Desire,* 235.

89. This, of course, is the sublime's connection to sublimation, especially if sublimation is understood as making something valuable that was not previously valued by exposing what is beyond the pleasure principle. The rest of this chapter will outline how these two modes of the sublime and the feelings they respectively evoke not only coincide with the Gothic sublime's distinction between terror and horror, but also how they correspond to Freud's two major forms of neurotic pathology: hysteria and obsessional neurosis.

90. Maggie Kilgour, *The Rise of the Gothic Novel,* 37.

91. Ibid., 38. Kilgour bases this claim on the aesthetic distinction inaugurated in Terry Eagleton, *Marxism and Literary Criticism.*

92. Ibid., 150.

93. Freud also makes this distinction between a primary anxiety and a secondary fear, between an internal and a projected external fear in *The Future of an Illusion:* "If the elements have passions that rage as they do in our own souls, if death itself is not something spontaneous but the violent act of an evil Will, if everywhere in nature there are Beings around us of a kind that we know in our own society, then we can breathe freely, can feel at home in the uncanny and can deal by psychical means with our senseless anxiety. We are still defenseless, perhaps, but we are no longer helplessly paralysed; we can at least react" (Sigmund Freud, "The Future of an Illusion," in *SE,* 21:16–17).

94. Williams, *Art of Darkness,* 72.

95. Ibid.

96. Ibid., 79.

97. Ibid., 76.

98. Ibid., 72. This misreading on Williams's part may stem from the fact that she relies on Kristeva's notion of the semiotic process, which is essentially a conflation of the Lacanian imaginary and real.

99. Ibid., 59.

100. Because Williams reads the "paternal order" of the symbolic as complete, her argument lapses into the usual misunderstanding of the gaze. In her easy characterization of Lacan as "the most recent of theorists to emphasize the power and importance of the gaze," Williams claims that through his metaphor of the "mirror stage," which represents the formation of a divided self, Lacan's theory of the gaze is implicitly male. Williams's exact words: "Lacan is only the most recent of theorists to emphasize the power and importance of the gaze as a sign of identity. His metaphor of the 'mirror stage' represents the formation of a self inevitably divided. While the mirror reflects a subject that is apparently unified and whole, the image is already split from the subject perceiving its own image: to be a self is

to be an alien and alienated. But the gaze so constituted is implicitly male, implicitly patriarchal" (ibid., 108). Although she is correct to contend that the "gaze so constituted" is invariably a male gaze, she assumes it is Lacan, and not herself, who constitutes the gaze as such. There may be no question that the gaze is male, that the male possesses the gaze, and that women become the object of this gaze, but there is a fundamental question of whether or not the gaze actually exists. Lacan's answer, of course, is that it does not. Because Williams uses Lacan's "mirror stage" to briefly develop a notion of the patriarchal gaze, she inevitably confuses what for Lacan is merely an imaginary image with the gaze. The gaze, as Lacan insists, is not constituted by how I see myself, nor by how others see me (Williams's notion of the gaze), but by how I see others seeing me — "a given-to-be-seen" (Jacques Lacan, *The Four Fundamental Concepts of Psychoanalysis*, 74). The gaze not only posits the Other, it is wholly virtual. What Williams simply forgets about the gaze, as Petit Jean points out to Lacan apropos the sardine can, is that "*it doesn't see you!*" (ibid., 95). Not only is its existence a strictly virtual existence — only possible because the symbolic order is never complete — but the gaze is the embodiment of the fundamental incompleteness of the symbolic. The symbolic order, then, is only oppressive for the subject to the extent that it does not offer guaranteed protection against the onslaught of enjoyment. The Gothic romances of Radcliffe and Lewis do not so much offer a radical critique of the "Symbolic" order from the "edge," as it were, as they do simply illustrate the insufficiency of the symbolic, to borrow the words of Lacan, to "say it all" (Jacques Lacan, *Television: A Challenge to the Psychoanalytic Establishment*, 3).

101. Bruce Fink, *The Lacanian Subject: Between Language and Jouissance*, 106.

102. Jacques Lacan, *Ecrits: A Selection*, 319.

103. Ibid., 324.

104. Sigmund Freud, "The Dissolution of the Oedipus Complex," in *SE*, 19:179.

105. Ibid.

106. Fink, *The Lacanian Subject*, 118.

107. "And why did Freud fall into the error at this point, whereas, if my analysis of today is to be believed, he only had literally to chew over what was being hand-fed to him? Why did he substitute this myth, the Oedipus complex, for the knowledge that he gathered from all these mouths of gold, Anna, Emma, Dora?" (Jacques Lacan, *Seminar XVII*, 113). Anna, Emma, and Dora, of course, were three of Freud's more famous hysterics.

108. For the neurotic, the *nom-du-père* is simultaneously the "no" uttered by the father and the "name" given to the mother's desire. Technically, if one hears both "no" and "name" in the

nom, one falls into a neurotic structure. As we saw in the last chapter, if one only hears the "no" and disavows the "name," one becomes perverse.

109. Men, in a sense, know where they "get off." Lacan states, "An equivalence is therefore drawn, in Freudian terms, between the dead father and *jouissance*. It is he who keeps it in reserve, if I can put it like that" (Lacan, *Seminar XVII*, 123). Enjoyment, for men, is locatable beyond the prohibition that was set up by the murder of the primal father.

110. The father's prohibition is, in fact, the emergence of the superego. This will explain, contra certain feminist complaints, why Freud thought that women do not have a very developed superego.

111. Lacan, *Seminar XVII*, 101.

112. Ibid., 123.

113. It will be recalled that both Lacan's notion of masculine sexuality and Kant's dynamical sublime are articulated around a prohibition. Likewise, Lacan's notion of feminine sexuality and Kant's mathematical sublime are articulated around a fundamental impossibility.

114. That there is a pre-symbolic entity like the Primal Father–enjoyer, the non-lacking Mother, the exceptional Lady or plentitude of enjoyment beyond the prohibition is just a masculine fantasy. See Slavoj Žižek, "'Woman is one of the names-of-the-father' or, How Not to Misread Lacan's Formulas of Sexuation," 24–39.

115. Lacan, *Seminar XVII*, 123.

116. For an account of the subtle distinction between psychosis and the Other *jouissance*, see Linda Belau's unpublished manuscript, *Encountering Jouissance: Trauma, Psychosis, and Psychoanalysis*.

117. Žižek, "'Woman is one of the names-of-the-father,'" 26.

118. Fink, *The Lacanian Subject*, 197.

119. Fink, *A Clinical Introduction to Lacanian Psychoanalysis*, 128.

120. Sigmund Freud, "The Aetiology of Hysteria," in *SE*, 3:210.

121. Colette Soler, "Hysteria and Obsession," in *Reading Seminars I and II*, 251.

122. Freud, "The Aetiology of Hysteria"; and "Obsessions and Phobias: Their Psychical Mechanism and Their Aetiology," in *SE*, 3:71–84.

123. See Jacques Lacan, *Seminar III*, 173–182.

124. Lacan. *Seminar VII*, 109.

125. Ibid., 112.

126. Alenka Zupančič, *The Shortest Shadow*, 165.

127. Jacques Lacan, *Seminar VII*, 301.

128. Jacques Lacan, *Seminar X: Anxiety*, Unpublished Seminar, March 13, 1963.

129. See Jan Cohn and Thomas H. Miles, "The Sublime: In Alchemy, Aesthetics and Psychoanalysis," 289.

130. Zupančič, *The Shortest Shadow*, 180.

Chapter 5

1. Robert Whytt, *Observation on the Nature, Causes, and Cure of Those Disorders which have been commonly called Nervous, Hypochondriac, or Hysteric: To which is prefixed Remarks on the Sympathy of the Nerves,* 206–07.

2. William Cullen, *First Lines in the Practice of Physic,* 121.

3. Ilza Veith, *Hysteria: The History of a Disease,* 178.

4. Claudia Iddan argues that "to believe in the words of love, in something they say to the subject that concerns its whole being, creates a path that enables it to approach what rests beyond any signification and concerns it as the 'subject' of drive." She concludes, "Indeed, symptom and love overlap in such a way, that love turns the symptom into a social function" (Claudia Iddan, "Symptom and Love—Points of Suspension," 106). This claim intimates what will be illustrated below, namely, that love functions in the female Gothic as a mode of desublimatory sublimation.

5. Sigmund Freud, "Family Romances," in *SE,* 9:237.

6. Ibid., 240.

7. Ibid., 241.

8. According to Bruce Fink, neurosis is characterized by the instating of the paternal function, the assimilation of the essential structure of language, the primacy of doubt over certainty, considerable inhibition of the drives, the tendency to find more pleasure in fantasy than in direct sexual contact, the mechanism of repression as opposed to disavowal or foreclosure, and the return of the repressed from within in the form of symptoms (Bruce Fink, *A Clinical Introduction to Lacanian Psychoanalysis,* 112). Unlike the pervert who acts as the object of the Other's enjoyment, the neurotic acts as that which wards off the Other's enjoyment. Because of sexual difference, the neurotic takes up either the hysterical or obsessional position. In hysteria—the topic of the present chapter—the subject undergoes a forgetting of thought that results in an accompanied persistence of affect. In obsessional neurosis, however, a persistent thought is present but is divorced from any affect whatsoever. In obsessional neurosis, therefore, the repressed returns in the mind as "impure" thoughts. In hysteria, the repressed returns on the body as a psychosomatic symptom.

To fully explain the structural difference between the two neuroses, Fink draws a distinction between the fundamental fantasy pertaining to each. Since the fundamental fantasy develops as a pathological defense against the encroachment of enjoyment (*jouissance*—that which was given up upon the entry into language), it is inaugurated as a reaction to castration. Therefore, Fink uses the simplified Freudian figure of the mother's breast—the infant's primary source of satisfaction—to illustrate the fundamental difference between a hysterical and an obsessional reaction to enjoyment. Initially, the infant draws no distinction between itself and the breast; it simply sees the breast as part of itself. Since it has yet to apprehend objects, the world exists as a big blob—unobstructed enjoyment. Once the infant proceeds through the "mirror stage," once the infant notices a distinction between itself and its mother, it can never have full access to its own satisfaction again. The initial satisfaction, Fink points out, was tied to a time prior to the self-other, or subject-object, distinction. With separation comes loss. But, as Fink is quick to point out, it is not so much the mother that the child loses in separation as the erotic object, the object that provided so much pleasure.

The child compensates for this loss by developing unconsciously the fundamental fantasy which promises something as compensation. The obsessional's fantasy overcomes separation by taking the breast as the object cause of desire. The obsessional refuses to acknowledge the breast as belonging to the Other, thereby refusing to recognize the Other's existence. In the hysteric's fundamental fantasy, according to Fink, separation is overcome "as the subject constitutes herself, not in relation to the erotic object she herself has 'lost,' but as the object the Other is missing" (ibid., 120). Unlike the obsessional who registers the loss as its own, the hysteric registers the loss on the side of the Other. She senses that the Other is somehow incomplete, and she therefore seeks to become that object necessary to fill out the Other's incompleteness. As far as the male is concerned, castration points to his own incompleteness. Castration for the female, however, points out the fundamental incompleteness of the Oedipal project itself: "The obsessive attempts to overcome or reverse the effects of separation on the subject, whereas the hysteric attempts to overcome or reverse the effects of separation on the *Other*" (ibid., 120). Because psychic reality, not material reality, is the decisive constituent of neurosis, fantasy always displays the wish fulfillment of a recovered plentitude, the recovery of what the neurotic lost upon acquiring the ability and need to fantasize. For the obsessional, fantasy fills in a self-lack while fantasy, for the hysteric, compensates for the lack in the Other. It must, of course, be kept in mind that the breast only becomes the object cause of desire once it is symbolized; that is, once it is lost and only exists as lost. According to Darian Leader, "the breast is not an original primary object, but takes on its value *as* a primary object due to the symbolic background in which the child relates to it" (Darian Leader, *Promises Lovers Make,* 157; italics in original).

9. Ann Radcliffe, *A Sicilian Romance*; italics added. Hereafter cited parenthetically in the text as *SR*.

10. That *Civilization and Its Discontents* should be read as Freud's Gothic romance has been argued by Mark Edmundson (*Nightmare on Main Street*, 34–36). Reading *The Interpretation of Dreams* as Freud's Gothic romance is the subject of Robert Young, "Freud's Secret: *The Interpretation of Dreams* Was a Gothic Novel," 206–31.

11. Sigmund Freud, "Fragment of an Analysis of a Case of Hysteria," in *SE*, 7:18.

12. Ibid., 40.

13. Ibid., 120.

14. Slavoj Žižek, *The Sublime Object of Ideology*, 187.

15. Darian Leader, *Why Women Write More Letters Than They Send*, 4.

16. Ibid.

17. In *Seminar XI*, Lacan says, "Man's desire is the desire of the Other" (Jacques Lacan, *The Four Fundamental Concepts of Psychoanalysis*, 235). Even though Lacan does not explicitly make this statement about the hysteric, my claim is that Lacan is indeed referring to the hysterical nature of human desire.

18. Jacques Lacan, *Feminine Sexuality*, 67. See also, Jacques Lacan, *Seminar XVII*, 96–97.

19. For the woman's lack of *savoir-faire* concerning femininity, see Collette Soler, *What Lacan Said about Women: A Psychoanalytic Study*.

20. Leader, *Why Women Write More Letters Than They Send*, 7.

21. Freud, "Fragment of an Analysis of a Case of Hysteria," in *SE* 7:96.

22. For an argument indicating that Austen based Elinor and Marianne Dashwood from *Sense and Sensibility* on Radcliffe's Emilia and Julia Mazzini, see Elizabeth Nollen, "Ann Radcliffe's *A Sicilian Romance*: A New Source for Jane Austen's *Sense and Sensibility*," 30–37; and Nelson C. Smith, "Sense, Sensibility and Ann Radcliffe," 577–90.

23. In her intriguing inter-textual reading of *A Sicilian Romance*, Ruth Bienstock Anolik claims, "in the real, natural world in which women live, the human male is a far greater threat than any supernatural presence" (Ruth Bienstock Anolik, "'There Was a Man': Dangerous Husbands and Fathers in *The Winter's Tale*, *A Sicilian Romance* and *Linden Hills*," 87).

24. Radcliffe offers the reader a clue to Julia's affinity with that which is excessive to the domestic realm by describing this excessiveness as terror-producing. While it is true that Radcliffe appears to use the terms "terror" and "horror" interchangeably and indiscriminately in this early romance, one can, on closer scrutiny, observe precisely how she uses each term quite strategically. For instance, during all the late-night episodes

when the southern wing of the castle becomes spectrally animated, the narrative consistently describes the characters' affect as overcome with terror. Terror, much aligned with the concept of anxiety, springs from an unknown source. On the other hand, horror, as used by Radcliffe's narrative, usually arises as a feeling of repugnance toward something one encounters. When Julia's brother Ferdinand queries his father regarding the late night terrors emanating from the mysterious southern wing of the castle, the marquis, in an effort to quell Ferdinand's terror and cover his own powerlessness regarding his sovereignty, fabricates a tale to explain these supposedly cryptic happenings. Reportedly, two generations previously, the marquis' grandfather — Ferdinand's great-grandfather — kidnapped a territorial rival, entombed him in the southern wing, and tortured him to death. Because of the dastardly act, the murderous Mazzini ancestor forever locked these southern buildings as a symbolic gesture of suturing his power over Sicily. By the time the current fifth marquis of Mazzini assumed rule, rumors were rampant that these same southern buildings of the castle were haunted. At first the marquis disbelieved these superstitious conjectures. But, as the marquis confesses to Ferdinand, "one night, when every human being of the castle, except myself, was retired to rest, I had such strong and dreadful proofs of the general assertion, that even at this moment I cannot collect them without *horror* ... and the circumstances I have mentioned, is the true reason why I have resided so little at the castle" (*SR* 53; italics added). The terror felt by every other resident of the Castle of Mazzini registers as horror for the marquis because he, in a sense, knows the cause of the haunting. Even Ferdinand, when hearing his father's explanation, is described to have "listened to this narrative in silent *horror*" (*SR* 53; italics added). It appears terror metamorphoses into horror when the one afflicted with fear acquires knowledge of a repugnant external object causing this feeling. As Ferdinand reflects on his father's rationalization, he "remember[s] the temerity with which he had dared to penetrate those apartments — the light, and figure he had seen — and, above all, his situation in the staircase of the tower. Every nerve thrilled at the recollection; and the *terrors* of remembrance almost equaled those of reality" (*SR*, 53–4; italics added). Once the mysterious aspect of the haunting is erased by what turns out to be the marquis's concocted fiction, the original terror Ferdinand felt becomes merely a memory. The open-ended aspect of the southern apartments, which cause terror as a specific affect associated with the feminine Gothic supernatural, becomes closed-up and renounced through the marquis's rationalized fabrication of a ghost as external supernatural object.

25. Radcliffe's narrative itself also parallels a certain narrative distinction made explicit in the literary writings of Virginia Woolf. In *A Room of One's Own*, Woolf dramatizes the contrast between what she refers to as constative and performative uses of narrative. Constative narrative, which characterizes Mr. A's writing as a synecdoche for all male writing, claims to echo only that which is already present outside the writing itself. This type of writing then, following Woolf, purports to dwell in the truth. On the other hand, performative narrative, epitomized by Mary Charmichael as synecdoche for female writing, characterizes itself as a means of doing things with words that is not to be measured by its truth of correspondence to any pre-existing pattern. This distinction is best highlighted in a single passage from Woolf's later novel *The Waves*. Toward the end of the novel, the narrative mysteriously moves from Bernard's perspective to a sort of confusing collective perspective embodying a general, but not universal, claim. The reader is told indirectly of Rhoda's suicide in the following words: "I see far away, quivering like a gold thread, the pillar Rhoda saw, and feel the ru*sh of* the wind of her flight when she leapt" (Virginia Woolf, *The Waves*, 289; italics added). Even though on the constative level this passage lets the reader know that Rhoda leapt to her death, on the performative level, spotted within the interstices of the words themselves, highlighted by the italics, the reader is told that Rhoda was *shoved* to her death by language. By this point in the novel, the reader is already privy to the fact that Rhoda has always had a tremendous time recognizing the gaps between words. So even though the narrative ostensibly tells the reader that Rhoda leapt from the tall building, it also performs that fact, heard in the space between the words "rush" and "of," that language itself is the perpetrator of death. The male constative narrative is nominal-oriented while the female performative remains verbal-oriented. In other words, the male narrative privileges objects whereas the female privileges relation. Woolf's and other writers' use of the "trans-segmental drift" is the subject of Garrett Stewart's *Reading Voices: Literature and the Phonotext*.

26. In her reading of Ann Radcliffe's third Gothic, *The Romance of the Forest*, Elisabeth Bronfen argues that the language of hysteria is, indeed, characterized by "the refusal of closure." Bronfen also argues not only that hysteria is a "malady of the imagination" but that the Gothic hysteric possesses an "imagination gone awry" (Elisabeth Bronfen, *The Knotted Subject*, 170, 140, 149). While Bronfen's analysis focuses on Radcliffe's romance as a "mise-en-scène" of hysterical desire and similarly argues that "the social space within which the hysterical heroine wanders

emerges as the scene where unconscious phantasies can be materialized," she focuses exclusively on *The Romance of the Forest* and not specifically on hysteria as a Lacanian clinical structure (ibid., 153, 155).

27. Robert Miles, *Ann Radcliffe: The Great Enchantress*, 97.

28. Anolik also makes a compelling case that Radcliffe's romance is an implicit critique of the laws of coverture and primogeniture as defended by William Blackstone's 1765–1769 *Commentaries of the Laws of England*: "Radcliffe's revelation of the dangerous husband and father demystifies and denaturalizes the legal metaphors, revealing the horror that lurks beneath the neutral language of Blackstone" (Ruth Bienstock Anolik, "'There Was a Man,'" 91).

29. Darian Leader, "The Not-All," 46.

30. Ibid.

31. See Leader, *Why Women Write More Letters Than They Send*.

32. Veith, *Hysteria*, 123.

33. Ibid., 153.

34. For more on the importance of the interspersed verse throughout Radcliffe's prose romances, see Ingrid Horrocks, "'Her Ideas Arranged Themselves': Re-membering Poetry in Radcliffe," 507–27.

35. J.M.S. Tompkins, *The Popular Novel in England, 1770–1800*, 257.

36. Ibid., 261.

37. Ann Ronald, "Terror-Gothic: Nightmare and Dream in Ann Radcliffe and Charlotte Bronte," 179.

38. Cynthia Griffen Wolff, "The Radcliffean Gothic Model: A Form for Feminine Sexuality," 208–09.

39. Patricia Yaeger designates the mode of incorporation which characterizes the female sublime as the "failed sublime": "In texts where it occurs, we witness a woman's dazzling, unexpected empowerment followed by a moment in which this power is snatched away—often by a masculine counter-sublime that has explicit phallic components. What remains in our minds after such scenes is not simply a sense of feminine failure, but a double burden. First we learn that women, like men, are capable of joining the great. Second, we learn that something in the social order (either something external, or a set of beliefs internalized by the actant herself) intervenes, and the heroine finds herself not only stripped of transcendent powers, but bereft, in a lower social stratum than before" (Yaeger, "Toward a Female Sublime," 201). Without really knowing it, Yaeger is articulating the basis of the Lacanian feminine side of sexuation. Woman, just like man, has access to phallic sexuality, is "capable of joining the great." The woman, however, finds herself stripped of her transcendental

powers because the signifier necessary for such powers is, for her, inadequate. The "lower social stratum" she finds herself in correlates to the non-all nature of the symbolic order for the feminine subject. The feminine sublime exposes the subject to this non-all aspect of the symbolic without, however, offering an adequate way to avoid encountering the Thing.

Yaeger seems to recognize this failure when she insists that the female sublime is non–Oedipal. In fact, she insists the female sublime is pre–Oedipal. Where the masculine sublime, based on what Yaeger considers a primordial Oedipal confrontation, is a reaction rooted in aggression, the female sublime, confronted with the same primordial desire, resists repressing the confrontation. According to Yaeger, "in the pre-oedipal sublime these libidinal elements are not repressed; they break into consciousness and are welcomed as a primary, healthful part of the writer's experience, as part of the motive for metaphor" (ibid., 205). The masculine sublime is based on subsuming the object as dependent on the subject's imagination. In the female sublime, on the other hand, subject and object enter into what Yaeger calls an "intersubjective dialectic of grandeur" in which the poet refuses to annex what is alien, but revels, for a brief poetic moment, in a pre–Oedipal longing for otherness and ecstasy. The Oedipal, for Yaeger, has nothing to do with the female sublime. However, according to my analysis, the failed sublime, as she refers to it, fails because the Oedipus complex remains fundamentally incomplete within the feminine side of sexual difference. But this does not necessarily mean that the so-called female sublime is more in touch with the maternal. Rather, what Yaeger refers to as the female sublime — or what I am referring to as Kant's mathematical sublime — exposes the subject to only the inconsistency of the signifier, not something maternal that has been repressed by the signifier. It is the masculine sublime that is tied to the prohibited, incestuous, pre-oedipal mother: the Lady of Courtly Love, for instance. After all, it is Victor Frankenstein who makes the Freudian slip by calling, via a pun, his creature "mummy" immediately after awakening from his incestuously necrophilic dream about his mother. See Mary Shelley, *Frankenstein or The Modern Prometheus*, 58. The son wants what the father has, and the Maternal Thing is what haunts him throughout life. The daughter, on the other hand, wants what the father does not have, that to which the signifier is inadequate. As Lacan states in *Seminar VII*, the ultimate neurotic desire of a man is the possession of all women, and the ultimate neurotic desire for a woman is an ideal man. See Lacan, *Seminar VII*, 303. In either case, this fundamental fantasy prevents the subject from encountering *das Ding*. The sublime,

whether masculine or feminine, exposes the subject to the Thing that the neurotic fantasy conceals. For the masculine, it is the prohibited object. For the feminine, it is the impossibility of the fantasy itself. For an extended explication of the female sublime, see Barbara Claire Freeman, *The Feminine Sublime: Gender and Excess in Women's Fiction*. For an analysis of how the female sublime emerges in male writers, see Catherine Maxwell, *The Female Sublime from Milton to Swinburne*. For an understanding of the particularly Gothic female sublime, see Anne K. Mellor, *Romanticism and Gender*, 65–106; Anne Williams, *Art of Darkness*, 66–79; and Kathy Justice Gentile, "Sublime Drag."

40. Leader, *Why Women Write More Letters Than They Send*, 47.

41. Ibid.

42. This in no way should assert that feminine sexuality is primarily masochistic. As we see with Julia's wandering in the wilds of Sicily, she is far from playing a subordinated role. Gothic heroines do not so much enjoy being subordinated as their enjoyment needs to be subordinated in the name of sovereignty. For an analysis of the Gothic heroine and her desire to be subordinate, see Michelle A. Massé, *In the Name of Love: Woman, Masochism, and the Gothic*. For an analysis of feminine sexuality and the issue of absence in popular romance fiction, see Renata Salecl, "Love and Sexual Difference: Doubled Partners in Men and Women," 297–316.

43. Isn't reading Gothic romances, especially as a pleasurable, escapist practice, when compare to studying serious, more productive reading material, often viewed implicitly as a masturbatory intellectual exercise?

44. Willy Apollon, "Four Seasons in Femininity or Four Men in a Woman's Life," 104.

45. Ibid., 105.

46. Ibid.

47. Ibid., 106.

48. Ibid., 110.

49. The institution of the convent acts as the second lawful place of refuge for Radcliffe's wandering hysteric. Radcliffe erroneously situates 17th-century convents within the walls of monasteries to dramatic effect. Although her anti-Catholic bias rears its ugly head in this ignorant displacement, it reveals something untimely concerning sexual difference. By situating the convent within the space of the monastery, Radcliffe highlights how the convent functions solely as a place for housing woman who are seeking refuge from the Other *jouissance*. As Apollon insists, "in this logical period of solitude where she faces the void, the quest for love is that with which woman questions the failure of the signifier to contain jouissance and arrest the wandering where she is carried away" (ibid., 108). A woman, outdone by

the limitlessness of the Other *jouissance*, the enjoyment associated with being non-all to the signifier, will seek love to prop up the inadequacy of the signifier. But once exposed to this Other *jouissance*, she cannot but question any discourse of love aimed at her. She will, therefore, tend to seek the love of God as that one unconditional love which can never betray her.

50. Alenka Zupančič, "Kant with Don Juan," 114. *Don Juan*, another story of feminine enjoyment, is also, not accidentally, set in Sicily.

51. Ibid.

52. Ibid.

53. At the end of the novel when everyone is harmoniously reunited, the lighthouse, much like the one in Woolf's famous novel, stands as a point of stability within the rhythmic sassy waters of the Mediterranean, which themselves figure as the Woolfian rhythm of feminine enjoyment. While Woolf's writing proceeds from the partial stability of the narrative of *To the Lighthouse* to the chaotic, indeterminate narrative of *The Waves*, Radcliffe's, it appears, proceeds the other way: from the tumultuous waves of unlimited *jouissance* to the stable fragility of marriage figured in the lighthouse. Julia's, and Radcliffe's, desire to condescend enjoyment to the level of love betrays a particular sublimation of women.

54. For a fuller analysis of Lacan's conception of love outside the limits of the law, see Juliet Flower MacCannell, *The Hysteric's Guide to the Future Female Subject*, 235–58.

55. I would contend that Julia's discovery of her long-lost mother at the end of the romance only indirectly influences her decision to cede her desire and marry Hippolitus. In other words, unlike most critical accounts, I would contend that Julia's actual discovery of her mother is not as important for the romance's meaning as much as the place where she finds her mother. One minute Julia is wandering into a deep cavern from the indeterminate wilds on the margin of her father's sovereignty, and the next minute she accidentally discovers her incarcerated mother. Once this discovery is made, not only are all the supernatural occurrences from earlier in the novel explained, but Julia realizes that she is now within the confines of the Castle de Mazzini. Finding her mother, whom she had long since thought dead, is one thing, but realizing that the locked southern wing of the castle is actually a segue to the realm of enjoyment is a much more profound experience for Julia. For the first time, she directly realizes that the enjoyment of solitude in the woods was part and parcel of the domestic, canny space itself. Her father's sovereignty was always already open-ended. This discovery of her mother also reveals to Julia and the reader the fact that Maria, the desire of Julia's desire, was never, at least legally, a "wife." Because of bigamy,

the signifier is inadequate to Maria. Once Julia realizes this, she can make her enjoyment condescend to the level of a certain domesticity; she is able to marry the man she loves.

Chapter 6

1. One is here reminded of Eino Railo's hypothetical frustrated reader of Radcliffe's romances: "As her [Radcliffe's] imagination fails to supply what the reader has been led to await, and most of her enigmas are explained away as insignificant auxiliary details capable of perfectly natural solutions, the final state of the reader is one of irritation and chagrin" (Eino Railo, *The Haunted Castle: A Study of the Elements of English Romanticism*, 72).

2. Fred Botting, *Gothic*, 76.

3. I will follow the tendency of reality by referring to the obsessional neurotic in the masculine.

4. See Jacques Lacan, *Seminar XX*. Although Lacan's feminine and masculine formulas of sexuation do not necessarily correspond directly to hysteria and obsessional neurosis, there is a great deal of coincidence.

5. In *Totem and Taboo*, Freud mentions how one of his obsessional patients coined the phrase "omnipotence of thought" in order to account for "all the strange and uncanny events by which he, like others afflicted with the same illness, seemed to be pursued" (Sigmund Freud, *Totem and Taboo*, in *SE* 13:86).

6. Bruce Fink, *A Clinical Introduction to Lacanian Psychoanalysis*, 130.

7. Ibid., 131.

8. To show how the obsessional's fantasy substitutes *a* for the Other, therefore nullifying the Other, Serge Leclaire recounts an amusing tale — what amounts to a psychoanalytic "urban myth" — of the perfect psychoanalytic session for an obsessional: "It concerns an analyst of great renown, who hour after hour is generous to receive and to listen to his illustrious clients. One day he was a little weary and did not get up from his easy chair. A charming secretary, used to this, ushered each patient out at the end of his session. It was five o'clock, and the obsessional who was lying there was speaking a great deal. When the session was over, the patient, particularly satisfied with himself, concluded with these words: 'I think this has been a good session.' Then, echoing the words habitually spoken by the analyst, he added, 'We are going to leave things there.' He looked at the therapist, who appeared to be colder than usual; he seemed to be asleep. But no, he was very pale, really cold. The patient was concerned and summoned the secretary, who became agitated. They called in a colleague, who

ran right over, listened, and said that the analyst had died three hours earlier" (Serge Leclaire, "Jerome, or Death in the Life of the Obsessional," 95). The obsessional is most likely not willing to come to analysis by his own volition. For the very presence of the analyst, as the Other who knows, horrifies the obsessional. Even if the obsessional does eventually come to analysis, the initial preliminary meetings where analyst and analysand face each other are almost unbearable. The Other is too present. But if the obsessional does manage to survive the preliminary meetings, he is much more likely than the hysteric, who depends on the Other's desire, to enjoy his sessions on the couch speaking to a blank wall and ignoring the Other. The point of Leclaire's psychoanalytic "urban myth" revolves around the literalization of the death of the Other. There is, perhaps, nothing more satisfying for the obsessional than this death. Therefore, the obsessional in Leclaire's little tale feels like his session was particularly good because the Other was absent. The analysand was literally left in the room for 50 minutes alone with his fantasy. Since there was no one there to punctuate his free association, he was never forced to confront the horrifying unfathomable desire of the Other. Leclaire tells another story about a patient of his who is compulsively overcome by the word "crocodile" during a session one day. He remembers a documentary film in which a crocodile that appears to be asleep, floating in the water, suddenly leaps out of the water and swallows a fisherman faster than one can imagine. Leclaire realizes that for his patient, playing dead can permit one to eat the Other. Obsessionals, in fact, especially hypochondriacs, constantly act like they are dead precisely so the Other will not kill them and, thus, enjoy at their expense. This is why Leclaire formulates the notion that "the obsessional structure can be conceived of as the repeated refusal of the possibility of one's own death" (ibid., 107). Death, as the ultimate harm the Other can enact on the subject, the ultimate form the Other's enjoyment takes, is primarily what the obsessive, through his compulsive actions, attempts to ward off. As mentioned previously, Lacan even formulates the fundamental question of the obsessional neurotic as "Am I alive or dead?"

9. Laurie Langbauer, *Woman and Romance*, 94.

10. Half-man/half-woman is the very Freudian definition of hysterical desire: "Am I a man or a woman?" One might even conclude from this bit of Lewis household gossip that only a hysterical woman could give birth to an obsessional son. The obsessional, indeed, fears the unsatisfied woman.

11. Sigmund Freud, "Notes Upon a Case of Obsessional Neurosis," in *SE*, 10:160.

12. Charles Melman, "On Obsessional Neu-

rosis," in *Returning to Freud*, 131. Freud's analysis of the Rat Man case, and particularly this episode, is most likely responsible for Jane Marie Todd's critique of the connection between women and the uncanny in Freud: "women ... are *unheimlich*, either because the sight of their genitals provokes the male's fear of castration or because women's gaze reminds men of the 'valuable and fragile thing' they fear to lose, or because the desire to be female resurfaces as a fear of death" (Jane Marie Todd, "The Veiled Woman in Freud's *Das Unheimlich*," 520).

13. See Jacques Derrida, *Dissemination*, especially 1–59.

14. Matthew Lewis, *The Monk*, 3. Hereafter cited parenthetically in the text as *M*.

15. For more on Lewis and his reported plagiarisms, see E. J. Clery, *The Rise of Supernatural Fiction*, 142–43.

16. Jacques Lacan. *The Seminar of Jacques Lacan, Book II: The Ego in Freud's Theory and in the Technique of Psychoanalysis*, 205.

17. For more on Lewis's literary borrowings and possible plagiarisms, see Louis F. Peck, *A Life of Matthew Lewis*, 292–3; Syndy M. Conger, *Matthew Lewis, Charles Robert Maturin and the Germans*, 12–125; Andre Parreaux, *The Publication of The Monk*, 26–31; and Michael Gamer, *Romanticism and the Gothic: Genre, Reception, and Canon Formation*, 73–79.

18. Even though Lewis is supposedly ridiculing and criticizing the religious practices and excesses of Catholicism, his description of the Monk's sermon (monks do not give sermons) with all its fire and brimstone better approximates certain Protestant practices. For more on *The Monk's* anti–Catholicism, see Victoria Nelson, "Faux Catholic: A Gothic Subgenre from Monk Lewis to Dan Brown," 87–107; and Melanie Griffin, "'Is Nothing Sacred?' Christ's Harrowing through Lewis's Gothic Lens," 167–74. Through an analysis of Lewis's inversion of Christ's harrowing of hell, Griffin insinuates that Lewis turns Protestantism into the uncanny of Catholicism. My argument, of course, is that the Gothic romancer's fixation on a Catholic aesthetic uncannily haunts their Protestant ethic.

19. Sigmund Freud, "Obsessive Actions and Religious Practices," in *SE*, 9:118.

20. Jacques Lacan, *Seminar XX*, 76.

21. Sigmund Freud, "A Special Type of Choice of Object Made by Men," in *SE*, 11:165.

22. Ibid.

23. Sigmund Freud, *Three Essays on the Theory of Sexuality*, in *SE* 7:171.

24. Darian Leader, *Why Do Women Write More Letters Than They Send?* 22.

25. Freud, *Three Essays*, in *SE* 7:207.

26. Leader, *Why Do Women Write More Letters Than They Send?* 18.

27. Neurosis is the mark of castration.
28. Leader, *Why Do Women Write More Letters Than They Send?* 19.
29. Ibid.
30. Ibid., 21.
31. Jacques Lacan, *The Four Fundamental Concepts of Psychoanalysis*, 56–60.
32. For an analysis claiming that Ambrosio's angry destabilization results from Matilda's unsettling transgender performative, see William D. Brewer, "Transgendering in Matthew Lewis's *The Monk*," 192–207.

Conclusion

1. Robert Hume maintains that Poe, Hawthorne, and Brockden Brown belong to the genre of Gothic. But because American literary fashion ran about a generation behind Europe, two of these three writers are not exactly contemporary with their British counterparts. Robert D. Hume, "Gothic Versus Romantic: A Revaluation of the Gothic Novel," 282. For a further analysis of the distinction between Gothic as a genre and gothic as a mode, see Frederick Garber, "Meaning and Mode in Gothic Fiction," 155–69.
2. For the progress and authors of these other genres, see David H. Richter, *The Progress of Romance*.
3. Frederick Frank compares Hogg's novel to a case study of a schizophrenic. Frederick Frank, *The First Gothics*, 151. Frank and I are far from the only critics to privilege the mad over the bad, or anthropological over the supernatural, configuration of Wringhim's character. Barbara Bloedé argues that Wringhim's condition is a precursor to paraphrenia with multi-personality disorder, comparing Hogg's antihero to the real cases of both Sybill and Eve White/Eve Black. See Barbara Bloedé, "The Confessions of a Justified Sinner: The Paranoiac Nucleus," 15–28. In a separate article, Bloedé speculates that Hogg may even have been influenced by the true story of the multiple-personalities of Mary Reynolds when conceiving Robert Wringhim's psychological disorder (Bloedé, "A Nineteenth-Century Case of Double Personality: A Possible Source for *The Confessions*," 117–27). Psychiatrist Allan Beveridge has contended that Wringhim's pathology appears very similar to the rare disorder Fregoli Syndrome, named after nineteenth-century Italian actor Leopoldo Fregoli. See Allan Beveridge, "*The Confessions of a Justified Sinner* and the Psychopathology of the Double," 344–45. David Petrie compares Wringhim's plight to his own personal struggle with autoscopy. See David Petrie, "The Sinner Versus the Scholar: Two Exemplary Models of Mis-re-membering and Mistaking Signs in Relation to Hogg's *Justified Sin-*

ner," 57–67. Joel Faflak claims that Wringhim's mental state is the product of mesmeric madness. See Joel Faflak, "'The Clearest Light of Reason': Making Sense of Hogg's Body of Evidence," 94–110. Finally, Scott Brewster makes a compelling argument that Wringhim's disturbed condition can best be understood as a borderline experience, as outlined by Julia Kristeva. See Scott Brewster, "Borderline Experience: Madness, Mimicry and Scottish Gothic," 79–86. The current chapter can be seen as supplementing these various readings with a novel interpretation, strictly adhering to a Lacanian diagnostic. For an analysis of Hogg's Wringhim that favors the "sinner" interpretation over the "psychotic" interpretation, see Jill Rubenstein, "Confession, Damnation and the Dissolution of the Identity in Novels by James Hogg and Harold Frederic," 103–13. For an examination of *Justified Sinner* explicitly critical of psychological interpretations, see Douglas Jones, "Double Jeopardy and the Chameleon Art in James Hogg's *Justified Sinner*," 164–85.
4. Hogg even names young Robert Wringhim's doppelgänger "Gil-Martin," an anagram for "margin lit." For an alternative and more elaborate analysis of the significance of Gil-Martin's name, see Douglas Gifford, *James Hogg*, 158–70; and Philip Rogers, "'A Name Which May Serve Your Turn': James Hogg's Gil-Martin," 89–98.
5. Bruce Fink, *A Clinical Introduction to Lacanian Psychoanalysis*, 79.
6. Jacques Lacan, "On a Question Prior to Any Possible Treatment of Psychosis," in *Écrits*, 481.
7. The editor describes Lady Dalcastle as "the most severe and gloomy of all bigots to the principles of the Reformation. Hers were not the tenets of the great reformers but theirs mightily overstrained and deformed. Theirs was an ungent hard to be swallowed; but hers was that ungent embittered and overheated until nature could no longer bear it" (James Hogg, *The Private Memoirs and Confessions of a Justified Sinner*, 2; Hereafter cited parenthetically in the text as *JS*).
8. Russell Grigg considers this the consequence of the name-of-the-father failing to substitute properly for the mother's desire (Grigg, "From the Mechanism of Psychosis to the Universal Condition of the Symptom: On Foreclosure," 55.
9. Early in Robert's own narrative portion of the novel, Robert refers to his reverend Robert Wringhim Sr., who is most likely Robert's biological father, as *father*, the italics qualifying the title and confirming the lack of a name-of-the-father in Robert's universe (*JS* 99).
10. The name of young Robert's schoolmate M'Gill is what Lacan would call an "enigmatic prefiguration" of the appellation Gil-Martin used for the doppelgänger and of young Robert's psychosis. See Jacques Lacan, *Seminar III*, 103. For a further elaboration of the connection between

M'Gill and Gil-Martin, see John Herdman, *The Double in Nineteenth-Century Fiction*, 78. Furthermore, according to Claire Rosenfield, Robert "reveals several psychotic symptoms. He hates women; he suffers from some nervous disease which he attributes to witchcraft" (Rosenfield, "The Shadow Within: The Conscious and Unconscious Use of the Double," 335).

11. Kevin Cameron, "Sovereignty of the Perverse: Democratic Subjectivity and Calvin's Doctrine of Predestination," 18.

12. Ibid., 29.

13. According to Freud's famous analysis of the psychotic Daniel Paul Schreber's *Memoir of My Nervous Illness*, Schreber, much like the young Robert Wringhim of Hogg's narrative, was brought up by strict principles, was convinced he was a redeemer, and also sought for his lost "father" in the grand and the sublime. See Sigmund Freud, "Psycho-analytic Notes on an Autobiographical Account of a Case of Paranoia," in *SE*, 12:3–82. Likewise, Jacques Lacan's quote from Schreber's memoir also bears a direct relation to Robert's claims of justification: "Enlightenment rarely given to mortals has been given to me" (Jacques Lacan, *Seminar III*, 31).

14. Nelson Smith has pointed out the numerous instances of character doubling within Hogg's romance: Robert as George's double; George as Robert's double; Arabella Logan and Lady Dalcastle; the two Arabellas (Logan and Calvert); George Colwan, Sr. and Robert Wringhim Sr.; and, of course, Gil as both Robert's and George's double (Smith, *James Hogg*, 150). For sake of argument, this chapter focuses solely on the only truly psychological case of the doppelgänger phenomenon in Hogg's narrative: Gil as Robert's double.

15. Grigg, "From the Mechanism of Psychosis," 58.

16. Lacan, *Seminar III*, 41.

17. Freud, "Psycho-analytic Notes on an Autobiographical Account of a Case of Paranoia," in *SE* 12:71.

18. Fink, *A Clinical Introduction to Lacanian Psychoanalysis*, 106.

19. For a clinical elaboration of this motif, see Marcel Czermak, "The Onset of Psychosis," 171–83.

20. Sigmund Freud discusses the nature of the delusion used by psychotics to repair their loss of reality when they are overcome by the id and torn away from reality in "Neurosis and Psychosis," in *SE*, 19:148–53.

21. Lacan, *Seminar III*, 45.

22. Lacan, "On a Question Prior to Any Possible Treatment of Psychosis," in *Écrits*, 481.

23. Dylan Evans, *An Introductory Dictionary of Lacanian Psychoanalysis*, 156.

24. In *Seminar III*, Lacan says *apropos* Schreber, "while he may be a writer, he is no poet. Schreber does not introduce us to a new dimension of experience. There is poetry whenever writing introduces us to a world other than our own and also makes it become our own, making present a being, a certain fundamental relationship. The poetry makes us unable to doubt the authenticity of St. John of the Cross's experience, or Proust's, or Gérard de Nerval's. Poetry is the creation of a subject adopting a new order of symbolic relations to the world. There is nothing like any of this in Schreber's *Memoirs*" (Lacan, *Seminar III*, 78).

25. Andrew Webber indicates that conventionally, the doppelgänger is the product of a broken home: "*Doppelgänger* are more-or-less invariably the products of dysfunctional families. They embody a symptomatic breakdown in the family romance of a cosy home-life" (Webber, *The Doppelgänger*, 46). This convention accords well with Robert's situation, considering the fact that he is most likely and especially thought to be by his legal father, George Colwan, a product of his wife's adulterous affair and the fact that Robert grows up with his mother in Glasgow instead of at the family seat with his father and brother. The doppelgänger, it appears, is an embodiment of the once homey turned strange.

26. Mladen Dolar, "'I Shall Be with You on Your Wedding Night,'" 12. Rogers argues the same, claiming that the double is altogether a reflection of narcissism, a projected wish fulfillment, and a conscience figure. Robert Rogers, *A Psychoanalytic Study of The Double in Literature*, 30.

27. Ibid., 15.

28. Otto Rank, *The Double: A Psychoanalytic Study*, 40. In her examination of Charlotte Dacre's strategic use of the double, Cynthia Murillo also claims that in the romantic era, the doppelgänger "became associated with a monstrous self" (Murillo, "Haunted Spaces and Powerful Places," 75).

29. Jacques Lacan, "The Mirror Stage as Formative of the *I* Function: as Revealed in Psychoanalytic Experience," in *Écrits*, 79. For Lacan's clinical analysis of the inevitable rise of aggressivity within the imaginary transferential relation between analysand and analyst, see his essay "Aggressiveness in Psychoanalysis," in *Écrits*, 82–101.

30. Jacques Lacan, *Seminar X: Anxiety*. Unpublished seminar, Nov. 28, 1962.

31. Rank, *The Double*, xx.

32. Ibid., 48.

33. John Todd and Kenneth Dewhurst maintain that narcissism is one of the leading non-somatic causes of autoscopy, the psychiatric term for seeing one's double (John Todd and Kenneth Dewhurst, "The Double: Its Psycho-Pathology and Psycho-Physiology," 50). N. Lukianowicz

provides a definition of autoscopy: "a complex psycho-sensorial hallucinatory perception of one's own body image projected into the external visual space" (Lukianowicz, "Autoscopic Phenomena," 199). Although most psychologists use the term autoscopy when examining the doppelgänger phenomenon in both its literary and clinical manifestations, the term heautoscopy has recently come into favor as the appropriate term for the doppelgänger phenomenon. Arguing that autoscopy is really just a purely visual encounter with one's double, Peter Brugger contends that heautoscopy is the more overwhelming and disturbing encounter with the alter ego that we are familiar with in doppelgänger literature. Heautoscopy consists of "a reduplication not only of bodily appearance, but also of aspects of one's psychological self." Therefore, the heautoscopic experience is felt by the subject much more profoundly and has a much greater emotional impact than the autoscopic experience. The heautoscopic double is also not a mirror reverse image like the autoscopic double, making its actual existence more certain. Incidentally, Brugger uses a Peter Pendrey illustration of young Robert Wringhim encountering Gil-Martin from an illustrated edition of Hogg's novel to pictorially demonstrate the difference between the autoscopic and heautoscopic double (Brugger, "Reflective Mirrors: Perspective-taking in Autoscopic Phenomena," 179, 183).

34. Robert Rogers makes the connection between psychosis and the doppelgänger phenomenon by noting an extreme narcissism running through both: "The results of the taking of one's own ego as an object can be seen in their most morbid form in the psychoses, with their radical megalomania and marked withdrawal of interest in the external world" (Rogers, *The Double in Literature*, 19).

35. See Mortimer Ostow, "The Metapsychology of Autoscopic Phenomena," 622–24.

36. C. F. Keppler, *The Literature of the Second Self*, 11.

37. Stanley M. Coleman, "The Phantom Double: Its Psychological Significance," 266. Coleman's borrowed description of Dostoevsky could almost apply to young Robert Wringhim from Hogg's novel: "the introvert who compensates himself for habitual self-control by violent sallies of self-assertion" (266).

38. Freud, "Neurosis and Psychosis," in *SE* 19:153.

39. Fink, *A Clinical Introduction*, 89–90.

40. Ibid., 90.

41. Ibid., 94.

42. Julie Fenwick argues that the "riddling ambiguity" of Gil-Martin's speech, together with Hogg's narrative manipulation "enmeshes Robert deeper in his self-delusion and further entangles him in his fate" (Fenwick, "Psychological and Narrative Determinism in James Hogg's *The Private Memoirs and Confessions of a Justified Sinner*," 64).

43. Fink also points out that, unlike the neurotic who needs to be in an altered state in order to act, the psychotic lacks control over his or her drives. According to Fink, "neurosis is generally characterized by extensive ego and superego control over the drives. When the neurotic engages in truly physically aggressive acts, he or she usually has to be drunk or in some other altered state (for example, repeatedly angered by someone, pushed to the limit, sleep deprived, or on drugs); only then are the restraints of conscience lifted sufficiently for the neurotic to take direct action. To act directly and effectively is, indeed, one of the hardest things for a neurotic to do.... The psychotic is more prone to immediate action, and plagued by little if any guilt after putting someone in the hospital, killing someone, raping someone, or carrying out some other criminal act. The psychotic may manifest shame, but not guilt. Guilt necessitates repression: one can feel guilty only if one knows one secretly wanted to inflict harm or enjoyed doing so" (Fink, *A Clinical Introduction*, 97–98). Otto Rank, in fact, refers to the doppelgänger as a "detached personification of instincts and desires" (Rank, *The Double*, 76). For a more thorough development of the psychotic's *passage à l'acte* and murder, see Linda Belau, "Killing the Object: Psychosis and the Criminal Act," 2229–53.

44. Otto Rank, *Beyond Psychology*, 81.

45. N. Lukianowicz, "Autoscopic Phenomena," 205. Andrew Webber also claims that the doppelgänger displaces the present onto the past (Webber, *The Doppelgänger*, 11).

46. Keppler, *The Literature of the Second Self*, 69.

47. Rank, *The Double*, 75.

48. Karl Miller argues that Robert's narrative captures his desire for a father: "Robert, an imaginary orphan, the son of estranged parents who, having been rejected by his natural father, the laird, dreams for himself a resplendent 'real' father. The role of the preferred or imaginary father is successfully played by the predestinarian divine, Wringhim, and by the friend Gil-Martin, who is therefore both Robert himself and the father he seeks" (Miller, *Doubles: Studies in Literary History*, 7). I would add that the success of these substitute fathers has only been in evidence in those moments when young Robert can successfully keep his sense of reality together through his delusion. During his many aggressive acts and his numerous blackouts, his delusional metaphor seems to have reached its limit.

49. For an argument in favor of maintaining this ambiguity, see Gifford, *James Hogg*, 139. For

an argument in favor of separating these two mutually exclusive understandings of the status of Gil-Martin, see Herdman, *The Double in Nineteenth-Century Fiction*, 85.

50. David Eggenschwiler correctly argues that, by the end, Robert's narrative has "move[d] into the realm of folk legend and chapbook superstition" (Eggenschwiler, "James Hogg's *Confessions* and the Fall into Division," 38). Eggenschwiler is primarily concerned with the numerous flagrant demonic visitations and the more explicitly supernatural torments that follow Robert during his feeble attempt to reach England. But, with some elaboration, one could even argue that the "The Editor's Narrative" always has at least one foot in this Scottish folkloric tradition. This would explain why Gil-Martin is often seen in this part of Hogg's narrative as a possessing devil, the traditional folkloric understanding of insanity.

51. David Oakleaf claims that the folk tradition, in which the editor's narrative openly indulges, is implicitly excluded in Robert's narrative. After hearing of the folktale of the "Devil of Auchtermuchty" from his servant Penpunt, Robert's "folkloric expectations" of finding cloven hoofs when examining Gil-Martin's feet are denied when he uncovers "the foot of a gentleman" (David Oakleaf, "'Not the Truth': The Doubleness of Hogg's *Confessions* and the Eighteenth-Century Tradition," 60).

52. Hogg refers to "Gil-Moules," a traditional Scottish folkloric demonic figure, in several of his verses, including "A Witches Chant" and *Mador of the Moor*.

53. Sigmund Freud, "A Seventeenth-Century Demonological Neurosis," in *SE* 19:72. L. L. Lee has argued that Hogg's romance "serves as a kind of watershed between ... two artistic attitudes towards the devil. The devils of the Gothic novel, even the Mephistophcles [sic] of Goethe, will no longer suffice — for example, Charles Maturin in that last of the Gothics, *Melmoth the Wanderer* (1820), cannot let us see the actual Devil; and the demonic human figures such as Heathcliff or the 'psychological' Satans such as Dostoyevsky's or Mann's are yet to come" (L. L. Lee, "The Devil's Figure: James Hogg's *Justified Sinner*," 230).

54. For instance, Angela Wright argues that Hogg's appearance in his own romance "serves to cast doubt upon the integrity of the editor's version" of events (Wright, "Scottish Gothic," 76).

55. Just as allegories were the rage of the day for Robert, Richard Jackson has argued that "confessional" literature was very fashionable when Hogg published his *Private Memoirs and Confessions of a Justified Sinner* (Richard D. Jackson, "The Devil, the Doppelgänger, and the Confessions of James Hogg and Thomas De Quincey," 91).

56. Webber, *The Doppelgänger*, 7.

57. Fink, *A Clinical Introduction*, 97.

Bibliography

Addison, Joseph. *Essays in Criticism and Literary Theory.* Edited by John Loftis. Northbrook, IL: AHM, 1975.

Adriano, Joseph. *Our Ladies of Darkness: Female Demonology in Male Gothic Fiction.* University Park: Pennsylvania State University Press, 1993.

Aikin, J., and A. L. Aikin. *Miscellaneous Pieces in Prose.* London: J. Johnson, 1773.

Anolik, Ruth Bienstock. "'There Was a Man': Dangerous Husbands and Fathers in *The Winter's Tale, A Sicilian Romance* and *Linden Hills,*" in *Horrifying Sex: Essays on Sexual Difference in Gothic Literature,* edited by Ruth Bienstock Anolik, 83–101. Jefferson, NC: McFarland, 2007.

Apollon, Willy. "Four Seasons in Femininity or Four Men in a Woman's Life." *Topoi* 12.2 (1993): 110–15.

Arata, Stephen. *Fictions of Loss in the Victorian Fin de Siècle.* Cambridge: Cambridge University Press, 1996.

Auerbach, Erich. *Mimesis: The Representation of Reality in Western Literature.* Princeton: Princeton University Press, 1953.

Azari, Ehsan. *Lacan and the Destiny of Literature.* London: Continuum, 2008.

Baldick, Chris, and Robert Mighall. "Gothic Criticism," in *A Companion to the Gothic,* edited by David Punter, 209–28. Oxford: Blackwell, 2000.

Bayer-Bernbaum, Linda. *The Gothic Imagination: Expansion in Gothic Literature and Art.* Madison, NJ: Fairleigh Dickenson University Press, 1982.

Beattie, James. *Dissertations Moral & Critical.* London: Stahey, Cadell & Creech, 1783.

Beer, Gillian. *The Romance.* London: Methuen, 1970.

Belau, Linda. *Encountering Jouissance: Trauma, Psychosis, and Psychoanalysis.* Unpublished Manuscript, 2010.

_____. "Killing the Object: Psychosis and the Criminal Act." *Cardozo Law Review* 24.6 (2003): 2229–53.

Berek, Peter. "Interpretation, Allegory, and Allegoresis." *College English* 40.2 (1978): 117–32.

Bergland, Renée. *The National Uncanny: Indian Ghosts and American Subjects.* Hanover: University Press of New England, 2000.

Bergler, Edmund. *The Writer and Psychoanalysis.* New York: Doubleday, 1950.

Beveridge, Allan. "*The Confessions of a Justified Sinner* and the Psychopathology of the Double." *Psychiatric Bulletin* 15 (1991): 344–45.

Bloedé, Barbara. "The Confessions of a Justified Sinner: The Paranoiac Nucleus," in *Papers Given at the First James Hogg Society Conference,* edited by Gillian Hughes, 15–28. Stirling: James Hogg Society, 1983.

_____. "A Nineteenth-Century Case of Double Personality: A Possible Source for *The Confessions,*" in *Papers Given at the Second James Hogg Society Conference,* edited by Gillian Hughes, 117–27. Aberdeen: Association for Scottish Literary Studies, 1988.

Bloom, Harold. "Freud and the Poetic Sublime: A Catastrophe Theory of Creativity," in *Freud: A Collection of Critical Essays,* edited by Perry Meisel, 211–31. Englewood Cliffs: Prentice Hall, 1981.

Bloomfield, Morton W. "Allegory as Interpretation." *New Literary History* 3.2 (1972): 301–17.

Botting, Fred. *Gothic*. London: Routledge, 1996.

_____. *Gothic Romanced: Consumption, Gender and the Technology in Contemporary Fictions*. London: Routledge, 2008.

Bowie, Malcolm. *Freud, Proust, and Lacan: Theory as Fiction*. Cambridge: Cambridge University Press, 1987.

Brewer, William D. "Transgendering in Matthew Lewis's *The Monk*." *Gothic Studies* 6.2 (2004): 192–207.

Brewster, Scott. "Borderline Experience: Madness, Mimicry and Scottish Gothic." *Gothic Studies* 7.1 (2005): 79–86.

Bronfen, Elisabeth. *The Knotted Subject: Hysteria and its Discontents*. Princeton: Princeton University Press, 1998.

Brown, Marshall. *The Gothic Text*. Stanford: Stanford University Press, 2005.

Brugger, Peter. "Reflective Mirrors: Perspective-taking in Autoscopic Phenomena." *Cognitive Neuropsychiatry* 7.3 (2002): 179–94.

Burke, Edmund. *A Philosophical Enquiry into the Origin of our Ideas of the Sublime and Beautiful*, edited by Adam Phillips. Oxford: Oxford University Press, 1990.

Burley, Stephanie. "The Death of Zofloya; or, The Moor as Epistemological Limit," in *The Gothic Other: Racial and Social Constructions in the Literary Imagination*, edited by Ruth Bienstock Anolik and Douglas L. Howard, 197–211. Jefferson, NC: McFarland, 2004.

Cameron, Ed. "The Moral Value of Gothic Sublimity," in *Morality and the Literary Imagination*, edited by Gabe Ricci, 119–37. New Brunswick: Transaction, 2009.

Cameron, Kevin. "Sovereignty of the Perverse: Democratic Subjectivity and Calvin's Doctrine of Predestination." *Literature and Psychology* 49.3 (2003): 16–44.

Carter, Margaret L. *Specter or Delusion?: The Supernatural in Gothic Fiction*. Ann Arbor: UMI Research, 1987.

Castle, Terry. *The Female Thermometer: Eighteenth-century Culture and the Invention of the Uncanny*. New York: Oxford University Press, 1995.

Chapin, Sue. "'Written in Black Letter': The Gothic and/in the Rule of Law." *Law and Literature* 17.1 (2005): 47–68.

Chase, Cynthia. *Decomposing Figures: Rhetorical Readings in the Romantic Tradition*. Baltimore: The Johns Hopkins University Press, 1986.

Clery, E. J. "The Genesis of 'Gothic' Fiction," in *The Cambridge Companion to Gothic Fiction*, edited by Jerrold E. Hogle, 21–39. Cambridge: Cambridge University Press, 2002.

_____. *The Rise of Supernatural Fiction, 1762–1800*. Cambridge: Cambridge University Press, 1995.

Cohn, Jan, and Thomas H. Miles. "The Sublime: In Alchemy, Aesthetics and Psychoanalysis." *Modern Philology* 74.3 (1977): 289–304.

Coleman, Stanley M. "The Phantom Double: Its Psychological Significance." *British Journal of Medical Psychology* 14 (1934): 254–73.

Conger, Syndy M. *Matthew Lewis, Charles Robert Maturin and the Germans: An Interpretative Study of the Influence of German Literature on Two Gothic Romances*. Salzburg: University of Salzburg Press, 1977.

Copjec, Joan. *Read My Desire: Lacan Against the Historicists*. Cambridge: MIT, 1994.

_____. "The Tomb of Perseverance: On *Antigone*," in *Giving Ground: The Politics of Propinquity*, edited by Joan Copjec and Michael Sorkin, 233–66. New York: Verso, 1999.

Craft, Christopher. "'Kiss Me with Those Red Lips': Gender and Inversion in Bram Stoker's *Dracula*." *Representations* 41 (1990): 19–46.

Cullen, William. *First Lines in the Practice of Physic*. Vol. 3, 4th Ed. Edinburgh: C. Elliot, 1784.

Czermak, Marcel. "The Onset of Psychosis," in *Returning to Freud: Clinical Psychoanalysis in the School of Lacan*, edited by Stuart Schneiderman, 171–83. New Haven: Yale University Press, 1980.

Davenport-Hines, Richard. *Gothic: Four Hundred Years of Excess, Horror, Evil and Ruin*. New York: North Point, 1998.

DeLamotte, Eugenia C. *Perils of the Night: A Feminist Study of Nineteenth-Century Gothic*. Oxford: Oxford University Press, 1990.

de Man, Paul. *The Resistance to Theory*. Minneapolis: University of Minnesota Press, 1986.

Demata, Massimiliano. "Discovering Eastern Horrors: Beckford, Maturin, and the Discourse of Travel Literature," in *Empire and the Gothic: The Politics of Genre*, edited by Andrew Smith and William Hughes, 13–34. New York: Palgrave, 2003.

Derrida, Jacques. *Dissemination*. Translated by Barbara Johnson. Chicago: University of Chicago Press, 1981.

Doane, Mary Ann. *Femme Fatales: Feminism, Film Theory, Psychoanalysis*. New York: Routledge, 1991.

Dolar, Mladen. "'I Shall Be with You on Your Wedding Night': Lacan and the Uncanny." *October* 58 (1991): 5–23.

_____. "The Legacy of the Enlightenment: Foucault and Lacan." *New Formations* 14 (1991), 43–56.

Duncan, Ian. *Modern Romances and the Transformations of the Novel: The Gothic, Scott, Dickens*. Cambridge: Cambridge University Press, 1992.

Eagleton, Terry. *The Ideology of the Aesthetic*. Cambridge: Basil Blackwell, 1990.

_____. *Marxism and Literary Criticism*. Berkeley: University of California Press, 1976.

Edmundson, Mark. *Nightmare on Main Street: Angels, Sadomasochism, and the Culture of the Gothic*. Cambridge: Harvard University Press, 1997.

Eggenschwiler, David. "James Hogg's *Confessions* and the Fall into Division." *Studies in Scottish Literature* 9 (1972): 26–39.

Ellenberger, Henri F. *The Discovery of the Unconscious*. New York: Basic, 1970.

Ellis, Kate. *The Contested Castle: Gothic Novels and the Subversion of Domestic Ideology*. Chicago: University of Illinois Press, 1989.

Ellis, Markman. *The History of Gothic Fiction*. Edinburgh: Edinburgh University Press, 2000.

Evans, Dylan. *An Introductory Dictionary of Lacanian Psychoanalysis*. London: Routledge, 1996.

Faflak, Joel. "'The Clearest Light of Reason': Making Sense of Hogg's Body of Evidence." *Gothic Studies* 5.1 (2003): 94–110.

Fairer, David. "The Faerie Queen and Eighteenth-Century Spenserianism," in *A Companion to the Romance: From Classical to Contemporary*, edited by Corrine Saunders, 197–215. Oxford: Blackwell, 2004.

Farnell, Gary. "The Gothic and the Thing." *Gothic Studies* 11.1 (2009): 113–23.

Fenwick, Julie. "Psychological and Narrative Determinism in James Hogg's *The Private Memoirs and Confessions of a Justified Sinner*." *Scottish Literary Journal* 15 (1988): 61–9.

Ferguson, Frances. *Solitude and the Sublime: Romanticism and the Aesthetics of Individuation*. New York: Routledge, 1992.

Fink, Bruce. *A Clinical Introduction to Lacanian Psychoanalysis: Theory and Technique*. Cambridge: Harvard University Press, 1997.

_____. *The Lacanian Subject: Between Language and Jouissance*. Princeton: Princeton University Press, 1995.

Fletcher, Angus. *Allegory: The Theory of a Symbolic Mode*. Ithaca: Cornell University Press, 1964.

Foucault, Michel. *The Foucault Reader*, edited by Paul Rabinow. New York: Pantheon, 1984.

_____. *Power/Knowledge: Selected Interviews & Other Writings*, edited by Colin Gordon, translated by Colin Gordon, et al. New York: Pantheon, 1980.

Frank, Frederick S. *The First Gothics: A Critical Guide to the English Gothic Novel*. New York: Garland, 1987.

Freeman, Barbara Claire. *The Feminine Sublime: Gender and Excess in Women's Fiction*. Berkeley: University of California Press, 1995.

Freud, Sigmund. *The Standard Edition of the Complete Psychological Works of Sigmund Freud*. 24 vols. Edited and translated by James Strachey. London: Hogarth, 1955.

Frye, Northrop. *Anatomy of Criticism: Four Essays*. Princeton: Princeton University Press, 1957.

_____. *The Secular Scripture: A Study of the Structure of Romance*. Cambridge: Harvard University Press, 1976.

Fuchs, Barbara. *Romance*. New York: Routledge, 2004.

Gamer, Michael. *Romanticism and the Gothic: Genre, Reception, and Canon Formation*. Cambridge: Cambridge University Press, 2000.

Garber, Frederick. "Meaning and Mode in Gothic Fiction." *Studies in Eighteenth Century Culture* 3 (1973): 155–69.

Gentile, Kathy Justice. "Anxious Supernaturalism: An Analytic of the Uncanny." *Gothic Studies* 2.1 (2000): 23–38.

_____. "Sublime Drag: Supernatural Masculinity in Gothic Fiction." *Gothic Studies* 11.1 (2009): 16–31.

Gifford, Douglas. *James Hogg.* Edinburgh: Ramsey Head, 1962.

Griffin, Melanie. "'Is Nothing Sacred?' Christ's Harrowing through Lewis's Gothic Lens." *Orbis Litterarum* 64.3 (2009): 167–74.

Grigg, Russell. "From the Mechanism of Psychosis to the Universal Condition of the Symptom: On Foreclosure," in *Key Concepts of Lacanian Psychoanalysis*, edited by Dany Nobus, 48–74. New York: Other, 1998.

Grondin, Jean. *Introduction to Philosophical Hermeneutics*, translated by Joel Weinsheimer. New Haven: Yale University Press, 1994.

Gwynn, Stephen. *The Life of Horace Walpole.* London: Thornton Butterworth, 1932.

Haggerty, George. *Queer Gothic.* Chicago: University of Illinois Press, 2006.

Halberstam, Judith. *Skin Shows: Gothic Horror and the Technology of Monsters.* Durham: Duke University Press, 1995.

Harfst, Betsy Perteit. *Horace Walpole and the Unconscious: An Experiment in Freudian Analysis.* New York: Arno, 1980.

Hatlen, Burton. "The Return of the Repressed/Oppressed in Bram Stoker's *Dracula*," in *Dracula: The Vampire and the Critics*, edited by Margaret L. Carter, 117–36. Ann Arbor: University of Michigan Press, 1988.

Heiland, Donna. *Gothic and Gender: An Introduction.* Oxford: Blackwell, 2004.

Herdman, John. *The Double in Nineteenth-Century Fiction.* New York: St. Martin's Press, 1991.

Hoeveler, Diane Long. *Gothic Feminism: The Professionalization of Gender from Charlotte Smith to the Brontës.* University Park: Pennsylvania State University Press, 1998.

Hoffman, E.T.A. *Tales of Hoffman*, edited and translated by R. J. Hollingdale. New York: Penguin, 1982.

Hogg, James. *The Private Memoirs and Confessions of a Justified Sinner*, edited by John Carey. Oxford: Oxford University Press, 1995.

Horrocks, Ingrid. "'Her Ideas Arranged Themselves': Re-membering Poetry in Radcliffe." *Studies in Romanticism* 47.4 (2008): 507–27.

Hume, Robert D. "Gothic Versus Romantic: A Revaluation of the Gothic Novel." *PMLA* 84 (1969), 282–90.

Hurd, Richard. *Letters on Chivalry and Romance.* New York: Garland, 1971.

Iddan, Claudia. "Symptom and Love — Points of Suspension," in *Almanac of Psychoanalysis II: Psychoanalytic Stories After Freud and Lacan*, edited by Ruth Golan, et al., 102–06. Tel Aviv: G. I. E. P., 1998.

Jackson, Richard D. "The Devil, the Doppelgänger, and the Confessions of James Hogg and Thomas De Quincey." *Studies in Hogg and His World* 12 (2001): 90–103.

Jameson, Frederic. "Magical Narratives: Romance as Genre." *New Literary History* 7.1 (1975): 135–63.

Johnson, Samuel. *Samuel Johnson: The Major Works*, edited by Donald Greene. Oxford: Oxford University Press, 1984.

Johnston, Arthur. *Enchanted Ground: The Study of Medieval Romance in the Eighteenth Century.* London: Athlone, 1964.

Jones, Douglas. "Double Jeopardy and the Chameleon Art in James Hogg's *Justified Sinner*." *Studies in Scottish Literature* 23 (1988): 164–85.

Kallich, Martin. *Horace Walpole.* New York: Twayne, 1971.

Kant, Immanuel. *The Critique of Judgment*, translated by James Creed Meredith. Oxford: Oxford University Press, 1952.

_____. *Critique of Pure Reason*, translated by F. Max Muller. New York: Anchor, 1966.

_____. *Immanuel Kant: Philosophical Writings*, edited by Ernst Behler. New York: Continuum, 1986.

Karl, Frederick R. "Gothic, Gothicism, and Gothicists," in *A Reader's Guide to the Eighteenth-Century Novel*, by Frederick R. Karl, 235–74. New York: Noonday, 1974.

Kennedy, J. Gerald, and Lilian Weissberg. *Romancing the Shadow: Poe and Race.* Oxford: Oxford University Press, 2001.

Keppler, C. F. *The Literature of the Second Self.* Tucson: University of Arizona Press, 1972.

Kilgour, Maggie. *The Rise of the Gothic Novel.* London: Routledge, 1995.

Kristeva, Julia. *Strangers to Ourselves*, translated by Leon S. Roudiez. New York: Columbia University Press, 1991.

Lacan, Jacques. *Écrits*, translated by Bruce Fink. New York: Norton, 2006.

_____. *Écrits: A Selection*, translated by Alan Sheridan. New York: Norton, 1977.

_____. *Feminine Sexuality: Jacques Lacan and the École Freudienne*, edited by Juliet Mitchell and Jacqueline Rose; translated by Jacqueline Rose. New York: Norton, 1982.

_____. *The Four Fundamental Concepts of Psycho-analysis*, translated by Alan Sheridan. New York: Norton, 1978.

_____. "Homage to Marguerite Duras, on *Le ravissement de Lol V. Stein*," translated by Peter Connor, in *Duras by Duras*, 122–29. San Francisco: City Lights, 1987.

_____. "On Freud's '*Trieb*' and the Psychoanalyst's Desire," translated by Bruce Fink, in *Reading Seminars I and II: Lacan's Return to Freud*, edited by Richard Feldstein, Bruce Fink, and Maire Jaanus, 417–21. Albany: SUNY, 1996.

_____. *The Seminar of Jacques Lacan, Book II: The Ego in Freud's Theory and in the Technique of Psychoanalysis, 1954–1955*, edited by Jacques-Alain Miller, and translated by Silvana Tomaselli. New York: Norton, 1988.

_____. *The Seminar of Jacques Lacan, Book III: The Psychoses, 1955–1956*, edited by Jacques-Alain Miller, and translated by Russell Grigg. New York: Norton, 1993.

_____. *The Seminar of Jacques Lacan, Book VII: The Ethics of Psychoanalysis, 1959–1960*, edited by Jacques-Alain Miller, and translated by Dennis Porter. New York: Norton, 1992.

_____. *The Seminar of Jacques Lacan, Book XVII: The Other Side of Psychoanalysis, 1969–1970*, edited by Jacques-Alain Miller, and translated by Russel Grigg. New York: Norton, 2007.

_____. *The Seminar of Jacques Lacan, Book XX: Encore, 1972–1973*, edited by Jacques-Alain Miller, and translated by Bruce Fink. New York: Norton, 1998.

_____. *Seminar X: Anxiety*. Unpublished seminar, Nov. 28, 1962.

_____. *Television: A Challenge to the Psychoanalytic Establishment*, edited by Joan Copjec, and translated by Denis Hollier, Rosalind Krauss, and Annette Michelson. New York: Norton, 1990.

Langbauer, Laurie. *Women and Romance: The Consolations of Gender in the English Novel*. Ithaca: Cornell University Press, 1990.

Leader, Darian. "The Not-All." *Lacanian Ink* 8 (1994), 43–49.

_____. *Promises Lovers Make When It Gets Late*. London: Faber and Faber, 1997.

_____. *Why Women Write More Letters Than They Send: A Meditation on the Loneliness of the Sexes*. New York: Basic, 1996.

Leclaire, Serge. "Jerome, or Death in the Life of the Obsessional," in *Returning to Freud: Clinical Psychoanalysis in the School of Lacan*, edited by Stuart Schneiderman, 94–113. New Haven: Yale University Press, 1980.

Lee, L. L. "The Devil's Figure: James Hogg's *Justified Sinner*." *Studies in Scottish Literature* 3 (1996), 230–39.

Lewis, Matthew. *The Monk*, edited by Howard Anderson. New York: Oxford University Press, 1995.

Longinus. "On the Sublime," translated by Rhys Roberts, in *The Critical Tradition*, edited by David H. Richter. Boston: Bedford/St. Martin's Press, 1998.

Longueil, Alfred E. "The Word 'Gothic' in Eighteenth-Century Criticism." *Modern Language Notes* 38 (1923): 453–56.

Lukianowicz, N. "Autoscopic Phenomena." *Archives of Neurology and Psychology* 80 (1956): 199–220.

MacCannell, Juliet Flower. *The Hysteric's Guide to the Future Female Subject*. Minneapolis: University of Minnesota Press, 2000.

_____. *The Regime of the Brother: After the Patriarchy*. London: Routledge, 1991.

Malchow, H. L. *Gothic Images of Race in Nineteenth-Century Britain*. Stanford, CA: Stanford University Press, 1996.

Mannoni, Octave. "'I Know Well, but All the Same...'" translated by G. M. Goshgarian, in *Perversion and the Social Relation*, edited by Molly Anne Rothenberg, Dennis A. Foster, and Slavoj Žižek, 68–92. Durham, NC: Duke University Press, 2003.

Massé, Michelle A. *In the Name of Love: Woman, Masochism, and the Gothic*. Ithaca, NY: Cornell University Press, 1992.

_____. "Psychoanalysis and the Gothic," in *A Companion to the Gothic*, edited by David Punter, 229–41. Oxford: Blackwell, 2000.

Maxwell, Catherine. *The Female Sublime from Milton to Swinburne: Bearing Blindness*. Manchester: Manchester University Press, 2001.

McGowan, Todd. *The Impossible David Lynch*. New York: Columbia University Press, 2007.

McIntyre, Clara. "Were the 'Gothic Novels' Gothic?" *PMLA* 36.4 (1921): 644–66.

Mellor, Anne K. *Romanticism and Gender.* New York: Routledge, 1993.

Melman, Charles. "On Obsessional Neurosis," in *Returning to Freud: Clinical Psychoanalysis in the School of Lacan*, edited by Stuart Schneiderman,130–38. New Haven, CT: Yale University Press 1980.

Michasiw, Kim Ian. "Charlottes Dacre's Postcolonial Moor," in *Empire and the Gothic: The Politics of Genre*, edited by Andrew Smith and William Hughes, 35–55. New York: Palgrave, 2003.

Miles, Robert. "The 1790s: The Effulgence of the Gothic," in *The Cambridge Companion to the Gothic*, edited by Jerold E. Hogle, 41–62. Cambridge: Cambridge University Press, 2002.

———. *Ann Radcliffe: The Great Enchantress.* Manchester: Manchester University Press, 1995.

Miller, Jacques-Alain. "Commentary on Lacan's Text," translated by Bruce Fink, in *Reading Seminars I and II: Lacan's Return to Freud*, edited by Richard Feldstein, Bruce Fink, and Maire Jaanus, 422–27. Albany: SUNY, 1996.

———. "The Experience of the Real in Psychoanalysis." *Lacanian Ink* 16 (2000): 7–27.

———. "*Extimité*," translated by Françoise Massardier-Kenney, in *Lacanian Theory of Discourse: Subject, Structure, and Society*, edited by Mark Bracher, et al., 74–87. New York: New York University Press, 1994.

———. "On Perversion," in *Reading Seminars I and II: Lacan's Return to Freud*, edited by Richard Feldstein, Bruce Fink, and Maire Jaanus, 306–20. Albany: SUNY, 1996.

———. "Paradigms of *Jouissance*," *Lacanian Ink* 17 (2000): 10–47.

Miller, Karl. *Doubles: Studies in Literary History.* Oxford: Oxford University Press,1985.

Mishra, Vijay. *The Gothic Sublime.* Albany: SUNY, 1994.

Monk, Samuel H. *The Sublime: A Study of Critical Theories in 18th-Century England.* Ann Arbor: University of Michigan Press, 1960.

Moretti, Franco. *Signs Taken for Wonders: Essays in the Sociology of Literary Forms*, revised edition, translated by Susan Fischer, David Forgacs, and David Miller. London: Verso, 1988.

Morris, David B. "Gothic Sublimity." *New Literary History* 16.2 (1985): 299–319.

Mowl, Timothy. *Horace Walpole: The Great Outsider.* London: John Murray, 1996.

Murillo, Cynthia. "Haunted Spaces and Powerful Places: Reconfiguring the Doppelgänger in Charlotte Dacre's *Zofloya.*" *Studies in the Humanities* 32.1 (2005): 74–92.

Nelson, Victoria. "Faux Catholic: A Gothic Subgenre from Monk Lewis to Dan Brown." *boundary 2* 34.2 (2007): 87–107.

Nicholls, Angus, and Martin Liebscher, eds. *Thinking the Unconscious: Nineteenth-Century German Thought.* Cambridge: Cambridge University Press, 2010.

Nobus, Dany, ed. *Key Concepts of Lacanian Psychoanalysis.* New York: Other, 1998.

Nollen, Elizabeth. "Ann Radcliffe's *A Sicilian Romance*: A New Source for Jane Austen's *Sense and Sensibility.*" *English Language Notes* 22.2 (1984): 30–37.

Oakleaf, David. "'Not the Truth': The Doubleness of Hogg's *Confessions* and the Eighteenth-Century Tradition." *Studies in Scottish Literature* 18 (1983): 59–74.

Ostow, Mortimer. "The Metapsychology of Autoscopic Phenomena." *International Journal of Psycho-Analysis* 41 (1960): 619–25.

The Oxford English Dictionary, 2nd ed., vol. 18. Oxford: Clarendon, 1989.

Parreaux, Andre. *The Publication of The Monk: A Literary Event, 1796–1798.* Paris: Didier, 1960.

Paulson, Ronald. "Gothic Fiction and the French Revolution." *Journal of English Literary History* 48 (1981): 532–54.

Peck, Louis F. *A Life of Matthew Lewis.* Cambridge, MA: Harvard University Press, 1961.

Petrie, David. "The Sinner Versus the Scholar: Two Exemplary Models of Mis-remembering and Mis-taking Signs in Relation to Hogg's *Justified Sinner.*" *Studies in Hogg and His World* 3 (1992): 57–67.

Plato. *Lysis, Phaedrus, and Symposium*, translated by Benjamin Jowett. New York: Prometheus, 1991.

"Political Vampyres," in *Gothic Documents: A Sourcebook 1700–1820*, edited by E. J. Clery and Robert Miles, 24–26. Manchester: Manchester University Press, 2000.

Punter, David. *Gothic Pathologies: The Text,*

the Body and the Law. New York: St. Martin's Press, 1998.

———. *The Literature of Terror: A History of Gothic Fiction from 1765 to the Present Day*. London: Longman, 1980.

———. "Narrative and Psychology in Gothic Fiction," in *Gothic Fictions: Prohibition/Transgression*, edited by Kenneth W. Graham, 3–27. New York: AMS, 1989.

———. "Shape and Shadow: On Poetry and the Uncanny," in *A Companion to the Gothic*, edited by David Punter, 193–205. London: Blackwell, 2001.

———. "The Uncanny," in *The Routledge Companion to the Gothic*, edited by Catherine Spooner and Emma McEvoy, 129–36. London: Routledge, 2007.

Punter, David, and Glennis Bryon. *The Gothic*. Malden, MA: Blackwell, 2004.

Quilligan, Maureen. *The Language of Allegory: Defining the Genre*. Ithaca, NY: Cornell University Press, 1979.

Rabaté, Jean-Michel. *Jacques Lacan: Psychoanalysis and the Subject of Literature*. New York: Palgrave, 2001.

Radcliffe, Ann. *The Mysteries of Udolpho*, edited by Bonamy Dobrée. Oxford: Oxford University Press, 1998.

———. "On the Supernatural in Poetry." *New Monthly Magazine and Literary Journal* 16.1 (1826): 145–52.

———. *The Sicilian Romance*, edited by Alison Milbank. New York: Oxford University Press, 1993.

Radford, Jean, ed. *The Progress of Romance: The Politics of Popular Fiction*. London: Routledge, 1986.

Railo, Eino. *The Haunted Castle: A Study of the Elements of English Romanticism*. New York: Humanities, 1964.

Rank, Otto. *Beyond Psychology*. New York: Dover, 1958.

———. *The Double: A Psychoanalytic Study*, edited and translated by Harry Tucker. Chapel Hill: University of North Carolina Press, 1971.

Reeve, Clara. *The Old English Baron: A Gothic Story*, edited by James Trainer. Oxford: Oxford University Press, 2003.

———. *The Progress of Romance, through Times, Countries, and Manners with Remarks On the Good and Bad Effects on Them Respectively in a Course of Evening Conversations*. 2 vols. London: W. Keymer, 1785.

Regnault, François. "Art After Lacan," translated by Barbara P. Fulks and Jorge Jauregui. *Lacanian Ink* 19 (2001): 48–69.

Richtor, David H. *The Progress of Romance: Literary Historiography and the Gothic Novel*. Columbus: Ohio State University Press, 1996.

Rogers, Philip. "'A Name Which May Serve Your Turn': James Hogg's Gil-Martin." *Studies in Scottish Literature* 21 (1986): 89–98.

Rogers, Robert. *A Psychoanalytic Study of the Double in Literature*. Detroit: Wayne State University Press, 1970.

Ronald, Ann. "Terror-Gothic: Nightmare and Dream in Ann Radcliffe and Charlotte Bronte," in *The Female Gothic*, edited by Juliann E. Fleenor, 176–86. London: Eden, 1983.

Rosenfield, Claire. "The Shadow Within: The Conscious and Unconscious Use of the Double." *Daedalus* 92.2 (1963): 326–44.

Royle, Nicholas. *The Uncanny*. Manchester: Manchester University Press, 2003.

Rubenstein, Jill. "Confession, Damnation and the Dissolution of the Identity in Novels by James Hogg and Harold Frederic." *Studies in Hogg and His World* 1 (1990): 103–13.

Sabor, Peter, ed. *Horace Walpole: The Critical Heritage*. London: Routledge, 1987.

Sade, Marquis De. *The 120 Days of Sodom and Other Writings*, translated by Austryn Wainhouse and Richard Seaver. New York: Grove, 1966.

Salecl, Renata. "Love and Sexual Difference: Doubled Partners in Men and Women," in *Sexuation*, edited by Renata Salecl, 297–316. Durham, NC: Duke University Press, 2000.

Samson, John. "Politics Gothicized: The Conway Incident and *The Castle of Otranto*." *Eighteenth Century Life: British Literature and Culture* 10.3 (1986): 145–58.

Schmitt, Cannon. *Alien Nation: Nineteenth-Century Gothic Fictions and English Nationality*. Philadelphia: University of Pennsylvania Press, 1997.

Sedgwick, Eve Kosofsky. *Between Men: English Literature and Male Homosocial Desire*. New York: Columbia University Press, 1985.

Shelley, Mary. *Frankenstein* or *The Modern Prometheus*, edited by M.K. Joseph. Oxford: Oxford University Press, 1969.

Singh, Kalu. *Sublimation*. Cambridge: Icon, 2001.

Smith, Allan Lloyd. "'This Thing of Darkness': Racial Discourse in Mary Shelley's *Frankenstein*." *Gothic Studies* 6.2 (2004): 208–222.

Smith, Andrew. *Gothic Radicalism: Literature, Philosophy and Psychoanalysis in the Nineteenth Century*. New York: St. Martin's Press, 2000.

Smith, Nelson C. *James Hogg*. Boston: Twayne, 1980.

_____. "Sense, Sensibility and Ann Radcliffe." *Studies in English Literature 1500–1900* 13.4 (1973): 577–90.

Soler, Colette. "Hysteria and Obsession," in *Reading Seminars I and II: Lacan's Return to Freud*, edited by Richard Feldstein, Bruce Fink, and Maire Jaanus, 248–82. Albany: SUNY, 1996.

_____. "Literature as Symptom," in *Lacan and the Subject of Language*, edited by Ellie Ragland and Mark Bracher, 213–18. New York: Routledge, 1991.

_____. *What Lacan Said about Women: A Psychoanalytic Study*, translated by John Holland. New York: Other, 2006.

Stewart, Garrett. *Reading Voices: Literature and the Phonotext*. Berkeley: University of California Press, 1990.

Summers, Montague. *The Gothic Quest: A History of the Gothic Novel*. New York: Russell & Russell, 1964.

Szondi, Peter. "Introduction to Literary Hermeneutics," translated by Timothy Bahti. *New Literary History* 10.1 (1978): 17–29.

Tatar, Maria. "The Houses of Fiction: Toward a Definition of the Uncanny." *Comparative Literature* 33.2 (1981): 167–82.

Todd, Jane Marie. "The Veiled Woman in Freud's *Das Unheimlich*." *Signs* 11 (1986): 519–28.

Todd, John, and Kenneth Dewhurst. "The Double: Its Psycho-Pathology and Psycho-Physiology." *Journal of Nervous and Mental Diseases* 122 (1955): 47–55.

Todorov, Tzvetan. *The Fantastic: A Structural Approach to a Literary Genre*, translated by Richard Howard. Ithaca, NY: Cornell University Press, 1975.

Tompkins, J.M.S. *The Popular Novel in England, 1770–1800*. Lincoln: University of Nebraska Press, 1961.

Townshend, Dale. *The Orders of the Gothic: Foucault, Lacan, and the Subject of Gothic Writing, 1764–1820*. New York: AMS, 2007.

Trilling, Lionel. *The Liberal Imagination*. New York: Anchor, 1953.

Varma, Devendra. *The Gothic Flame*. New York: Russell & Russell, 1966.

Veith, Ilza. *Hysteria: The History of a Disease*. Chicago: University of Chicago Press, 1965.

Verhaeghe, Paul. "Causation and Destitution of a Pre-ontological Non-entity: On the Lacanian Subject," in *Key Concepts of Lacanian Analysis*, edited by Dany Nobus, 164–89. New York: Other, 1998.

Walpole. Horace. *The Castle of Otranto*, edited by W. S. Lewis. Oxford: Oxford University Press, 1996.

_____. *The Letters of Horace Walpole*. 16 vols. Edited by Paget Toynbee. Oxford: Clarendon, 1904.

_____. *The Works of Horatio Walpole, Earl of Orford*, edited by Mary Berry et al. London: Robinson, 1798.

_____. *The Yale Edition of Horace Walpole's Correspondence*. 48 vols. Edited by W. S. Lewis. New Haven: Yale University Press, 1937.

Webber, Andrew J. *The Doppelgänger: Double Visions in German Literature*. Oxford: Clarendon, 1996.

Whyte, Lancelot Law. *The Unconscious Before Freud*. New York: St. Martin's Press, 1978.

Whytt, Robert. *Observation on the Nature, Causes, and Cure of Those Disorders which have been commonly called Nervous, Hypochondriac, or Hysteric: To which is prefixed Remarks on the Sympathy of the Nerves*. 3rd Ed. Edinburgh: J. Balfour, 1767.

Williams, Anne. *Art of Darkness: A Poetics of Gothic*. Chicago: University of Chicago Press, 1995.

Williams, Ioan, ed. *Novel and Romance, 1700–1800: A Documentary Record*. New York: Barnes & Noble, 1970.

Wolff, Cynthia Griffen. "The Radcliffean Gothic Model: A Form for Feminine Sexuality," in *The Female Gothic*, edited by Juliann E. Fleenor, 207–23. London: Eden, 1983.

Woolf, Virginia. *The Waves*. San Diego: Harcourt Brace, 1931.

Wright, Angela. "Scottish Gothic," in *The Routledge Companion to Gothic*, edited by Catherine Spooner and Emma McEvoy, 73–82. London: Routledge, 2007.

Yaeger, Patricia. "Toward a Female Sublime," in *Gender and Theory: Dialogues on Feminist Criticism*, edited by Linda Kaufman, 191–212. New York: Basil Blackwell, 1989.

Young, Robert. "Freud's Secret: *The Interpretation of Dreams* Was a Gothic Novel," in *Sigmund Freud's* The Interpretation of Dreams: *New Interdisciplinary Essays*, edited by Laura Marcus, 206–31. Manchester: Manchester University Press, 1999.

Žižek, Slavoj. *Enjoy Your Symptom: Jacques Lacan Inside Hollywood and Out*. New York: Routledge, 1991.

———. "Grimaces of the Real, or When the Phallus Appears." *October* 58 (1991): 45–68.

———. "'In His Bold Gaze My Ruin Is Writ Large,'" in *Everything You Always Wanted to Know About Lacan (But Were Afraid to Ask Hitchcock)*, edited by Slavoj Žižek, 211–72. London: Verso, 1992.

———. "Psychoanalysis this Side of the Hermeneutic Delirium." *Lacanian Ink* 34 (2009): 139–51.

———. "The Spectre of Ideology," in *Mapping Ideology*, edited by Slavoj Žižek, 1–33. London: Verso, 1995.

———. *The Sublime Object of Ideology*. London: Verso, 1989.

———. "Surplus-Enjoyment Between the Sublime and Trash." *Lacanian Ink* 15 (1999): 98–107.

———. *Tarrying with the Negative: Kant, Hegel, and the Critique of Ideology*. Durham, NC: Duke University Press, 1993.

———. "'Woman is one of the names-of-the-father' or, How Not to Misread Lacan's Formulas of Sexuation." *Lacanian Ink* 10 (1995): 24–39.

Zupančič, Alenka. "Kant with Don Juan and Sade," in *Radical Evil*, edited by Joan Copjec, 105–25. London: Verso, 1996.

———. "The Logic of the Sublime." *The American Journal of Semiotics* 9.2–3 (1992): 51–68.

———. *The Shortest Shadow: Nietzsche's Philosophy of the Two*. Cambridge, MA: MIT, 2003.

———. "The Splendor of Creation: Kant, Nietzsche, Lacan." *Umbr(a)* 1 (1999): 35–41.

Index